MAD DOGS, ENGLISHMEN, AND THE ERRANT ANTHROPOLOGIST

MAD DOGS, ENGLISHMEN, AND THE ERRANT ANTHROPOLOGIST

Fieldwork in Malaysia

DOUGLAS RAYBECK

Hamilton College

WAVELAND

PRESS, INC.

Long Grove, Illinois

For information about this book, contact:
Waveland Press, Inc.
4180 IL Route 83, Suite 101
Long Grove, IL 60047-9580
(847) 634-0081
info@waveland.com
www.waveland.com

10-digit ISBN 0-88133-906-7
13-digit ISBN 978-0-88133-906-2

Printed in the United States of America

22   21   20   19   18   17

For Karen and Alethea

for reasons both obvious and obscure

"Mad dogs and
Englishmen go out
in the mid-day sun . . ."
– Noel Coward

Acknowledgments

This is a small book, yet there is a large debt of gratitude to be acknowledged. Although there is one name on the cover of the book, efforts of this nature are never simply the results of one person's contributions.

First, there is the issue of material support. I want to acknowledge gratefully grants from the National Institute of Mental Health (Grant MH 11486) and the London-Cornell Project, which, quite simply, made possible the field research on which this book is largely based. I want to thank Hamilton College for a variety of small research grants that contributed to the advancement of my work, and for the leave that gave me time to complete the manuscript. In particular the generosity of the Christian A. Johnson Endeavor Foundation helped to defray some of the expenses of that leave. I also want to thank both the Department of Anthropology and the Southeast Asia Program of Cornell University for accepting me as a Visiting Fellow during work on this manuscript. In particular the latter supplied me with a comfortable office and other amenities that greatly aided my labors.

Second, I wish to recognize the inspiration and support of former teachers and current colleagues. While nonmaterial, this support was just as crucial a contribution to the completion of this book, as were the more palpable essentials mentioned above. My instructors at Dartmouth—Professors Harp, McKennan, and Whiting—stimulated my early interest in anthropology. Later, professors at Cornell—notably Bernd Lambert, William Lambert, Lauristan Sharp, and Arthur Wolf—furthered my exposure to the ideas and intellectual excitement of this field and, not parenthetically, drew my attention to some of my anthropological weaknesses. I owe a particular debt to Thomas Gregor, who, when I was an intellectual orphan bereft of a committee chair, graciously agreed to undertake that task for me, even though he was not particularly conversant with the methods I employed or the field area in which I worked.

I have received both assistance and encouragement from a number of colleagues and friends. In particular the contributions of P. L. Amin Sweeney and Zainab Sweeney to my field research, and to the morale of both Karen, my wife, and I while in Kelantan, are enormous and are only sketchily indicated in the following pages. I also want to express my appreciation for the support and friendship Clive Kessler showed both of us during that same period. I also wish to acknowledge the support of Donald Brown, Carrie Chu-Brown, and Joel Savishinsky. They are colleagues and friends of long standing, and I have profited both intellectually and personally from our association.

I want to thank my daughter, Alethea, for accurately and efficiently transcribing Karen's journal to my computer, where the information could be electronically searched. I want to acknowledge my debt to Kathy Salzman, a good friend and better wordsmith than I, who read and commented upon a draft of this manuscript. Additionally I want to recognize and to thank Douglas Herrmann, a psychologist with whom I have worked for many years, and who also read and appraised an earlier version of this work. I am indebted to him for his continued professional assistance and especially for his almost flawless friendship. Indeed, excepting my brother, Bruce, he is my favorite Republican.

I also want to express my gratitude to my students, both former and current, who reacted to much of the following material. Their responses, both positive and negative, helped me to shape both the contents of this work and the manner of its presentation. In particular I am indebted to Thomas Galizia, Thad Mantaro, Michelle Bonitto, and Shawn Wells for their continuing friendship and their support.

Special debts are owed the Kelantanese villagers of Wakaf Bharu with whom we lived and worked. As the ensuing narrative will relate, a number of these people became, and still are, good friends. I will not name them here, as they are described later, but I do also wish to acknowledge my gratitude to other Wakaf Bharu villagers who are not named in this work, and to the many friends in Kota Bharu and elsewhere who were so helpful during the first period of fieldwork. In particular Sidique Merican and his family, and Len and Jean Crossfield provided welcome hospitality and considerable support. More recently, I am indebted to Amran bin Mohammed Arifin, Azahar bin Haji Yacob, and Azuddin bin Abdul Rahman for assistance and support during later fieldwork ventures. Finally, I owe a special debt to Dr. Anuar Masduki who quite literally saved my life. But that is another story best told elsewhere.

Then there is the small matter of the production of this book. I owe Waveland in general, and Tom Curtin in particular, a debt of sincere gratitude. They let me write my own book, in my own way and by my own means. Tom's frequent response to my various requests: "Sure. Do it." If people find out just how much fun it is to work with this press, Waveland will have its hands full.

There remains but one acknowledgment, that for the efforts and contributions of Karen Jones Raybeck. The following pages will give some indication of the debt I owe her for her observations on village life, for her continued help during the fieldwork on which this book is based, and especially for her companionship. She not only steadfastly endured an experience she found less than enthralling, but she also had the good sense to maintain a daily journal in which she noted many details that escaped my field notes. Much of the following derives as much from her journal as it does from my field notes.

Table of Contents

Wakaf Bharu, Kelantan Malaysia

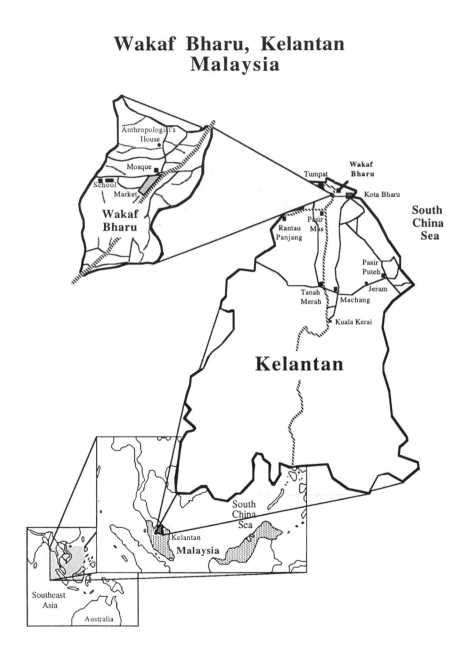

1

The Dawn of Interest

A nthropology is inherently interesting. At least I have always found this to be the case. It is a special lens through which we can view the world. And, like dark glasses used for fishing, anthropology can reduce surface glare, allowing one to see deeper into areas often cloaked in shadow. It can penetrate the iridescence of the exotic and mysterious, to reveal human commonalties among unfamiliar particulars. Just as importantly, by altering our view of the world about us, it can display the unusual in the mundane surroundings with which we are perhaps too familiar. If you are at all curious about humans and their behavior, anywhere and anywhen, anthropology is inherently interesting. Anthropology studies the full range of human behavior and beliefs. Its compass includes our cultures and thoughts, our languages, our prehistory, our environment, every aspect of existence that we have created or altered. Also, unlike any other social discipline that focuses on humans, anthropology includes a concern with our animal nature, with how we have evolved, and with some of the possible cultural and behavioral consequences of our physical makeup.

It is specifically because anthropology studies all of humanity, rather than simply a portion, that its comparative perspective is so valuable. Fish never know they are wet, because they lack a contrast. Likewise people unfamiliar with other patterns of belief and behavior can never realize the particular nature of their own patterns and customs, nor can they surmount them. To the extent that we take our cultural patterns for granted, we are captives of them. Intellectual and personal freedom begins with an awareness that alternatives are possible.

We are constrained to view the world in a narrow fashion by what are termed "cultural filters." Not surprisingly, people judge the world about them within the bounds of their own experiences and beliefs. Thus filters predispose us to assess situations in terms with which we are already familiar, rather than through novel concepts and associations. When we encounter people of different cultures, whose patterns of belief and experience are quite different from our own, the product of this meeting can easily be misinterpretation or, even worse, a violation of cultural relativity.

Cultural relativity is an argument that we should endeavor to assess the significance and meaning of any cultural element within the culture of which it is a part. Anthropologists are particularly sensitive to the dangers that cultural filters pose to attempts to understand others. Part of our training, including exposure to fieldwork, is intended to reduce the strength of cultural filters on our perceptions, though the abatement is seldom as great as we might like. Still we try, however imperfectly, to avoid fitting the meanings of others into our ideological pigeon-holes.

Perhaps more extensively than any other discipline, anthropology probes the human continuum and revels in both the differences and the similarities that it discovers there. The methods employed by anthropologists in pursuit of human understanding vary widely. They range from highly structured, quantified, and even experimental projects, to subjective apprehensions of the meanings and motives behind human behavior. Whatever the particular method used to pursue a question or concern, virtually all anthropologists do fieldwork.

Fieldwork is one of the defining aspects of anthropology, and despite some obvious shortcomings, it is vigorously defended by anthropologists. It represents some of our beliefs concerning how best to acquire information about others. We tend to distrust questionnaires and massive surveys, since it is our experience that people who have no reason to trust you also have no reason to be truthful. We also believe that people are complex, three-dimensional entities whose beliefs and behaviors are better understood if they are observed rather than studied. By that I mean we believe we should interfere and manipulate circumstance as little as possible, so that what we encounter is as representative and as (reasonably) honest as possible.

The best way to observe humans, while minimally influencing their behavior, seems to be to live with them and to avoid, as much as feasible, interference with their patterns of belief and behavior. Consequently fieldwork involves leaving one's own cultural and social surroundings, and going to live among the people one wishes to study. The location may be part of a block in the Bronx, or it may be the entirety of a tiny South Pacific island, but the demands and difficulties of fieldwork remain similar.

Anthropologists usually conduct their fieldwork using a method termed "participant observation." As the name suggests, the anthropologist is supposed to be a participant in the chosen setting, while at the same time observing the behavior of others. A moment's reflection will reveal that this simple methodological prescription creates a very schizoid situation. To the extent that anthropologists participate in social life, they can not step back and objectively observe the complexities of the world about them. Similarly, to the degree that anthropologists succeed in being objective social observers, they can not be participants. Thus all fieldwork involves compromise, and there is no accepted formula for conducting good field research.

Beginning fieldwork in a foreign culture is a bit like diving into an unfamiliar pond in which you expect there may be underwater hazards. You may examine the surface of the pond at length (and breadth and width for that matter). You may even review the observations of others who have swum in the pond. Yet, when you leap in yourself, you still have an excellent chance of landing headfirst on a submerged boulder.

This book describes several adventures and misadventures involving fieldwork, as well as the understanding, humility, and, of course, bruises that these experiences leave behind. Ultimately it also relates the process of becoming familiar with the uneven cultural terrain that lies below the seeming placidity of the surface. As fieldwork is a very personal experience, so will this be a personal tale of misperception and insight, innocence and guile, culminating in a bit of personal growth and some painfully acquired self-knowledge.

For those who may be studying fieldwork, I hope this little book will give you some additional insight into the human dimension of the undertaking, a sense of how one both builds rapport in a fieldwork setting and obtains reliable information.[1] For those who have already conducted fieldwork, I hope you will encounter resonances with your own experiences and, perhaps, some occasion for amused reflection.

2

In Search of Sunlight

People can be attracted to anthropology through various lures. Some find wonder in well-written descriptions of other peoples and other places. Others may have a chance encounter with a foreigner and be confronted with unanticipated contrasts. Still others experience some of the range of human behaviors through travel. Whatever the route, encountering these differences generally produces either fear and resistance or a profitable loss of innocence. The ethnocentric conviction that "the way I behave and believe is the only way to behave and believe" falls away to be replaced by a fascination with the range of human behaviors and beliefs.

I realize that the preceding sounds a bit abstract and ideal, but this is often inherent in the way we generalize about mundane particulars. All who choose to pursue anthropology must strive to surmount the barriers erected by their cultural baggage, knowing that they can never fully succeed in this endeavor. (Anyone who claims otherwise is either naïve, stupid, or mendacious.) Each of us also brings to anthropology a distinct cultural background, individual motives, and a variety of reasons for finding the discipline attractive. It is this collection of experiences and predilections that provides us with our initial strengths . . . and weaknesses.

I confess that my own attraction to anthropology drew from several sources, the first of which was hardly intellectual and involved a fascination with my uncle's collection of *National Geographic*s. After perusing the photographs, I found myself

reading the accompanying text and becoming increasingly surprised at and interested in the ways in which the rest of the world
seemed to differ from New Hampshire in the mid-fifties.

My own cultural filters were constructed largely from a
conservative, conforming New England base. I was raised in a
village of eleven hundred people that could quite reasonably be
characterized as homogenous. Everyone was white; the great
majority were Protestants who worshipped at the classically
severe, white church in the center of the village; and most were
farmers. Indeed, the only significant minority was an island of
eight registered Democrats who maintained a somewhat precari-
ous social existence amidst a sea of Republicans.

Village life was both remarkably supportive and very intru-
sive. People genuinely cared about one another, but the caring as
often took the form of gossip and interference as it did social and
emotional support. The definitions of the desirable and the
proper were narrowly determined, with significant social penal-
ties for those who departed from village norms. It is fair to say
that I felt some discontent with this undifferentiated and rather
repressive social environment, even though, in those days, I could
not have articulated my reasons. Although I had no means of
knowing it then, my experiences in this small agrarian village
would serve as excellent preparation for fieldwork in a peasant
village on the other side of the world.

My sensitivity to the constraints of my village environment
was eventually heightened by exposure to that most dangerous of
elements—ideas. In addition to the *National Geographic*, I read
rather widely, especially for that time and place. I generally found
that my reading led to conflicts with my environment. Having read
Darwin's *Origin of Species* and some related books on paleon-
tology obtained from the state, not the local, library, I queried the
village pastor concerning the absence of evolution and of dinosaurs in Genesis. He replied that evolution was a false doctrine
planted by the devil, that there never were any dinosaurs, and
that I should cease reading such books immediately. Now people
may be asked to believe or to disbelieve in a variety of things
concerning proper behavior and the world at large, and I might
well have surrendered the abstractions that constitute evolution,
but to require a young boy to accept that dinosaurs never existed
is asking a bit much.

I continued to read disapproved books and finally encountered one that introduced the field of anthropology, not a well-known subject in those days (nor, for that matter, in these days). *Man: His First Million Years* is a beautifully written book by Ashley Montagu. It is filled with both fact and wonder, as well as with an irreducible sense of the romance of humanity's past and a delight in its current variability. I have since discovered that many anthropologists of my generation were, at least in part, drawn to this profession through that remarkable work.

As an undergraduate at Dartmouth College, I was torn between two options: a rather romantic desire to study everything, and my interest in anthropology. Fortunately it was a small tear, as anthropology is in many respects a perfect refuge for the eclectic. You can study virtually any aspect of human behavior—past, present, and even future—under the rubric of anthropology.[2] Indeed, anthropologists seem to delight in creating new subfields ranging from the anthropology of dance to ethnoscience, the study of how different cultures perceive and categorize the world about them.

Anthropology at Dartmouth in the early sixties was represented by only two full-time professors; Robert McKennan, a social anthropologist who had conducted fieldwork among Northwest Coast Native Americans early in this century, and Elmer Harp, an archaeologist noted for his work in the Arctic and for the imaginative use of aerial photography to locate former Inuit campsites. In addition, there was a colorful ethnobotanist, Al Whiting, who had a part-time position managing the anthropology collection in the museum and running "labs" for the introductory anthropology course.

The initial course I took was long on facts and short on theory. The textbook was by Beals and Hoijer, a veritable encyclopedia of anthropological knowledge that, unfortunately, also read like one. Elmer Harp, who taught the course, was clear, well organized, and interesting, but I still had trouble bringing the discipline to life. Fortunately there was a component of the course that addressed exactly this problem: Al Whiting's labs that gave students some hands-on experience with anthropology.

The labs ranged from the interestingly experiential to fairly dry assessments of classification systems in which we were expected to discover principles different from those with which we were familiar. We succeeded nicely at this task, though the principles we articulated often had precious little to do with those used by the culture from which the exercise had been derived.

We also had occasion to knap flint, to examine and classify shards of pottery, to study real human bones, and, in one memorable instance, to conduct a tiny amount of fieldwork with a Hopi Indian informant. This was my first exposure, however modest, to some of the problems that surround this anthropologically central endeavor, and I still recall it clearly.

One morning when we students entered the room that served as a lab for our introductory anthropology course, we found Al Whiting dressed as a Hopi and sitting on a blanket in the center of the room. He proceeded to do a variety of mysterious things with a few bowls and implements, while stolidly ignoring us. We waited, expecting him to rise from his squatting position and to address us; we waited, anticipating an explanation of what was transpiring; we waited, hoping for some hint as to how to begin . . . we waited. Gradually it became apparent that Professor Whiting would continue his mysterious behavior indefinitely, unless we interrupted. Haltingly we began to ask questions and, in the process, to discover that asking useful questions was much more difficult than one might think.

We first asked all of the obvious and relatively unhelpful questions. These are the ones that generally begin with "what": "what" his name was—Mr. *Paska' Hopi*, (we later discovered this meant false Hopi); "what" he was doing—fixing lunch, a rather bland rabbit stew, as we discovered after some of us had joined him on the blanket and were encouraged to partake. Mr. Paska' Hopi answered all questions fully and accurately but volunteered no information, and we soon discovered that a full answer to many questions often did little to further understanding. The following exchange is characteristic of what occurred: Student: "What are you doing?" Paska' Hopi: "Preparing lunch." Student: "Why are you preparing lunch now?" Paska' Hopi: "Because I'm hungry."

The lab went by much too quickly, and when we later encountered the questions we were asked to address, we were discomfited to discover just how little we had learned concerning Mr. Paska' Hopi, the reasons for his behavior, and what he was doing among us. At another, more important level, each of us was made painfully aware that the ethnographic facts and observations we had encountered in our anthropology readings had not been easily acquired.

There was one other aspect of that fieldwork lab that was to haunt me in just a few years. Throughout the class period, I and others wallowed in a confusion that approached helplessness. We knew the circumstances of Mr. Paska' Hopi were different, and that they were supposed to be so, but that somehow failed to provide sufficient guidance for us to operate with any sense of efficacy. As the class period rapidly passed, I found intense frustration alternating with bouts of exhilaration. The former derived from a deep sense of anomic uncertainty; the latter, from the occasionally successful glimpse into a different world. These strong emotional swings help to explain the clear memory I have of that brief introduction to fieldwork. As I was to discover, fieldwork is as much an emotional experience as it is an intellectual one.

At Dartmouth I was torn between interests in both psychology and anthropology. I solved this dilemma in my usual decisive fashion, by developing an interest in psychological anthropology. I also defined an areal interest. Like early craftspersons who were identified both by their tools and by their construction specialities, anthropologists tend to be identified by two separate labels. We are known both by our major theoretical orientation and by the cultural area with which we are most familiar, almost always the same as the area in which we have carried out fieldwork.

My interest in Southeast Asia had begun years earlier in my uncle's study, and I found my research papers and my additional reading focusing upon the region of Indonesia and Malaysia, an area known as Insular Southeast Asia. Anthropologists believe that cultures are, however imperfectly, integrated entities. Thus occurrences that affect one aspect of life resonate with others as well and often have unforeseen consequences. Individuals can also encounter this phenomenon: I found that my interests in psychology and Southeast Asia influenced my decision to pursue graduate work, and even my choice of graduate schools.

The anthropology graduate programs to which I applied possessed both strong areal offerings in Southeast Asia and strong ties to psychology. At that time my two top choices were Yale and Cornell, as both possessed the features I was seeking. Once again I was to find my dilemma resolved by fate rather than by intellect: Yale refused me admission, while Cornell offered a handsome graduate fellowship. I "chose" to attend Cornell.

At Cornell I discovered something of which I had only a dim suspicion. My preparation in anthropology, while intellectually rigorous and eclectic, was quite spotty. I lacked course work in several subject areas, including such central anthropological concerns as kinship and social organization. Fortunately for me, anthropology's encompassing nature was often reflected in admissions to graduate programs. More than any discipline with which I am familiar, anthropology departments readily admit graduate students who lack significant training in the field. My cohorts consisted not only of undergraduate anthropology majors but also those who had majored in philosophy, history, and other subjects. Thus, in hopes of being better equipped to catch elusive anthropological meanings, I and several others devoted a portion of our first graduate year to repairing gaps in the nets of our knowledge.

The anthropology department at Cornell in the mid-sixties was remarkable, both for its personnel and for its flexibility. The roster of instructors included such luminaries as Victor Turner, Jack Roberts, Alan Holmberg, Robert Smith, Morris Opler, G. William Skinner, and others.[3] Each taught courses and trained graduate students in a very flexible program. Temporary advisors were assigned to entering graduate students, who, after their first semester, were expected to choose a three-person committee that would guide them to the completion of the Ph.D. Each committee was to include a chair representing the major field and two additional members, each responsible for a subfield.

My committee was chaired by Arthur Wolf, a young psychological anthropologist who had conducted some very innovative research during a lengthy five-year period of fieldwork in Taiwan. My areal interest in Southeast Asia was overseen by Lauriston Sharp, a senior anthropologist known for his work in Thailand and for some excellent papers on Australian Aborigines. Finally, for psychology I was fortunate enough to have Bill Lambert, one of the best cross-cultural psychologists of that time and a genuinely caring individual.

These three disparate individuals were supposed to guide my training in anthropology and to prepare me for the rigors of actually doing the stuff. Together we would discuss courses that I should elect and the best means of equipping me with the intellectual baggage necessary to successfully complete the Ph.D. journey. Since I professed an interest in Bali, it was recommended I take two years of Indonesian language training; since I was interested in psychology, it was suggested I take a variety of courses within the psychology department; and since I had successfully evaded mathematics during my undergraduate years, I was instructed to take a year of graduate-level statistics. Finally, my lack of training in kinship was noted, and I was gently informed that this made me something of an anthropological illiterate.

Many people familiar with anthropology wonder about the discipline's preoccupation with kinship systems, with who is related to whom and according to what principles. Other social scientists find our interests with kinship and kinship terminology inaccessible, abstruse, and curious. They are led to this perception by terms like "circulating connubium," "asymmetrical matrilateral cross-cousin marriage," and "ramages." Fortunately there is a ready and reasonable explanation for our concern with marriage and descent systems.

Anthropologists have traditionally studied simple rather than complex societies. Do not be misled by these terms. They refer to the degree of structural complexity that characterizes their respective social organizations. Simple societies possess fewer differentiated social institutions than do complex ones, but neither the people comprising them nor their conceptual systems are ever "simple." Simple societies often lack centralized forms of government or other complex means of ordering social life. Instead, in such societies, people relate to one another through the medium of kinship, which defines and reinforces the various rights and duties that individuals owe one another. An individual's place in a descent unit, such as a lineage, and connections to other lineages via marriage are the most important elements defining social identity. Anthropologists have also found that kinship is a major means of structuring interpersonal relationships in complex societies, even in American society, which makes less use of kinship than any with which we are familiar.[4]

I had come to Cornell to prepare myself as an anthropologist specializing in Southeast Asia, with the intention of doing field research in Indonesia, specifically, Bali. However, a political upheaval resulting in massive loss of life in 1965 made fieldwork in Indonesia impossible. At this point I had already invested more than a year of language study preparing myself for field research, and I had been reading intensively on Southeast Asian societies and cultures. It appeared that I would probably not be able to enter Indonesia to conduct fieldwork and that my academic preparation for this enterprise had indeed become academic. You could describe my initial reaction to this situation as somewhat disconsolate. Similarly you could describe Mount Everest as rather tall. I did not like the thought of having invested time and effort on seemingly irrelevant preparation, even though I knew that all knowledge is ultimately interlinked; and, in anthropology especially, knowledge garnered about one society is often apt to be useful in understanding aspects of another, if only by increasing the perception of contrast. Thus I sought a means to maximize the utility of my language and areal knowledge, while still meeting my intellectual interest in questions concerning psychological anthropology.

Happily the Indonesian language, both its grammar and most of its vocabulary, was based directly upon Malay, the major language of the Malay Peninsula. Further, there were significant similarities between Malay culture and society and that of Java, with which I was already somewhat familiar. Finally, the literature on Malaysia was not nearly as extensive as the literature on Indonesia; becoming familiar with it actually appeared quite possible. As you have probably surmised, I decided to switch my field site to somewhere in the Malay Peninsula.

My increasing familiarity with the literature on Malay society convinced me I had made a good choice. Malay society has been subject to many syncretic influences. In addition to a set of rich indigenous cultural traditions, there are clear influences from China and India in everything from language to religion. Further, Malaysia is strongly Islamic, and there are some intriguing conflicts between Islamic doctrine, and practices that are supported by traditional culture.[5] Finally, like Javanese society, the kinship system is bilateral. In bilateral kinship systems descent is traced through both men and women, much as it is in the United States, and descent does not form large corporate kinship groups that can often strongly influence, and even control, the behavior of members. This means that Malays often face complex kinship options in which choices motivated by political and economic considerations are freer than they would be in a society with a more constraining kinship system. Since I was developing interests in decision making and in the interplay between belief and behavior, these characteristics created a favorable field setting for research.

I believe it may be time for another awkward, but useful, confession. Many of you probably imagine this period of graduate preparation as arduous, demanding, dull, and tiresome. The first two adjectives are generally accurate, but seldom the latter two. One of the blessings of being a graduate student is that you are surrounded by cohorts who are variegated and interesting, and who share a common fascination with the chosen subject matter. Anthropology grad students are even more variegated than most, at least as interesting, and often well traveled. Further, they tend to be sociable, garrulous, and even somewhat eccentric. They are also the source of at least half one's graduate training.

One of the lesser known truths about graduate education is that half of it transpires in hallways, bars, and apartments, rather than simply in classrooms and libraries. Graduate students delight in discussing the latest theories, books recently read, lectures heard, and ideas encountered. They serve as useful stimuli to one another and, in the process, also save each other a great deal of firsthand research.

I was particularly fortunate in my graduate cohort. Not only did a very bright, personable, and attractive student of China, Karen Jones, become my wife, but I encountered many friends whose ideas and shared enthusiasm greatly increased the pleasure of the graduate experience. The importance of this kind of support is easily underestimated. Unlike undergraduate education, where the course work and expectations are carefully structured by the faculty, a great deal of graduate education is constructed by the student. This requires both motivation and a good deal of self-discipline, qualities that are not always prominent in early morning hours.

The majority of my course work was in anthropology, and the issue of fieldwork arose fairly often. Indeed, various members of the anthropology faculty took pains to impress me, and other graduate students, with the mystique of fieldwork. We were informed that it was a singularly important and necessary part of becoming an anthropologist (library theses were discouraged). We were given the impression that this experience served as a rite of passage, a transition that could transform one from a pedestrian scholar to a sensitive and perceptive observer of the human condition, possessed of increased wisdom and maturity.[6]

Despite the centrality of fieldwork to our chosen profession, we graduate students received no instruction in what it was or how to do it, a situation that has changed greatly since then. Indeed, when I, attempting to improve my grasp of this impalpable method, enrolled in a graduate seminar titled "Methods in Anthropology," I found that it involved reading most of the writings of Bronislaw Malinowski, an anthropologist famous for initiating fieldwork methods. Unfortunately, while such works as the *Sexual Life of Savages* were interesting and even edifying, they did little to dispel the mysteries surrounding fieldwork. Even reading the then recently published (and expurgated) field diary of Malinowski (1967) provided few pointers beyond the obvious: fieldwork was a difficult, lonely experience that could exacerbate personal problems.

In most graduate disciplines, students are divided into three categories: those who are newly entered, those who have passed their qualifying exams, and those who are working on their dissertations. In anthropology, however, there is an additional distinction that is at least as significant as the others: those who have completed fieldwork. There is a bit of a mystique attached to those who have gone out to a field site, lived there for a lengthy period, and successfully (or at least reasonably successfully) completed a program of research. Returning graduate students often add to the aura surrounding fieldwork with tales of personal adventures, culinary surprises (usually unsavory ones), and bouts of illness due to mysterious causes.

The actual process of conducting research is seldom described by returning students, except when there have been untoward, preferably colorful mishaps. However, since "Things go awry" is the one dictum that best characterizes the process of fieldwork, such events are not rare, and tales about them can yield instructive information. Unfortunately this information usually illustrates what one should not do rather than what one should.

New graduate students quickly gain the impression that no matter how well prepared for a field setting one is, no matter how much one has read, no matter what courses one has elected, in the field unanticipated complications nearly always arise. Irrespective of training, intelligence, and natural talents, things go awry. The year I entered Cornell, one of the advanced students was preparing for his fieldwork in American Samoa. He planned to make a comparative study of sexual arousal/anxiety between young adults in the United States and in Samoa. He chose, as his major research tool, a type of treated paper that could be applied to the palm to measure galvanic skin response, an indication of excitivity. Pretesting in the United States consisted of exposing willing volunteers to two series of slides in a darkened room. One series consisted of innocuous representations such as barns and country vistas, while the other series involved images of unclad men and women occasionally embracing. Following each series, subjects were tested with the treated paper, which did indeed indicate that the sexually oriented material produced a higher level of subject arousal.

Graduate students are seldom independently wealthy, and one of the usual prerequisites for fieldwork is adequate funding. This means that students must apply to a funding agency, either government or private. They attempt to persuade the agency that the fieldwork is worthy of support and that the applicant possesses the skills and knowledge to successfully complete the proposed research. Our senior graduate student applied to the National Institute of Health, and he did so with the assistance of one of anthropology's luminaries. Margaret Mead had conducted her initial fieldwork in Samoa, and she found the student's proposal sufficiently promising to warrant her endorsement. This seemingly well-prepared student obtained funding and left for Samoa, where, using slightly different materials adapted for Samoa, he hoped to replicate the study he had already conducted in Ithaca, New York.

Our apprentice anthropologist, a bright young man suitably trained and funded, arrived in Samoa, got situated, and began his research. Shortly thereafter he rather ruefully terminated his research. Despite the student's intelligence, preparation, and training, it seems that he had omitted one small factor from his research design: the weather. Samoa is a tropical island, and the weather is consistently hot and humid. When our student employed his treated paper to gauge baseline levels of arousal among Samoans, he found that either they perspired more than the Ithacans who enjoyed a temperate clime, or that Samoans were the most aroused people on record: possible but not likely. Our student was forced to abandon his prepared research program and instead carried out a study of Samoan family structure. Things go awry.

The anecdote illustrates how difficult it is to anticipate all of the possibilities that can impact a research program. It also demonstrates why anthropologists, as well as having a research speciality, are well trained in the basics of the field. It is fairly common for research objectives to alter once you are in the field. The alteration may be due to unforeseen difficulties or to the appearance of an equally unforeseen opportunity. Should either occur, one must be prepared to redesign completely the research program to meet new challenges that could not have been anticipated, and to continue research efforts in the absence of consultation with other anthropologists. Funding agencies are occasionally bemused by the strange turns that anthropology projects take, but they have (generally) learned that such changes are either necessary or desirable. Indeed, many of these unforeseen changes lead to serendipitous findings.[7]

Worried about my own choice of field sites, I read widely in the literature on Malaysia in an effort to become familiar with the culture. Kelantan, on the east coast of the Malay Peninsula, came to my attention because it met all of the requirements that I understood were necessary for a successful fieldwork experience. It was exotic, little studied, and reasonably accessible. Although Kelantanese were reputed to speak a somewhat difficult dialect of Malay, they were also supposed to be quite hospitable to strangers. Furthermore, compared to the states on the west coast, Kelantan was comparatively undeveloped and had a traditional Malay culture that elsewhere had been adulterated by modernization and exposure to other cultural influences.

I also read virtually all of the anthropology and much other literature written about Kelantan, a relatively modest task in the mid-sixties, and I obtained a field research grant from The National Institute of Mental Health. My research project proposed the use of a psycholinguistic device, the semantic differential, to study traditional values in Kelantan village life. The methodology would thus be a blend of experimental/empirical and interpretive/subjective. My hope was that the two approaches would compliment and strengthen one another, providing me with deeper and more reliable insights into Kelantanese culture.

Prior to departing for the field, I managed to arrange a semester in London. There I had the good fortune to study some Kelantanese dialect at the School of Oriental and African Studies with Amin Sweeney, at that time a graduate student about to undertake his dissertation research. Amin was and is a singular person who figured prominently in my fieldwork experiences. Finally, I contacted one of the doyens of anthropology, Raymond Firth, who, together with his wife, Rosemary, had worked in Kelantan in the early forties and again in the early sixties. I have a very high regard for Firth's unassuming brilliance and for his kind and gentle manner toward the most fumbling of graduate students. He generously provided me with assistance and my first real advice about the fieldwork process.

By now I was a well-trained graduate student in anthropology, steeped in the general literature on Southeast Asia, especially that on Kelantan. Further I had consulted two individuals who knew the area well and had even made some progress toward mastering the rather difficult local dialect. It might seem I was suitably armored against ignorance and error. That was my intent and my fervid hope, but . . . things go awry.

3

Arrival in the Sun Belt

Initial (dis)Orientation

E ntering the field can be a delicate matter. An anthropologist's presence needs to be acceptable to the authorities, as well as to those with whom one will work. However, it is also desirable to retain as much freedom of choice and movement as possible. One can either proceed "by the numbers," consulting each level of the bureaucracy from the national to the local levels and gaining written permission for research, or one can simply obtain a visa, enter the field site, sit down, and hope for the best. These two approaches offer contrasting strengths and weaknesses. Bureaucracies, especially those of developing nations, are notoriously slow and problematic in operation. Like an elephant's offspring, the production of a bureaucratic decision may take as long as two years and look rather strange once it has arrived. However, permits from authorities help to insure that one's work will not be called into question, and they provide safeguards against the disruption of research. In contrast, entering an area without permission saves a great deal of time and avoids government constraints but lacks the security that can be obtained through the more formal approach.

As with many dichotomous situations, the best choice is often a compromise. I decided to obtain the bare necessity—an entry visa. Karen and I spent two weeks in Kuala Lumpur, the capital of Malaysia, while I daily wrestled with bureaucrats in order to obtain an entry visa that would permit us to remain in Kelantan for three months. Malaysia had been a British colony, receiving its independence in 1957. The British left behind a sound infrastructure, a penchant for using English in both business and government affairs, and one of the more efficient and honest civil services in Asia. The permit was obtained in a span markedly shorter than the gestation period of an elephant.

Our stay in Kuala Lumpur gave us an opportunity to begin to acclimate to the change in weather. To envision an approximation of the climate on the Malay Peninsula, think of southern Florida during a heat wave. Peninsular Malaysia is just north of the Equator, and the phrase hot and humid only begins to hint at the reality of a day during the hot season (there is no cold season, just the rainy season, which trades temperature for even greater humidity). We were able to oscillate between periods of sweltering heat and the comfort of an air-conditioned hotel room, but we knew that an unremitting torrid reality awaited us in Kelantan.

Full of hope and slightly nervous, Karen and I arrived at Kota Bharu, the capital of Kelantan, on January 9, 1968. We took up temporary residence in the Hotel Rex, a cubical stucco compromise between comfort and going native, while I set about trying to familiarize myself with the city, buy a secondhand motorcycle, locate a suitable field site, and coincidentally, understand what was being said to me. It seems that people could understand my halting, standard Malay but insisted on answering in machine-gun bursts of plosives, fricatives, and sibilants that bore little relation to the language I had learned at Cornell, and which was both much more rapid and much less intelligible than the kindly paced and carefully articulated phrases to which Amin Sweeney had exposed me only months earlier.

Over the next few weeks we began to become familiar with our new location. Our experiences ranged from frustration with our insufficient language skills to exaltation when we actually accomplished something, such as buying an underpowered, secondhand Yamaha 125 cc. motorcycle. All this was accompanied by that hallmark of fieldwork in the tropics, persistent dysentery. Amidst these difficulties, which were complicated by occasional heat prostration (we were 6 degrees north of the equator) and continual bewilderment, there was one precious asset—an experienced pilot to assist in navigating these unfamiliar waters. Amin Sweeney had arrived in Kelantan a month before us and charitably provided his time, assistance, and friendship throughout the fieldwork period. Born in England, Amin had lived for years in Kelantan and had married a wonderful Kelantanese woman, Zainab. During his stay in Kelantan, Amin had learned the local language and customs and was exceptionally well suited to assist wandering would-be anthropologists in search of truth and beauty. One such individual was Clive Kessler, a graduate student from London, also conducting field research in Kelantan in an area well to the south of Kota Bharu. Clive was to become a good friend and occasional visitor to our new "home."

During these initial weeks, both Karen and I experienced a degree of culture shock—a sense of disorientation and intellectual insecurity as the result of exposure to patterns of behavior

Our friend, mentor, and occasional savior, Amin Sweeney, with his (then) young son Mubin.

markedly different from those in which one had been reared. The problem with fieldwork is not that *things* are different; one expects *things* to be different. The difficulty is that nearly *all things* are or can be different, and the neophyte has no means of anticipating which *things* will require special attention. It is not the big questions that exhaust you; those have been planned for and are, at least in part, anticipated. It is the little, commonplace experiences, which would ordinarily be taken for granted, that are the source of unending concern. People smile. Why did they smile? Are they simply being friendly, or did I do something foolish? Should I smile back? How long? How broadly? Am I too concerned about this? I cannot detail here the myriad ways in which Amin and Zainab eased the initial shock of fieldwork and provided a psychological haven from the storms of insecurity that attend such endeavors, but the debt is both significant and enduring.

The first two weeks were spent in search of an appropriate field site. The choice of a field site is among the most important decisions made in the initial stages of fieldwork. It takes months even to start becoming familiar with a community, to build rapport, and to develop a sense of mutual trust between anthropologist and community members. Choose an inappropriate setting and those months are largely wasted, and the whole process must be reinitiated somewhere else.

Since my research was to focus principally upon traditional values and deviance, I knew that I would have to invest a good deal of time gaining the acceptance and trust of those with whom I would be living for a year and a half. I also knew the qualities of the community I was seeking: it should be a reasonably typical, traditional peasant village subsisting on wet rice agriculture; it should possess a standard market and thus serve as a locus of activity for surrounding communities, and it should have a fair-sized Chinese population as interethnic relations was one of the topics in which I was interested. All of these were good, objective, professional considerations, but additionally my wife and I were hoping to be near the state capital, where we could buy such desirable provisions as film, canned food, pocket books, and ice cream, and where we could see the occasional movie and escape the confines of village life.

Admittedly these last concerns fall somewhat short of those recommended in texts on fieldwork, but they *are* important. As we will see, the demands of fieldwork are unremitting, and the need for occasional escapist pursuits is genuine and undeniable. It is far better to address one's human needs than to attempt to deny them in the service of an ill-considered image of a constant and sterling researcher.

On my well-used Yamaha, I began to explore roads, paths, and trails in search of an appropriate village (*kampong*). Motorcycles are better adapted to villages, with their winding footpaths, than are cars, which are constrained to roads. Motorcycles also allow air to cool the rider, enabling one to forget the equatorial location and to acquire a sunburn of impressive magnitude. I spent a full day in my bed, my badly sunburned arms stretched out to either side, vowing to pay greater attention to the little details of life in the tropics. Things go awry.

The desire to leave the city and enter a village was given new impetus in late January when Chinese New Year began. The Chinese in rural Kelantan are relatively inconspicuous and usually few in number, but as on the west coast of the peninsula, they congregate in urban centers where they wear traditional Chinese garb and openly practice their customs (Gosling 1964; Raybeck 1980). As many know, the Chinese welcome the New Year with fireworks and other noise-making devices. What you may not appreciate is just how this is done. Large strings of interconnected fireworks are set off day and night, outdoors and in. Karen and I were enjoying dinner in a Chinese shop (*kedai*) when two young men entered, hung a succession of forty strings of fifty firecrackers, lit them, and left. We quickly followed. Sleep became impossible for the next few evenings, and I redoubled my efforts to locate a suitable village setting for my research.

My search strategy was both simple and ineffective. When I came across what I judged to be a promising village, I would stop at a coffee shop, which both my reading and Amin assured me was a center for local gossip and information. I would make inquiries concerning the nature of the village and whether or not there was a house to rent. This slapdash approach led to numerous conversations with assorted villagers of a semi-intelligible nature. They could generally understand me; I seldom understood them. People were friendly, and there were many offers of houses to rent, but invariably one or more of the village characteristics I was seeking would be absent. Finally, in a fit of humility, I asked Amin for suggestions. He recommended Wakaf Bharu, a village that met my above-mentioned criteria and that was situated on Kelantan's lone railway, just across the Kelantan River and only eight miles from Kota Bharu, the state capital.

One of the few fieldwork recommendations with which I was familiar was to contact a local person of high status prior to entering a fieldwork setting. With the assistance of Amin I met with the local Imam, the Islamic priest, and learned that Wakaf Bharu possessed a mosque, a grade school, and a small police post that kept local demographic records (more or less, as I was to discover later). The population was just over two thousand, a bit large but not unmanageable since my research did not require detailed household registries and the like, and there was a nice, new house that could be rented for a reasonable sum. In short, the village appeared very appropriate for my research needs.

I was interested in traditional values, the relationship between these and behavior, and the manner in which these values changed over time. Thus I needed a population that could provide a good representation of established beliefs and customs, as well as access to younger people who would be exposed to both modernization and increased education. Enculturation, a process of cultural absorption that begins at birth, can vary with both time and location. I wanted to encounter both those who had been reared in the current and, especially, those who were steeped in the customary patterns. Happily Wakaf Bharu had been separated from the state capital by the Kelantan river until only a few years earlier, when a major bridge connected the two. Consequently, despite their proximity to Kota Bharu, a city of more than forty thousand, the residents of the village followed the very traditional, rural, agrarian culture characteristic of most Kelantanese peasants.

It is vitally important for anthropologists to be conscious of the way in which others view the appearance of strangers among them. Anthropologists, because of their participant observation methodology, usually take up residence in small-scale social units. Members of such units, such as peasant villagers, are invariably suspicious of strangers, often for good reason. Consider for a moment: a strange-appearing person with an imperfect command of your language appears, settles in nearby, and states an intention to study or to "get to know" people in the area. Further, this individual has no visible means of support, nor does this person seem to know the essentials of maintaining life and comfort. On the contrary, this individual goes about daily scribbling in a notebook and asking interminable questions, often of the sort that a typical three-year-old could answer. Who *is* this bozo, and why is this creature here? For all these reasons, the best means of presenting oneself is to be unremittingly honest, even when this can mean looking like a fool. (More on this theme shortly.)

Village Entry

With practically no acquaintance with the village, Karen and I, assisted by Amin and Zainab, moved in with our few belongings on a Thursday afternoon on February 1, three weeks after arriving in the country. Our initial discovery was easily made: the villagers of Wakaf Bharu were at least as interested in us as we were in them. We are both Caucasian, and my wife at 5'5" was taller than most Malay males, while I at 6'4" was an extreme oddity. People surrounded the house to watch us unpack. Little children ran through the house, checking our belongings and reporting back to their better-mannered parents (who, I uncharitably surmised, may have dispatched the children just for this reconnaissance). This was our first real exposure to what was to prove our most difficult cultural adjustment, the absence of privacy.

Many Western cultures, particularly that of the United States, are enamored of privacy. We have values that enshrine it, laws that insure it, and architecture that promotes it. In contrast, a stark and uncomfortable contrast, Kelantanese lack a word for privacy, let alone a value for it.[8] The closest word Kelantanese have for privacy, *sembunyi*, means hidden or secretive, and unlike the Western conception with its spatial connotations, it implies a withholding of information from the social stage. The root, *bunyi*, means sound, both natural and spoken. The concept of privacy is not one with which most Kelantanese villagers are comfortable. Indeed, attitudes about privacy range from ambivalence to disapproval. People who withdraw from village interaction are viewed with suspicion, as it is thought that good social members should have nothing to hide from their fellows. Kelantan village society is small scale and close knit. People are expected to be accessible to one another, and even strange-ap-

pearing newcomers are expected to be available for social interaction at all times.

We had not quite finished unpacking when I had to attend
to my first social obligation in the village. Prior to our arrival, I
had made an arrangement with the man whose house we had
rented that proved to be very valuable.

For complex current and historical reasons, Kelantanese
villagers distrust outsiders, especially representatives of authority, and prefer to address their own problems independently
(Chan 1965; Downs 1967; Raybeck 1974). During a nine-month
period preceding our arrival, Wakaf Bharu villagers had suffered
a number of break-ins and thefts. Unlike a U.S. community,
which would have summoned the police, they determined to deal
with the problem themselves. The village mounted a guard (jaga)
consisting of male volunteers, mostly younger married men, who
would give one or two evenings a week to safeguard the village.
Each night several Malay males armed with clubs would patrol
village pathways from ten in the evening to four in the morning
seeking evildoers. Since the man from whom I was renting the
house was scheduled to do guard duty on Tuesday and Thursday
evenings, I had (rather cleverly) arranged to take on his obligation, thereby making a statement to the village that I was not
simply an interloper but was willing to assume some responsibilities for the privilege of residence there.

At approximately ten o'clock on my first evening in the
village, four Malay males arrived at my front door and announced
in a quiet fashion that it was time to patrol the village. Two of the
four were to become close friends and valuable, if not always
subtle, sources of information. Yusof, a stolid, strongly built man
in his early twenties with an open and (for a Kelantanese)
somewhat assertive style, had been known for youthful misbehavior but, recently married, seemed to have settled down to a
degree. Mat, a clever, wiry, young man possessing a quick sense
of humor and an occasionally mischievous manner, was a frequent companion to Yusof, and the two, as I was to discover, were
still capable of the sporadic solecism.

The four young men introduced themselves, waited while I
located a suitable pickax handle, and then set off to escort me
through the twisting maze of arteries and capillaries linking the
houses and neighborhoods of the village organism. Thoroughly
lost and bemused by the barrage of questions I was continually

encountering, I was delighted to discover that the formidable jaga was, at least for the first two hours of its operation, largely a social affair. As we passed by houses, we were often invited to stop in for coffee and conversation. I don't doubt my presence increased the frequency of the invitations, but I found that this was customary even in my absence. Thus I was presented to villagers, not simply as a nosy busybody (it became clear later that such was my true calling) but as a visitor willing to share in the social life and responsibilities of the village. The continuing association with the young men of the jaga was to lead to my first real success in delving below the surface calm of Kelantanese village culture.

Arising early the next morning, I found my first hazard waiting outside our front door, wearing a broad grin and a dirty sarong. His manner was expansive and his language incomprehensible. Gradually he made it apparent that he wished to offer me a tour of the village and that his name was Cik Din. Quite reasonably I attributed our communication difficulties to my unfamiliarity with the Kelantanese dialect and with local customs. Pleased at the friendly offer and the prospect of beginning to become familiar with the tortuous network that comprised the village pathways, I told my wife that I would skip breakfast and headed off after Cik Din.

Very shortly I was thoroughly confused by the tangle of pathways that interconnect all areas of the village. I was also unable to decipher the barrage of comments that Cik Din kept up concerning people and houses we were passing. Wanting the villagers to view me as a sociable person, I nodded and smiled at everyone we passed or chanced across. Villagers returned my smile with broad grins and quizzical looks, probably, I thought, occasioned by my odd appearance. As we wound our way among the maze of trails, we came to a remarkably dilapidated house that had buckling sides and only part of its thatch roof. Cik Din indicated with some pride that this was his home and I nodded, confirming my initial and professionally sensitive judgment that he was not a wealthy man.

After more than an hour, with the sun suggesting that we were traveling back toward our point of departure, we came across three children playing in their yard near the path. The oldest boy looked up, pointed directly at my companion, laughed, and shouted, quite clearly, "orang nakal!" Now my reading had informed me that Malay parents took great pains to train their

Cik Din, looking much as he did when, on our first morning in Wakaf Bharu, he guided me about the village.

children to be very polite toward adults. Nonetheless a Kelantanese youth had just called my guide a "naughty person," raising the not inappropriate question: Just who the hell was I walking around with, anyhow?

Despite my increasing unease, nothing untoward transpired, and we arrived back at my house shortly after having encountered the children. With my thanks and to my relief, Cik Din soon took his leave, whereupon Hussein, my next-door neighbor, walked over with a smile and the inquiry, "Why were you going about the village with *tiga-suku?*" Tiga-suku translates as three-quarters and is a colloquial Kelantanese term for someone who is intellectually impaired. I had just been squired about the community by the village half-wit. So much for the carefully orchestrated presentation of self to members of the village. Things go awry.

What makes this occurrence particularly poignant, and perhaps even educational, is that I genuinely thought Cik Din was simply a poor Kelantanese. I had studied a closely related language for two years, read all of the anthropology written on the area, worked in a profession that sensitizes one to interpersonal behaviors, and I still couldn't perceive the difference between a typical Kelantanese and one who was mentally handicapped. Lacking a sound basis for comparison, I assumed that Cik Din was simply poor and perhaps a bit odd, but maybe many Kelantanese appeared a bit odd to outsiders.

Of Friends and Factions

Our next-door neighbors consisted of a husband and wife and their twelve-year-old son. The man, Encik Hussein bin Ahmad,[9] was small, wiry, and darkly complected. He had been born in another village and moved to Wakaf Bharu, where he had prospered and now owned a tiny (10' long x 4' deep) shop where he sold freshly grated coconut, an important component in nearly all Malay curries. His closet-sized shop also stocked one of nearly everything that a person might need, from sandals to toothpaste. Hussein was bright, observant, and very knowledgeable about traditional Kelantanese custom (*adat*). Over the next year and a half he was to become a close friend and valued colleague. Some anthropologists would term him a key informant—someone who is thoughtful, observant, and given to keen insights into his own culture.

Hussein's wife, Zainab, a somewhat heavy woman with light skin owing to her half-Chinese ancestry, was voluble, gregarious, and unstintingly generous with her time and attention. Perceiving that Karen was even more adrift on this unfamiliar sea than I was, Nab appointed herself my wife's chief companion and navigator. It was Nab who introduced Karen to the mysteries of Kelantanese cooking, bargaining in the marketplace, and appropriate comportment in public. My own training was to require the efforts of numerous individuals.

The son, Yusof, spoke some English and was attending high school in Kota Bharu some eight miles away. He was a bright, inquisitive boy who was experiencing some of the difficulties and dislocations occasioned by modernization. As a student, exposed to a Western-oriented education, Yusof was coming to value modern goals and, increasingly, to devalue those traditional aspects of Kelantanese culture that he found constraining. The

My mentor and neighbor, Hussein, preparing coconut for grating at his shop in the marketplace. Arrayed behind him is a wide assortment of merchandise. Immediately behind him is an electric grinder that shredded coconut and facilitated the extraction of coconut milk, a staple in Malay curries. The roof providing shade folds down to form a wall that is locked in place at the end of the workday.

result was a growing disparity between his worldview and that of his parents, a classic generation gap exacerbated by significantly different enculturation experiences. Yusof was to prove a valuable and rather representative guide to the experiences of educated young males in Kelantan.

Wakaf Bharu, due to its size and location on the rail line, was a low-level administrative unit within the district of Tumpat. As such, it had a village clerk; a lively, literate, pleasant, and highly intelligent man, Yusof bin Daud, whom villagers also termed Yusof Kerani, or Yusof the Clerk. Yusof immediately grasped the purpose of my study and displayed more good will and provided more assistance than I had any right to anticipate. On one occasion, after we had discussed the complex customs surrounding Kelantanese wedding ceremonies, he arrived at our house with a single-spaced, four-page document detailing the consecutive steps involved in a traditional wedding. Yusof became both a close friend and a valued colleague. He, his wife, Cik Gayah, and his children figured prominently in the success of my work, and I shall always be grateful for their helpfulness, for their understanding, and for their friendship.

Yusof bin Daud at his place of employment, the Regional Council. As a literate member of the community, Yusof had significant influence and his position gave him a broad perspective on village affairs. He was an excellent source of information and advice, and remains a close friend.

I soon became aware that Wakaf Bharu was unusual, not only because of its large Chinese minority, but also because it was strongly divided along political lines. Most rural villages were strongly committed to PAS, a conservative, Malay rights party opposed to Chinese interests and distrustful of the actions of the national government. In Wakaf Bharu there were a large number of PAS supporters, but perhaps owing to the increased mercantilism of the area, there were a slightly greater number of people who favored UMNO, the United Malay Nationalist Organization. UMNO, in turn, was the major component of the Alliance party, a coalition of Malay, Chinese, and Indian parties, which controlled both houses of Malaysia's bicameral legislature and every state, save Kelantan.

Like a husband and wife discovering an unexpected and divisive difference, this situation became both personal and problematic when I learned that Hussein and his family were ardent supporters of PAS (also known by its English acronym, PMIP), while Yusof Daud and his relatives were equally committed to UMNO. The next year, in 1969, Malaysia would have its second national election, and feelings about politics and political affiliations were high. This type of factionalism is feared by field researchers for simple, easily understood reasons. To the extent that Karen and I became identified with the members of one faction, the others would probably be less interested in interacting with us, and certainly they would hesitate to confide in us.

I strongly wished to avoid offending or alienating any member of the village, yet I was frequently asked my position on local political matters and what I thought of both local and national governments. Eventually I learned to deal with this sensitive issue as a Kelantan villager would. They neither wish to give offense, nor do they needlessly alienate fellow villagers. Instead there are a variety of verbal ploys and metaphors that are invoked to avoid taking public positions. What we would regard as "waffling," they view as appropriately circumspect behavior. I began to behave like a good villager, responding to queries about my political preferences with, "My head is gray" (*Kepala saya kelabu*), or with, "I'm still on the fence" (*Saya duduk atas pagar*), or the ever popular "I don't know" (*Tahu*). I marveled at the parallels between their obfuscations and our own, and with a combination of waffling, wavering, hesitating, and omitting, Karen and I managed to remain on good terms with supporters of both political parties.

Settling In

As Karen and I prepared to enter the village, Amin Sweeney recommended I adopt a Malay name to facilitate interaction, and he suggested Abdullah, as it was not too dissimilar to Douglas. I demurred, in part because I thought that action might be misconstrued as a misrepresentation. However, after arriving in the village and speaking with several people, I found that I had inadvertently acquired a Malay name . . . Abdullah. The process was simple. People would ask my name and I would respond with Douglas, as Raybeck is phonetically strange to Kelantanese ears. Individuals with whom I had spoken would inform others of my name, and therein lay the transformation. In Kelantanese, *g* is often treated as a glottal stop and a final *s* is aspirated. Thus Douglas became Dou'lah, which is very close to Dullah, an abbreviated form of Abdullah. My father's name was Joseph, and thus I became Abdullah bin Yusof, or Cik Lah, the more informal mode of address. Karen, despite the fact that her name did not lend itself to the same transformation, was given a Malay name, Cik Ren, derived from the last syllable of her first name.

Moving about the general area meant using my often reliable Yamaha and dealing with what might charitably be termed a traffic problem. As is well known, Malaysia has adopted the British convention of driving on the left. I worked hard to accommodate to this pattern, normally without difficulty. However, lacking a steering wheel on the right to remind me of my appropriate position on the left, I discovered that turning corners could be hazardous. The tendency was to end the corner in the right (wrong!) lane, often facing a bemused driver of a much larger vehicle. As I was to learn, the size of a vehicle in Kelantan was directly proportional to its road privileges. We are familiar with complex traffic ordinances that clearly define the rules of the road and matters such as "right of way." In Kelantan it seems that they have simplified matters to the point where, instead of "right of way" it is "fright of weight." The pecking order is thus made clear to anyone on the road. Large trucks and buses have precedence over smaller trucks and cars, which are ascendant over motorcycles and trishaws. Bicycles and pedestrians are on their own. If a bit slow to regularize my driving on the left, I rapidly learned the conventions concerning vehicle size. Terror is a fine teacher.

Trishaws (*beca*) are a common and colorful accompaniment to traffic throughout Southeast Asia. A trishaw consists of a bicycle to which is attached a sturdy sidecar that sports a small awning as protection from the sun, and a rear platform on which can be stacked a range of goods. Trishaws are often brightly painted and decorated in a somewhat less than subtle fashion with multiple mirrors, photographs in frames, and assorted bits of statuary, some of which originated on the hoods of trucks and automobiles. They are generally driven by older men who, for reasons surpassing understanding, seem convinced that traffic will yield them right of way. Their unjustified expectations allow them to dispense with hand signals or other indications of driving intent, and to play the role of yet another independent variable in the stochastic patterns that constitute Kelantanese traffic.

Watching out for the often curious behavior of other motorists included paying particular attention to taxi drivers. These were usually Malays who had acquired their driving skills in the army, and whose concept of speed limit was defined by the best velocity that their Chinese-owned Mercedes could maintain. Local and long-distance taxis were a common feature in Malaysia at that time, and taxi drivers were somewhat romantic figures associated with modernization. Lacking formal education, they nonetheless managed to participate in a "modern activity," dress in Western fashion, and behave somewhat like their Western idols, who, as far as I could determine, must have been cowboys. Wearing open shirts with turned-up collars and swaggering perceptibly, they would hang out in groups in front of coffee shops, waiting to acquire a sufficient number of fares to make their trip worthwhile. Fully loaded—often overloaded—they would depart for a destination that might be as much as three hundred miles distant. Karen and I had occasion to take several long-distance taxis, and we discovered that they believed themselves to be exempt from what we had thought was the ironclad "fright of weight" rule. Apparently they believed they could substitute speed, maneuverability, and panache. Unfortunately the newspapers carried weekly reports of drivers whose speed and panache seemed to have exceeded their maneuverability.

While the roads featured a variety of vehicles and driving styles, they were also congested by local fauna. Occasionally a valuable animal may be tied to a post and allowed to forage, but more often animals are allowed to wander about seeking sustenance and shade. Ducks, goats, cattle, chickens, the occasional sheep, and water buffalo could all be found on the streets of Kelantan. Chickens were particularly problematic because they were both stupid and fast, often darting out into the road in a frantic effort to answer the question of why the chicken crossed the road. The answer was clear—because it was suicidal. If the chickens were worrisome, there was yet a larger problem. There are few things more disconcerting than rounding a sharp corner on a motorcycle and coming upon a large water buffalo standing stolidly in what you thought was your right of way. It seems that, unlike taxi drivers, the water buffalo did subscribe to the Kelantanese rules of the road, and the weight was theirs.

All anthropologists, recognizing the doctrine of cultural relativity, are supposed to respect and acknowledge the values and practices of the people with whom they live and study. This often means engaging in behaviors that one might not normally undertake, and foregoing actions that might provide offense to others. Thus, despite the tropical heat and my frequently desiccated condition, I engaged in one of the greatest sacrifices of my first fieldwork experience. Six degrees north of the equator, enduring a temperature and humidity greater than any described by Tennessee Williams, I gave up cold beer! Again, the reason was simple. Kelantanese are deeply committed to Islam, which forbids the imbibing of alcoholic beverages. While people knew I was not a Muslim, they would still have been disturbed by a pattern of open drinking, simply because it did not seem to respect their beliefs. I was candid about my drinking preferences but assured people that I would not have beer while residing in the village. (As you will soon find, this assurance was not wholly maintained, but for very good reasons having to do with my research.)

If beer was undesirable, pork was an anathema. Karen and I both wanted villagers to feel free to drop by our house to visit and chat. The custom in village Kelantan, as in many other peasant societies, is to provide a guest with some refreshment, often coffee and a pastry or a bit of curry. Our problem was the manner in which villagers viewed pork. This is difficult for some Westerners to appreciate, but pork is not simply something forbidden by Islam—it is seen as something filthy. As we would be reluctant to eat from a clean plate that had once held dog excrement, no Kelantanese would knowingly eat off a plate that had been in contact with pork. Thus, had we cooked pork in our house, many villagers would have been reluctant to come by for social visits.

One major change in our situation occurred as a response of others to our behavior. One week after we moved in, we found our landlord, Mat Kadir, a sturdy, industrious, and intelligent man, hard at work with Hussein erecting a fence about our house. He cheerfully informed us that the fence would reduce the problem with prying children and afford us some privacy. Years later I discovered this was only a part of the rationale. Kelantanese rules concerning modesty are quite restrictive, and husbands and wives are not expected to display affection toward one another, except in private (wherever that is). It seems that body contact between husband and wife, however innocuous, was to occur in the dark of night. Karen and I had occasionally embraced within the confines of what we thought of as our privacy (yes, some of us are slow learners), but we had been seen by local children and a few others. Thus the fence was intended both to increase our privacy and to reduce the likelihood that our behavior would offend others.

The Privacy Issue—Again

In the small, rural, agricultural villages of Kelantan, people, not surprisingly, take a great deal of interest in the behavior of their coresidents. They are cross-connected to one another through ties of kinship, friendship, work, shared worship, and a variety of common experiences ranging from the floods of the rainy season to the traditional entertainments of the dry season (Raybeck 1992a). As in many other peasant communities, gossip is a social constant, serving both as a form of entertainment and as an element of social control (Campbell 1967; Gaffin 1991: 1538).

Villages are nucleated, with a series of roads and paths leading through the village to the rice fields beyond. Houses, elevated on pilings, invariably face the trails, with front porches providing a location from which residents may watch and interact with passersby. In this context the traditional greeting is not "hello" or "how are you?" rather it is "*gi mana*" ("Where are you going?" meaning "What are you up to?"). This query is often treated in a cavalier fashion (not unlike our response to "how are you"—"fine"), and the typical response is "*Jalan*" ("Going for a walk"). However, it is possible for the inquirer to press the issue and to seek a more specific answer. In such circumstances there is pressure on the respondent to answer truthfully, if not necessarily fully, since covillagers owe one another a degree of respect that entails veritable interactions.

If this direct social visibility were not enough, there is also a high degree of indirect visibility. Like the residents of small New England villages who know what car each person drives, Kelantanese are familiar with one another's footwear. Custom dictates that a person enter another's house barefoot, leaving sandals or shoes either at the bottom of the steps leading up to the house or on the porch landing outside the front door. Neighbors and passersby can readily identify many visitors by the footwear arrayed in plain view. Such information often provides material to neighbors and friends for subtly probing questions about visitors, their purpose, and so forth. Additionally, if there is reason to suspect that the visitor has dropped in for a socially significant purpose, the visit, with accompanying surmises, may immediately enter the gossip network. Visits of interest to villagers can range from those that are thought to involve debt collection, collusion in a deviant activity, or even an approved-of act, such as a filial visit to a parent.

If the layout and conventions of villages make it difficult to obtain privacy, the structure of houses and customs concerning their use only exacerbate the problem. For instance when villagers are at home, they are expected to have a door or window open. This signifies to the village that visitors are welcome. While the sleeping portions of a house should not be entered without invitation, the front area of all houses is, to some extent, part of the public domain. Visitors may appear, settle themselves, and hold converse without the "host" being immediately aware that there are guests about. On several occasions I entered our main room from my study and was surprised by the presence of several quiet visitors who were simply waiting for my appearance. This sort of social accessibility is expected of all villagers and is part of *budi bahasa*, a code of courtesy I will describe shortly. Guests are always welcomed and will be offered refreshments, minimally coffee and perhaps food.

The architecture of traditional Malay houses allows some visual privacy but impedes auditory privacy both within the structure and between it and neighboring houses. As figure 1 indicates, traditional houses are constructed of light materials, including woven pandanus walls that are permeable to both wind and sound. While contemporary houses now use wooden planks, the air vents near the roof are almost always retained so that air may circulate to help cool the structure. Further given the nucleated structure of the village, houses are frequently within ten to thirty feet of one another. This household proximity, coupled with their permeability to sound, means that any argument or occasion of raised voices will likely be heard by neighbors who will, should it prove interesting, promptly enter the information into the gossip network.

Typical Kelantanese House

Open space for escaping smoke

Atap leaf roof

Gaps for ventilation

Woven pandanus mat walls

Wooden or cement pilings

Neighbors to either side at distances of 10 to 35 feet

Two Common Floor Plans

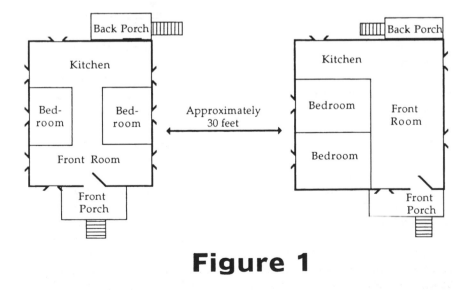

Back Porch

Kitchen

Bedroom

Bedroom

Front Room

Front Porch

Approximately 30 feet

Back Porch

Kitchen

Bedroom

Bedroom

Front Room

Front Porch

Figure 1

If Kelantan villagers are visible to one another, how much more so the lanky anthropologist and his wife. Our consistent problem was that we were always on display, even in our home. This means our performance for others either had to be unfeigned or be constantly monitored. We opted for what I believe to be the better choice and were honest in most of our behaviors. However, much of our genuineness was a reflection of the limitations of our privacy and thus unavoidable, even when it resulted in significant embarrassment.

Kelantanese are much more casual about basic bodily functions than are most Westerners. They are not sensitive about such matters, and it is not uncommon to find someone discussing the state of their bowel tract in a public setting. Further, as I discovered to my considerable discomfiture, my own bodily processes could become a source of village-wide concern . . . even entertainment.

My problem was not simply that I was white, tall, and strange. I was also unfamiliar with the local dialect, with local custom, and, very importantly, with local intestinal flora. This last unfamiliarity was painfully resolved through a series of awkward "introductions." As those who have traveled in the tropics know, dysentery is one of the world's more cunning disorders. It seldom strikes when one is in easy reach of toilet facilities, preferring to wait until the victim is well distanced from any easy means of relief.

I should note here that throughout much of Asia, the term "toilet facilities" does not connote the comfortable seating that we attribute to the good Mr. Crapper. Asian toilets, while usually ceramic, are essentially holes over which one squats in what, for Westerners, is a perilous position calling for both balance and endurance. In village circumstances, added tension is created by thoughts of errant millipedes and other small fauna that might threaten one's exposed nether regions. All in all, a rural Asian toilet is not a place to read the Sunday paper.

Many of my early forays through the local environs were interrupted by unanticipated bouts of diarrhea. The power of dysentery to shape behavior is impressive. Given the usually rudimentary nature of village toilet facilities, I felt strongly compelled to return home where there was a proper outhouse and an adequate supply of toilet paper, a substance not then common in village Kelantan. When summoned in such a fashion, I would quickly mount my underpowered motorcycle, crank the engine up to something approaching five thousand rpm, and tear down the dirt trails toward home at the best speed I could manage. Arriving, I would leap from the bike, run through the house and out to the privy in back, where I would spend a rueful half hour or so contemplating the competing calls of science and of nature.

I trouble to reveal this because of the impact it had on villagers and on me. This pattern of behavior, coupled with my desperate haste, was soon noted and the cause accurately diagnosed. Thereafter when I tore down village paths, small children would come to the edge of their front yards to cheer me on and wish me well. Shortly thereafter, people I met in the market and elsewhere in the village would comment (in what seemed to me an overly loud voice) on my predicament, ask after the state of my bowels, and frequently suggest home remedies. I don't doubt that my difficulties helped humanize me in the eyes of villagers, for intestinal difficulties are not uncommon in Kelantan and, like the weather, are a frequent source of light conversation. However, the clash between Kelantanese attitudes toward bodily functions and those with which I had been reared in New Hampshire was severe, and one that I never fully overcame.

Anthropologists, despite their respect for cultural relativity, their training in professional doctrine, and their (usually) broad acceptance of variety, still carry with them their own cultural baggage. This must be acknowledged for reasons both personal and professional. At the personal level, people attempting to deny their own preferences and values greatly increase the difficulty of field research, which generally lasts for a year or more. Professionally any anthropologists who forget that they actively filter the information they acquire often incur the cost of hubris—and accept without reservation their own misinterpretations. It is always better to be insecure in one's assessment of a different culture. The passage of time invariably succeeds in revealing interpretive blunders, allowing anthropologists to make far more sophisticated explanatory errors and to deepen their appreciation of the difficulty of the task of understanding another culture.

Out in Public

In the initial stages of fieldwork, the anthropologist appears to be a cross between a precocious child and an idiot savant. It was clear that I was an educated foreigner and therefore, presumably, intelligent. Nonetheless I was unaware of basic cultural elements known to any Kelantanese five-year-old. In many respects I behaved like a bright but untutored child, badly in need of enculturation. Happily the villagers of Wakaf Bharu proved to be tolerant and helpful parents who undertook my education with enthusiasm and good humor.

Their good humor was usually occasioned by one of my gaffes, which tended to be of two sorts: those that could be attributed to absolute ignorance, often coupled with a tendency to transpose assumptions from U.S. to Kelantanese culture, and those that arose from well meaning, but imperfectly executed, efforts to adapt to village society. Two examples will illustrate the differing ways in which I learned humility, though I would entreat the reader not to view these as typical of my fieldwork.

Very early in my fieldwork I was invited to attend a traditional Kelantanese wedding. Following the wedding I was seated cross-legged on a woven pandanus mat in a circle of five males preparing to enjoy the postwedding feast. There was a shallow bowl before me and a glass of clear, cool water by my right hand. I was the only one in the circle so equipped, but I assumed that my companions were simply making life easy for me as they had done several times already. As it was a hot afternoon (it seemed they all were), I picked up the glass and took a long drink, noticing gradually the somewhat curious looks my associates were giving me. Finally one of my companions leaned toward me and whispered some useful information. It seems Malays eat with their right hands and prior to meals (why wasn't this in any of the ethnographies I had read?) they wash the right hand by pouring water over it into a shallow bowl. I had just drunk the wash water, an act akin to sipping from a finger bowl. Things go awry.

The second class of gaffe is illustrated by a series of events that occurred after two months in Wakaf Bharu, when some of our village friends suggested Karen and I might be more comfortable wearing a local sarong (*kain*) rather than the hotter and more confining Western-style clothing we had worn to that point. Attracted by an invitation that seemed to suggest increasing acceptance of us (it did), we both decided to don traditional village garb . . . unfortunately with very mixed results.

Karen and I went with a friend to purchase several kain, or sarong, at the local market. Most sarongs are imported, preferably from India but increasingly from Japan, and are a standard

length of approximately four feet. They are sewn longitudinally forming a tube which is donned over the head, and, in the case of women, folded and then tied on the side with a knot that is then tucked under the taut fabric. For males the sarong is snugged with two center tucks and then folded down until a roll of fabric forms a natural belt. Kelantanese males pull their kain up just under their armpits and then roll the fabric down to their waists, where it supplies stability and insurance against embarrassment. This leaves them with the bottom of the kain just brushing the top of the foot; only a crude and uneducated hick (*orang darat*) would wear his kain halfway up his ankles.

Karen, at 5'5," looked quite attractive in her colorful collection of sarongs, and she garnered a number of compliments on her appearance. I, on the other hand, was not quite as well adapted to the long, flowing sarong. Adding fuel to a well-tended fire, I further agreed to wear a *baju Melayu*, a Malay-style overshirt of light cotton, which is cut full with a belled waist and belled sleeves. Kelantanese, being of modest stature, look quite attractive in such garb. However, I am long and lanky, and when attired in sarong and baju Melayu my mirror informed me that, despite the compliments I received from villagers, I most closely resembled a becalmed sailing ship.

Nor was appearance the worst of my travails. The average Kelantanese male is about 5'4" tall, and I am a foot taller. This simple fact created a dilemma. Being tall, I could not begin to roll my kain under my armpits and still have the bottom anywhere in the vicinity of my feet. I could either wear my kain according to the dictates of fashion or I could wear it securely, but not both. I opted for social acceptance and wore my kain as low as possible, allowing myself only two fragile rolls of the material to secure my modesty. In the process of accustoming myself to wearing a kain, I made some important and expensive discoveries: sarongs are remarkably poorly suited for motorcycle riding, and as most

◄ A *bersanding*, a traditional part of a Kelantanese wedding in which the bride and groom are literally King and Queen for a day (Raja sa-hari). Bersanding has its origins in India and follows the less elaborate but essential Islamic Nikah, in which the couple are actually wed. The bride appears lightly complected because she has been powdered. Malays have a distinct preference for light skin, especially in women.

women already know, when climbing stairs the hem of a long garment should be lifted. My discoveries were invariably accompanied by a good deal of amusement on the part of villagers, but they seemed to appreciate that I was making a genuine, if frequently inept, attempt to adapt to their mores.

If my vicissitudes provided the principle form of entertainment for our village friends, Karen was not wholly immune to error. Although we had rented a small half-size refrigerator, it was usually necessary for Karen to visit the market each morning to purchase food for the remainder of the day. She genuinely hated this daily undertaking. Part of her displeasure arose from her limited knowledge of the language, which was based on only three months of study in London just prior to our arrival; part of the problem derived from her normally reticent nature, but the greatest difficulty was due to the pressure she encountered to engage in bargaining.

As I shall detail, Malays in general and Kelantanese in particular are very sensitive to interpersonal relations, and they are quite concerned with maintaining interpersonal harmony within the village context (Firth 1966; Raybeck 1974; Raybeck 1975; Raybeck 1980; Raybeck 1986b; Wilson 1967). To facilitate harmonious relations, all villagers are schooled in a well-developed courtesy code (budi bahasa). This involves not only a set of rules for proper behavior but also the cultivation of a proper demeanor characterized by humility and indirection.

Practicing budi bahasa promotes village harmony (*sesuai*), an extremely important value, and it helps people to avoid embarrassing situations. Embarrassment only hints at the power of the emotional state. The Malay term is *malu*, and it is to embarrassment as tsunamis are to wavelets. It is a state of intense emotional discomfort usually occasioned by some social gaffe, and Kelantanese will normally go to considerable trouble to avoid malu-producing situations. Thus social life in Kelantan is complex, delicate, and sensitive. Residents are continually processing a wealth of information concerning their position vis-à-vis one another, and they are invariably conscious about the possibility of giving affront to others. There is only one area of life where these concerns do not fully obtain . . . bargaining.

Bargaining, or *tawar-menawar*, is a valued skill at which villagers strive to excel. To be known as a good haggler is to gain a measure of respect for a useful (and often highly entertaining) prowess. Prices in village markets are not fixed and can fluctuate from day to day. Nonetheless the range of fluctuation is narrow and it is known to both participants. Further, sellers commonly have a collection of "regulars." This patron-client relationship generally works well for both parties, with the seller obtaining a predictable market, while the purchaser usually gets a final price that is slightly under the market norm for that day.

Kelantanese treat the concept of pricing and sales quite differently than we do. It is viewed as a game between seller and buyer, a game in which the conventions are well established and known to both participants. The artistry appears both in the bargaining process, where verbal flourishes and expostulations are well regarded, and in the achievement of a final price, which usually manages to make both parties look good. A good haggling session will frequently draw spectators who will watch the proceedings and, upon their conclusion, invariably observe that they could have gotten a better price.

On one occasion I was returning from the market with a rolled mattress perched on my shoulder. As I walked along the dusty path toward home, several people called out to me from their front steps, inquiring how much the mattress had cost me. In the United States such a question would be highly impolite, but in Kelantan it is both proper and neighborly to make such a query. It opens possibilities to play the game. I had bargained to get the price of the mattress down from M$55 to M$37, a figure of which I was quite proud, but two of my three inquirers were quick to inform me that they could have gotten a better price.[10]

In the United States, bargaining occurs only at the occasional garage sale or similar venue. For the most part prices are fixed, and a suggestion to a clerk that an item might be worth less than it is marked will only garner surprise and perhaps amusement. Karen was accustomed to this pattern, which strictly limits interaction to functional exchanges between customer and salesperson. Indeed, in many establishments it is possible to locate and buy several items, pay for them, and never exchange a word. Karen regarded this as an eminently sensible approach to the task of shopping. She was quite unhappy with the necessity of purchasing goods in the local market.

Cik Nab, believing that Karen was unskilled at bargaining—rather than simply unwilling to engage in the practice—usually gave her a list of approximate prices for common foodstuffs to insure that she would not be overcharged. Indeed, she often accompanied Karen to the marketplace to oversee the purchasing process. This worked reasonably well, save that Karen still hesitated to enter into a real bargaining situation. Her reluctance to bargain eventually became a matter of wider concern.

Karen often purchased chicken in the market, and like a good villager, she frequented one particular seller, a wizened but lively old woman who sold chickens in a variety of guises: live on a string (lead it home and do it in yourself), dead—both with and without feathers—and cooked. The woman would suggest an inflated price that Karen would promptly pay, taking the chicken and returning home. (Unlike Kelantanese, Karen did not find the few pennies' difference between the real and suggested prices worth the trouble of bargaining.) This continued for some time until the old woman began to hint to my wife that the price could be lowered through bargaining. Karen continued to pay the price asked, taking the chicken and returning home. Finally, one morning the seller, having exhausted her store of subtleties, invited Karen to sit beside her on a woven mat where the elderly woman proceeded to laboriously explain the niceties of bargaining: "First, I ask much more than the chicken is worth, then you offer less than the chicken is worth. We continue until we arrive at a price with which we are both pleased." Karen recognized that she would have to participate, and I was later informed by villagers, concerned with our economic well being, that she was actively bargaining in the marketplace.

This anecdote illustrates both a basic anthropological point and an important aspect of Kelantanese culture. Cultural relativity suggests that one cannot assume that one's own values are easily exported to other cultural contexts. This can include basic assumptions about economic behavior. In the 1950s there was a dispute between anthropologists and classical economists, the latter arguing that many non-Western peoples did not behave in an economically rational fashion; that is, they did not strive to maximize their gains and minimize their losses. Anthropologists took pains to demonstrate that economists were defining value in too narrow a fashion, and that, once nonmaterial values were taken into account, all peoples behaved rationally.

In Kelantan the value associated with skillful bargaining is such that the elderly woman was willing to give up some profit in order to engage my highly visible wife in bargaining. True to her expectations, while she made less money, she, much to Karen's dismay, did succeed in drawing an appreciative audience to the interaction.

Probably our greatest public performances occurred during the holidays, especially Hair Raya Haji, the holiday that celebrates the successful conclusion of the pilgrimage to Mecca by those who can afford it. On major holidays it is the custom of Kelantanese and other Malays to visit friends, neighbors, and relatives and to receive people at home. These celebrations provide a means of reaffirming solidarity among the individuals involved and can also be used to repair damaged interpersonal relationships (Banks 1983; Raybeck 1992b). Our first Hari Raya Haji was in early March. By that time we were somewhat adjusted to our locale, had donned Malay clothing, and had gotten to know a number of people in the area. Virtually all our friends and acquaintances, as well as some people

A holiday picture. On the far left is Yusof Ismail (my friend from guard duty), myself, Karen, and our neighbors Zainab, Hussein, and their son Yusof. Five of the six look quite attractive in Malay garb as we prepare for a round of holiday visiting. Note that Hussein's sarong touches his instep as is proper, while mine ascends halfway to my knees. Perhaps you thought the phrase, "becalmed sailing ship" was a hyperbole?

who had simply heard of us, invited us to visit for Hari Raya. Naturally one is expected to accept an invitation. To refuse risks offending the person making the offer.

Early on the morning of the holiday, a Saturday, Karen and I mounted the Yamaha and set off on a marathon effort to visit many, if not all, of those who had invited us. We were wearing our finest Malay outfits, Karen appearing quite attractive, while I, attired in what Karen uncharitably termed my "baggy finery," simply flapped in the breeze. We went to three places in Kota Bharu, including Amin and Nab's, our constant sources of support, and we followed tradition at each stop. That is, we ate, we consumed, we devoured, we ingested, we partook of sustenance beyond what we had thought possible. In the process, we furthered our familiarity with Malay foods and beverages, which, like most cuisines, range from delicious to unpalatable. Happily most Kelantanese food is excellent and consists largely of delicious curries with a coconut-milk base. Unfortunately one of the favorite beverages is a mixture of water, condensed milk, and rose syrup. Given its rather singular odor and flavor, we thenceforth referred to it as "the dirty socks drink."

Midway between visits, I once again tore my kain when straddling the motorcycle. Nonetheless I was continually informed how good I looked in my Malay garb and that people were pleased we were dressed appropriately. We returned home just after noon to hide our swollen bodies from the sun and from the gaze of others. Later, that afternoon, we courageously reappeared and visited another four houses. As these visits were within the village, we walked from house to house. Unfortunately this had an undesired effect that I should have foreseen. People seeing us pass by would invite us in to "eat just a little" (*makan sedikit saja*). By late afternoon we were in actual pain from overeating and were making a slow trek homeward when we passed some children who, unlike the well-mannered adults with whom we had been interacting, pointed at me and burst into laughter, thereby confirming my suspicions about my real appearance.

◀ A major figure in the curing ceremony, *main puteri*, this man is playing a three-stringed viol. Later he will interrogate the curer (*bomoh*) when the latter is in trance and is consecutively inhabited by an assortment of spirits. A staunch traditionalist, the interrogator is not beyond wearing a wrist watch.

Late that afternoon, we took our turn entertaining friends and neighbors and took particular delight in foisting ever more food on those who had been similarly generous to us.

Our increasing acceptance, as well as our appearance in traditional garb, led to some unanticipated difficulties when it became apparent that many of our friends hoped/expected that we might convert to Islam. After all, we were obviously trying to fit in; we respected Kelantanese custom and acknowledged local leadership positions, including the Imam, the Islamic priest. Finally, we were both becoming more proficient with the local dialect, which entailed frequent utterances drawn from the Koran. We took pains to explain that, while we had great respect for Islam, we were already committed to another belief system . . . a slight shading of the truth. This seemed to satisfy most people, though we then received queries as to why we never attended service at the Chinese Presbyterian church located in the village. Wrong denomination.

Fielding questions about personal beliefs can also be awkward. When I began making initial inquiries about a local curing ceremony in which spirits are involved, I was asked whether or not I believed in *hantu*, the term for local spirits that are often mischievous, sometimes dangerous, and something like our ghosts. This simple question was more problematic than it might appear, for I wished to do research on this subject and feared that a negative response might exclude me from some conversations, while a positive response could involve me in an increasingly awkward spiral of fabrications. Happily my recent training in the niceties of politics came to my rescue, and I summoned up my favorite all-purpose obfuscations. I said that I didn't know (tahu) and hadn't yet made up my mind (Saya duduk atas pagar—literally, "I'm sitting on the fence"). However, I did add that there were people in America who claimed they had seen ghosts, and I went on to detail some of the differences between the beliefs.

As you may have noticed, the first stages of fieldwork are disorienting and mysterious. One encounters problems for which there can be no specific preparation. Happily the rewards that occur during the period of acclimatization are often as unanticipated as the costs. On many occasions both Karen and I were befriended by people whom we hardly knew and who had little reason to regard us as anything more than curious interlopers.

Part of our kind reception is clearly due to the hospitality of the Kelantanese, but part also seems due to the manner in which we behaved in the village.

We were honest both about our purpose in being there and about our own predilections. Researchers must remember that they are highly visible, that privacy is often scant, and that the people with whom they reside will often possess strong interpersonal skills. Attempts to dissemble or to misrepresent may not be doomed to failure, but they are bound to interpose a degree of distance and caution between the anthropologist and others. This distance can easily interfere with the development of mutual trust, one of the most important elements of successful field research.

Villagers responded positively to my explanation that I was a student of their culture who would return to the United States to teach others about the customs of the Kelantanese. Kelantanese are aware and proud that they maintain a rich, traditional Malay culture that elsewhere on the peninsula has largely succumbed to other cultural influences and to modernization. Indeed, many thought it only sensible that others would wish to know about their customs so that they might emulate them.

Finally, insofar as possible, Karen and I strove to respect the beliefs and practices of those around us. We knew we were dependent on the good will of others and we acted accordingly. Our conscious efforts at adapting to local customs were well received, often with more good humor than we had anticipated . . . or, in my case, wanted.

4

Beginning to Tan

Bureaucrats and Boggles

If the process of adjusting to an unfamiliar culture bore its challenges, so too did efforts to begin the acquisition of an anthropological understanding of what was going on. Prior to entering the field, I had made an assessment of what I would be able to accomplish and how much time the investigation might involve. Indeed, to acquire funding, I was required to submit a schedule of research. It is now my firm conviction that such submissions should be labeled fiction, perhaps science fiction, and treated that way. There is no feasible way a schedule, especially one drawn up in the comfort and blissful ignorance of an office far removed from the realities of a field situation, can adequately anticipate the problems that will intrude upon one's time.

My initial difficulty, as I have indicated, derived in large part from my inadequate grasp of the local dialect. My efforts to acquire information on the subtle and complex topics of village values and shared beliefs were apt to be as successful as the efforts of an ant to capture an elephant: the closer you get, the more you realize that encompassing the entire beast may be beyond you. I decided to undertake tasks that required relatively little language skill, like map making.

For several weeks I walked about measuring distances, assessing angles, and making rough sketches in my notebook. These activities were judged by villagers to be largely harmless, if not entirely comprehensible. Everyone already knew where everything was. Why would I want to make the easy chore of becoming familiar with a locale so laborious? Once again, Yusof Daud understood what I was trying to accomplish and why and suggested to me that I try obtaining extant maps of the area and village from a government office in Kota Bharu. Willing to heed transparently good advice, and only slightly chagrined at not having thought of this myself, I headed off to the state capital to pick up my maps. Yeah, right . . . I thought I would be able to just *get* them.

I first went to the State Secretary's Office, partly because it dealt more often with foreigners and partly because I had already met an assistant secretary there who seemed quite willing to be helpful. He welcomed me into his office, we had a lengthy chat, and he finally got around to informing me that my request might better be dealt with at the Ministry of Education (presumably because I was in education?). At the Ministry of Education I met with a friendly assistant minister. He welcomed me into his office, we had a lengthy chat, and he finally got around to informing me that my request might better be dealt with at the Ministry of the Interior. Arriving at the new location, somewhat sweatier than usual given the late-morning temperature, I met with yet another assistant minister. He welcomed me into his office, we had a lengthy chat, and he finally got around to informing me that my request might better be dealt with by a "friend" of his at the Survey Department. I went, somewhat resignedly, to the Survey Department, where I met with a young man who promised to be helpful. He welcomed me into his office, we had a lengthy chat, and he finally got around to informing me that my request might be met for a price. Since by now I would have cheerfully chartered a fleet of planes to map the local environs, I agreed to a reasonable amount, which, as it eventuated, consisted of a series of quite proper fees.

Two days later, I approached the young man at the Survey Department to inquire after my maps. He welcomed me into his office, we had a lengthy chat, and he finally got around to informing me that a conversation he had with a superior had changed his mind about the wisdom of granting my request.

Discouraged and mildly upset by this train (very slow train!) of events, I once again approached the assistant minister of education, since he had seemed most impressed with my mission. He welcomed me into his office, we had a lengthy chat, and he finally got around to informing me that we might appeal the situation to the head of the Survey Department. With his encouragement and a precursory phone call, I returned to the Survey Department, where I met with the department head. He welcomed me into his office, we had a lengthy chat, and he finally got around to informing me that my request could probably be granted assuming only that the appropriate paperwork was completed. My spirits immediately rose, my perspiration began to evaporate, and I looked forward to the completion of what I had naively thought would be an easy task . . . yes, I can be a slow learner.

It was to take another two days to complete the paperwork, replete with new letters of permission and an assortment of copies forwarded to anyone who might possibly have an interest in my presence in Kelantan. Finally I obtained several maps of Kelantan, after signing a series of guarantees that I would protect them, not copy them, and return them before leaving the state. It seems that many of the precautions I had encountered were due less to the formidable Malaysian bureaucracy than to a fear of Communists. Ever since the end of a Communist challenge about 1960, somewhere between one and three hundred Chinese had reportedly been moving back and forth between Thailand and Malaysia. No doubt a cadre of these Communists had been seeking maps in Kelantan, but they had been thwarted by the ever vigilant bureaucracy—or perhaps they simply lacked my stamina.

In Search of Information

Having achieved mapness and an increasing fluency in Kelantanese, I began the practice of actually asking nosy questions and found that this undertaking had grown no easier than it was with Paska' Hopi during my undergraduate days. There is an acquired skill to fieldwork that avoids both questions that call for a single simple response and what are termed leading questions.

It is all too easy to ask questions that call for what might be termed a "dead-end" answer: "What time do you usually eat?" Not a terrible question, but it leaves out context and why one might have a meal at that particular time. (Actually, as I was to discover, there are no particular times in Kelantan. All times are approximate, to within a day or so.) It is far better simply to begin talking about food, dining, and so forth, while trying to keep in mind the specifics one wants to record. Throughout the conversation, information is exchanged, not simply acquired, so that both participants learn something from the interaction and come away having had a positive experience. This avoids the "me anthropologist, you informant" structure that can promote an asymmetrical relationship and impede the development of trust. It is also a far more pleasant means of acquiring information, and as I will relate later, it can result in serendipitous discoveries. Some of the most valuable insights come from unexpected responses and unguided conversations. After all, if we knew just what we were looking for, we wouldn't need to do fieldwork.

Leading questions are a problem because they suggest to the listener the direction one wants taken. They frequently result from anthropologists' mistaken assumption that they understand what is going on and merely need to acquire some details in support. A question about a choice between two alternatives omits other possibilities: "Do you prefer eating with a spoon or with your hands?" omits the possibilities of chopsticks, bread, knives, forks, and so on. A question that asks how much one likes or wants something puts the respondent under some pressure to answer in a positive rather than a negative fashion. That is, a response such as "I don't really like anise" is not the same as saying "I hate anise." Better questions are generally open-ended, even if that means being a bit clumsy and having to spiral in to the chosen focus.

Acquiring information takes time, patience, and some interpersonal skills. It helps if you are genuinely interested in the subject matter and in the people with whom you speak. Questionnaires and interview schedules are appropriate for acquiring certain kinds of information, but when you want to get close to people and to learn from them, such devices generally interfere with the process of developing rapport.

Many of my initial efforts in pursuit of truth and beauty were ably assisted by Yusof Daud and by my neighbor Hussein, but it is hazardous to rely on only two or three sources of information, as there are always a variety of perspectives on events and differential access to various kinds of information. Therefore I sought out a variety of other villagers to pester. My usual strategy was to drop by in the late afternoon or early evening to chat about my topic of the moment. However, many of my more valuable conversations occurred unexpectedly, as I moved through the village.

I have described how people spend much of their time on the front porch, watching the comings and goings of neighbors and friends. Passersby may often be called to a house and invited to have coffee and conversation, especially if they are entertainingly attired in the local garb and reputed to make amusing mistakes at irregular intervals. Thus it was that much of my more valuable information was acquired at the instigation of others, while I had thought I was on my way to somewhere else. For such reasons flexibility is absolutely essential for fieldwork. Adhering to a schedule or plan can be quite costly in terms of opportunities forgone. Indeed, attempting to follow a schedule rigidly invites a variety of frustrations and can actually cost time.

Of Time and Indirection

Kelantanese attitudes toward time, like those of many peasant societies, are much looser than our own. We are the future-oriented ones who invented digital watches, capable of telling time to the second. Kelantanese possess a present-time orientation that is characteristically inexact. There are few pressures for temporal precision in the social life of the village. Annual cycles arc loosely defined, related largely to agriculture, and reflect such ecological features as the coming of the monsoons (Latif and Spencer 1981; Raybeck 1992a). Divisions of the day also reflect both ecological and religious influence. Although the Kelantanese day is formally ordered by the cycle of five Islamic prayers, it is informally ordered by the work routine, which in turn reflects the influence of the sun and changes in temperature throughout the day.

In Kelantan village life, time is something experienced, not something hoarded, calculated, or squandered. Given the experiential nature of time reckoning, village time is treated very flexibly. Indeed, the common daily markers for time, the prayer periods, are structured in a loose fashion that promotes a flexible rather than a precise approach to appointments, whether social or business. A farmer may agree to help a neighbor, promising to arrive before the second prayer of the day, which may mean early or mid morning, or even midday. As Latif and Spencer have noted, even designating a prayer time for an appointment can result in a window of over two hours (1981:212).

Not surprisingly, given such conventions, the Kelantanese concept of lateness differs from that characteristic of Western cultures. There is a term for lateness, *lewat*, and even a term that refers to having missed an appointment, *kelewatan*, but the use of these terms less accurately reflects the actual amount of time passed than the likelihood that someone may have been inconvenienced. Thus arriving two hours behind schedule to assist a fellow farmer would not make a villager late, but the same interval involving an engagement with a busy and high-status village elder might well do so. However, even in such circumstances, there might at most be a veiled allusion to lateness, partly because this would risk making the tardy embarrassed (malu) and partly because such an observation could make the observer appear too concerned with punctuality.

Villagers value their pace of life, and this pace is leisurely (Ong 1987). The orientation of villagers is toward present time, yet a present time in which different events and activities do not compete with one another for primacy. What is not done one day will be done the next, or the day after that. There is a strong ethic that haste is unseemly, the mark of a person too concerned with material advances who may not be paying sufficient attention to social obligations. People who hurry their activities are often the subject of gossip. They are regarded as less refined (*halus*), an important indication of a civilized nature, and it is also suspected that they may have something to hide.

Clearly the concepts of time and punctuality were somewhat removed from what I had experienced in my New England village. After some irksome lessons, I discovered that arranging to meet someone at four o'clock was virtually meaningless. The individual might arrive half an hour early but was far more likely to be two hours late . . . and pleased with his punctuality! I gradually learned to adjust to this system by carrying extra work with me and by seeking other opportunities for interaction when waiting.

As it was, there were a number of villagers who believed me to be simply too obsessed with time for my own well-being.

As my familiarity with Kelantanese culture and good manners (budi bahasa) grew, I learned a painful lesson in politeness. Kelantanese, and indeed most Malays, do not like to be put in a situation where they must deny a request. When I asked for an appointment or a favor, I was never refused. Interestingly, however, many of my requests were never granted. It took a while to learn the conventions, but it seemed there were rules for such affairs—they simply differed from those I had been raised with in New Hampshire. It seems that in addition to translating the language, one also needs to translate the idiom. Thus, "I'll see about it" means "forget it"; "I'll do it tomorrow" translates as "Not in your wildest dreams"; and "soon" equals "never." Things go awry.

Once I became aware of these delicate nuances, I noted that Kelantanese hardly used them among themselves. Instead they were adept at indirect requests that were so subtle, a clumsy Westerner might easily miss them. The nice thing about oblique requests is that they never need to be denied. They may, however, be cheerfully ignored. The amount of attention and preparation that attends these matters is quite impressive, as the following two excerpts from my field notes demonstrate:

> Hamid often borrows the car of Haji Hassan who runs the local gas station, but Hamid stated that, each time he asks Hassan, he looks into his face first to ascertain whether he is in a good or a bad mood. If he's in a bad mood, Hamid won't hint that he needs the car.

> Hussein [my neighbor] mentioned that before he ever asked to borrow anything from someone or asked a favor he always carefully sized up the person first, to see whether or not the person was apt to grant the favor or refuse it. He said that if there were a probability, or a likelihood, or even a possibility of a refusal he was reluctant to ask and usually wouldn't. He said that it was because a refusal would make him malu. He said that this pattern held even with people from whom he was accustomed to borrow things. . . . He said that to this date he has not yet asked his nephew for the loan of his car. He says the relationship is part of the reason he hasn't asked: "If a person who isn't a relative refuses something, then you are not too embarrassed and don't take it too hard. But if a nephew refuses, it is very awkward and creates a problem."

My own social efforts often fell notably short of subtle and occasionally moved my neighbor Hussein to offer me some assistance. He was also one of few villagers willing to give me advice concerning social matters, a mission that he carried out with great sensitivity and tact. Rather than provide direct advice, a behavior that risks embarrassing both the giver and the receiver, Hussein would use personal references of transparent relevance. On one occasion when he wished to suggest that my behavior was not as tactful as it might have been, he made the following observation:

> I was not born here and I do not have my relatives here. I have to be careful of my behavior. When you go to live in a place where you weren't born, you behave like a hen, not like a rooster. This is proper. In my own kampong I can behave more importantly, but here I must be careful not to give offense.

I got the idea.

Conversations, Chess, and Kinship Conundrums

As I continued to improve my language skills, I began to obtain information by the best means possible: listening to the conversations of others. I would note that this is not the same as eavesdropping, though the two bear some resemblance. When listening to others, the development of the subject and the degree of candor involved proceed without the intervention of the anthropologist. One actually hears people discussing matters they regard as important (though the weather figures just as prominently in Kelantan conversations as it does anywhere else).

In Kelantan, the coffee shop (*kedai kopi*) is a place where males congregate to discuss village matters, to gossip, and to encounter the news of the day. Any moderate-sized village will have several such shops, and each will have its regulars. I began to frequent one that was owned and run by a middle-aged woman. Her position was unusual, given the strictures of Islam that constrain the public activities of women, but in Kelantan and elsewhere on the east coast of the peninsula, women have been both prominent and powerful since well before the advent of

Islam (Raybeck 1980–81; Strange 1981). The shop, like most, was small, had a few tables and chairs, and had a view toward the major path, the better to interact with passersby. It opened for the morning market trade and remained open until well after midnight, serving coffee, soft drinks, and assorted edibles.

It was at this shop where I gained my greatest proficiency with the dialect, though the beginnings of this venture were disappointing in the extreme. Villagers, knowing my Kelantanese was limited, took some pains to clarify and even repeat their utterances. At the coffee shop, however, villagers spoke to one another with machine-gun rapidity, employing an arsenal of local metaphors, idioms, and similes. I will not pretend that I understood most, or even half, of what transpired about me, but I do think I gained insights into village life that would otherwise have eluded me.

As I became familiar with the regulars at the shop, one of them, a toothless, elderly man, whom I later discovered was illiterate, invited me to join him in a game of chess. I did so happily as the rules of chess are the same everywhere, participation requires little language skill, and I had been a fairly good chess player at home . . . or so I believed. Our first game was brief, exciting, and crushing. I lost to him within fifteen minutes. Resolved to bear down, I asked for a second game, which he was pleased to play. This time I fared much better, lasting nearly thirty minutes before acknowledging an insurmountable difference in board strength—he had pieces, I didn't. I was learning in a practical fashion a lesson that had hitherto simply been an academic abstraction: intelligence is often independent of formal education. One can have an abundance of the former without any of the latter.

My chess forays also served to improve my access to interaction. Such was my fame that people I had not yet met dropped by the kedai to challenge me to a friendly game. In the process of giving me yet another drubbing, they would engage in conversation, and often I received invitations to visit homes in other villages. Of course the price of accepting one of these invitations was later to be regaled with tales of my ineptitude at a game at which many villagers are *very* proficient.

One of my early fieldwork projects was the collection and analysis of genealogies. This material can be used to ascertain patterns of residence, inheritance, and marriage. At least that is what my reading of texts and ethnographies had assured me was the case. However, I soon discovered that collecting genealogies among Kelantanese involved some unanticipated problems.

Kelantanese, as mentioned earlier, use Arabic naming conventions; thus, there are no surnames to assist the anthropologist in developing an understanding of descent lines. Instead the family members of a single generation share a last name that will disappear in the next generation, and that last name is likely to be as undistinctive as Mat or Yusof, for example. In short, there were a limited number of names, which only faintly differentiated between individuals—at least from the poor anthropologist's perspective. In addition, the divorce rate in Kelantan is one of the highest in the world, having averaged 77 percent over a ten-year period (Raybeck [n.d.]; Raybeck 1980–81). I often found it necessary to record several marriages for an individual, along with an assortment of step-relations and various fractional siblings; i.e., half sister, half step-sister, etc. The emerging kinship charts took on the appearance of a Kandinsky painting, with lines running every which way and splashes of color designating different kinds of relationships. It was extremely difficult to develop an accurate genealogy suitable for analysis. Question: "Is this the same Abdul who married Yayah and fathered Mat, before divorcing Yayah and marrying first Ro'fiah and then Lah?" Answer: "No this is the Abdul who works in Tumpat, who married Ro'fiah and had Fatimah, Mat, and Minah."

If this were not enough of a burden, I discovered that Kelantanese men frequently change their names. It is a sign of gender equality that middle-aged Kelantanese village men will frequently adopt their wife's first name as their surname. Thus my landlord, who was Mat Kadir when I first knew him during this period of fieldwork, is currently Mat Mizin, and many people are nowadays unaware of his former surname.

Despite my difficulties acquiring accurate genealogical information, I discovered that villagers often possessed a detailed and accurate knowledge of very extensive kin networks. In an agrarian society, kin relations are important as sources of both emotional and material support. This importance is reinforced in Kelantan by strong social values concerning appropriate behavior between relatives (Raybeck 1975). The result is that most villagers are enmeshed in a web of kin relations that both offers aid and makes demands. One of my village friends was a man who, with his wife, had been childless for fifteen years and who consequently became more interested in kinship than most villagers. Despite being illiterate, he was able to identify 184 relatives, their places of residence, means of livelihood, and approximate ages. The additional detail was not simply because of human interest but because it was necessary in identifying specific individuals . . . the Kelantanese naming system can be problematic for them as well as for bemused anthropologists.

The above example of prodigious memory is imposing, but the reader should not take it to be an indicator of some mythic skill possessed by Kelantan villagers. It is simply a reflection of how important that information is to them on an everyday basis. We need to recall that we live in a society where people do not agree on the definition of what constitutes a second cousin, let alone treat kinship as a significant cultural element. Our own feats of memory are reserved for those cultural components to which we attach importance . . . notably sports and television schedules.

Things seemed to be going well. My note cards multiplied at an appropriate rate, and people were quite helpful in addressing many of my questions. I quickly discovered, however, that there were distinct limits on the kinds of questions with which I could expect assistance.

Those questions that concerned factual minutiae pertaining to such mundane activities as planting, family life, and common rituals were answered readily and fully. However, since my major interests dealt with values and deviant behavior, I also somewhat naively asked about the existence of misbehaviors such as gambling, drinking, premarital sex, and so forth. My friends and acquaintances gave me to believe that Kelantanese were among the most law-abiding and proper individuals on the planet. No one drank, gambled, fooled around, or, it seemed, even spoke ill of others.

My suspicions that people were being less than candid with me were exacerbated one day when I attempted to ascertain the reasons behind a heated and loud quarrel between a man and woman that I had heard the preceding evening. I inquired of a variety of villagers, whom I knew to be closer to the disturbance than I had been, what the argument concerned and who the principles were. I received a notably uniform reply: "What argument? Sorry, but I didn't hear any argument." I realized that I was still not sufficiently trusted to be made privy to the sensitive and sometimes less-than-ideal social life of the village. Access to such information would give me a means to harm village interests, and as I was still seen largely as an outsider, villagers could not be certain I wouldn't use such means against their interests.

I had encountered a formidable obstacle that anthropologists refer to by a variety of terms, often as the difference between the real and the ideal. Villagers were giving me an idealized picture of themselves and of their culture. I needed a means to delve below the surface boundaries of village life, where I might encounter the muddiness and unevenness that constitutes a portion of all human relationships. As in most aspects of fieldwork, the solution to my problem came in an unforeseen manner, from an unexpected source, and owed little to the anthropologist's intelligence.

Getting Backstage

Gaining the trust of those with whom you work is a slow process generally characterized by numerous small exchanges that gradually add to mutual understanding and acceptance. Seldom are there breakthroughs in trust of the sort to which one can point. Nonetheless I can date exactly when I was enabled to gain access to the backstage of village society: Monday, March 18, 1968.

Throughout the early months of fieldwork, I continued to participate in the evening guard (jaga) twice a week. This regularly placed me in the company of married males a few years younger than myself, with whom I shared several interests. As time progressed and they, especially Mat and Yusof, grew more comfortable with me, they asked questions about that preeminent concern of young males—sex. They wished to know about the sexual mores of contemporary U.S. society, which in the sixties had rather a lurid reputation. I answered their questions candidly and responded with queries of my own. They began giving me my first evidence that Kelantanese were as frailly human as the rest of us.

Eventually we even exchanged swearwords, an extremely important aspect of language, curiously absent from language classes. They traded Kelantanese curses for English profanities and seemed pleased with the secret power the words conferred. Mat, the more playful of the two, delighted in approaching young women, smiling, and saying "Fook!" (his pronunciation lacked total accuracy) before cackling and running away.

After months of this sort of banter, we had become quite comfortable with each other and seemed to be developing close friendships. I became more confident of this when, walking through the village, Yusof started to hold hands with me. Kelantan Malays avoid intergender contact, and as mentioned earlier, even husbands and wives do not touch in public. Yet, within gender, body contact is common and serves as both a source of comfort and as a social reinforcer of a friendly relationship. I had witnessed this behavior among young Kelantanese women and men and understood the cultural significance attached to such acts.

However, I soon discovered that understanding the significance of hand-holding and participating in the behavior were two very distinct things. Despite my awareness that Yusof was paying me a compliment and being friendly, I have to confess that my initial reaction was a slight pause followed by a small but perceptible feeling of unease. Throughout New England (and elsewhere in the United States, save football fields), straight men generally do not come in physical contact with one another, and they certainly do not hold hands. Nonetheless, in contrast to my experiences with dysentery, after a few weeks I found I could genuinely relax with this custom and even initiate it with Yusof, Mat, and a few others.

One Thursday evening as we were ending our jaga, Yusof asked me if it would be possible for three people to travel on my motorcycle. I remarked that it probably was feasible and asked why he wished to know. His response was both opaque and promising: he asked me to meet Mat and him Monday evening on the main road at the edge of the village and commented that there was something he wanted to show me.

That Monday night I met Mat and Yusof at the designated location, and the three of us set off on my motorcycle under Yusof's direction. Questions concerning our destination were greeted with smiles, and directions were confined to immediate turns. I was guided into the capital, Kota Bharu; down a side street; through a maze of paths; and into a dark, dead-end alley where we dismounted. Yusof beckoned me to follow him, which I did with only a slight frisson of apprehension.

My friend, Mat (Mohammed bin Su), from guard duty days with some of his children. He currently runs a shop in Wakaf Bharu, and has a total of twelve children.

We approached the side of a darkened building where Yusof opened a door and ushered me into a noisy, dingy, low-ceilinged room occupied by both men and women. Within three minutes, Yusof had purchased beers for all of us and had a "waitress" sitting on my lap. With both he and Mat watching me closely, I realized the significance of the risk they were taking and the importance of my response. I drank the beer, joked with the waitress, and thanked them for both opportunities. After I declined their kind invitation to retire with my waitress to a loft over the room, we settled in for some pleasant drinking and conversation.

It seems that there were numerous bars of the same sort throughout Kota Bharu. People from a given village tended to patronize a single location, thus assuring a degree of confidentiality. Villagers engaged in similar deviance at a shared locale were unlikely to inform on one another, partly due to bonds of solidarity and partly because doing so would raise questions regarding how one knew of the behavior. Indeed, I learned later that Yusof and Mat were very interested in compromising me as soon as possible and were somewhat disappointed that I hadn't taken the waitress upstairs. Had I done so, they would have had even greater insurance that I would not mention our recent activities upon returning to the village.

That evening perceptibly changed my relationship with Yusof and Mat. I now had two friends who had taken me behind the scenes and who counted on me to be circumspect about the experience. They had invested their trust in me, and we had shared solecisms. Each possessed information that could be detrimental to the others, were it to enter the ever-active village gossip network. That evening also represented a major breakthrough in my fieldwork. Soon I could approach Yusof and Mat with questions concerning subsurface elements of village behavior, and they would delight in telling me whatever relevant gossip they knew. As gossiping is a favored pastime, they usually had useful information concerning any event about which I might ask.

Information garnered from Yusof and Mat allowed me to ask very different and far more successful questions of other villagers. Instead of asking open-ended questions betraying my near total ignorance of a situation, I could now inquire about events in a manner suggesting I was already privy to the main issues and only wished clarification of details. Instead of asking, "What was that argument last night about, and who took part in it?" I could now inquire, "Were Minah and Dir arguing about her sister's inheritance again?"

This approach immediately placed me backstage, for I could not be familiar with such information unless other villagers already trusted me. In this fashion I rapidly increased my access to information that hitherto had been denied me, and as it became increasingly apparent that I neither disclosed nor abused this knowledge, other villagers began to accord me a trust similar but not identical to that which Yusof and Mat had displayed.

From this point forward, my work progressed nicely. Among other things, I had learned that the evolution of trust involves mutual vulnerability. Reciprocity is widely regarded as the most fundamental of social expectations, and it obtains in fieldwork fully as much as it does in everyday life. I can never forget that I owe much of my fieldwork success not to my own professional acumen but to a night out on the town in the company of good friends.

5

The Midday Sun and Other Hazards

or
Cobras in the Kitchen, Rats in the Rafters, and
Ants Everywhere

Those who have read ethnographies—those anthropological descriptions of others cultures, brimming with facts and insights—probably have the impression that anthropologists fill most of their days with interviews, surveys, observations, and other forms of professional engagement. This is something less than wholly accurate. While there may indeed exist anthropologists who can lay claim to such work schedules, I have never encountered them. Instead most of us fill much of our days with the mundane tasks associated with keeping clean, feeding ourselves, looking after health concerns, staying sane (for the most part), and so on. In my case I must confess that only about 35 percent of my available research time was actually devoted to research. This is certainly not the way one conceives of research practices when writing up proposals in the comfort of an office. It also helps to explain why anthropologists seldom adhere to the detailed schedules with which they enter the field, and why fieldwork often takes more than a year to accomplish.

The continuing theme is a simple one. Anthropologists have needs that must be addressed if they are to continue working effectively in what can be rather trying circumstances. There is benefit in devising a schedule for research, but it can be unwise to attempt to follow it slavishly in the field. Anthropologists are often surprised to discover that some experiences that were expected to be difficult are not, while others anticipated to be easy can be surprisingly problematic. This is particularly true for those who, like my friend Clive Kessler, are in the field alone. I was fortunate to be accompanied by my wife, Karen, who proved to be an invaluable helpmeet both with professional and domestic tasks (the latter in which she was far more active than I), a source of information on the women's perspective on affairs, and a major buttress of sanity. She figures prominently in the following description of daily fieldwork problems for the simple reason that she figured prominently throughout the day-to-day reality of fieldwork.

Climate Concerns

I had been apprised that the climate of Malaysia was tropical, and I expected both heat and humidity. However, having been raised in New Hampshire, it seems my expectations were a bit too abstract and intellectual. I thought that I would simply sweat a bit more. Well, I was partially correct—as a candle is to a forest fire, so was my expectation of the heat to its reality. I sweated, I flowed, I bloody well streamed. In a period of ten months I went from a rather lean 180 pounds to 154. Karen, who also suffered this climate, was pleased with her weight loss but quite concerned about mine. She took to referring to me in her journal as "the bony one."

In addition to weight loss, the heat and humidity created a set of daily problems that taxed both endurance and ingenuity. It seems that anything made of leather quickly grew a green patina of mold, cloth tended to suffer accelerated decomposition, exposed food often started to decay in a matter of hours, and moisture relentlessly attacked metals, particularly those that were part of delicate and expensive instruments, like cameras. However, the biggest daily difficulty arrived with the hot season in mid-March—unrelievedly high temperatures that refused to dissipate properly in the evening hours. Sleep became difficult and the daily schedule had to be reshaped.

Unlike mad dogs, Englishmen, and the occasional anthropologist, Malays do not go out in the midday sun. They have more sense than that. Instead they take a nap after lunch and stay out of the sun until approximately three o'clock or so for very good reason (Raybeck 1992a). The heat of the midday sun is exceptional and can easily lead to hyperthermia and even sunstroke. However, this practice of sleeping at midday led the British colonialists to perceive Malays as lazy, a perception that was strengthened by the reluctance of Malays to participate in wage-labor situations. The British assumed that Malays were uninterested in employment because they shunned work, not recognizing that the structured circumstances of work were unintentionally designed to create malu situations for Malays. Traditional Malays neither give nor receive orders directly. Instead, as I have indicated earlier, communication is subtle and indirect, though nonetheless clear. Further, being called to account for a lack of

Mat Halimah demonstrating how rubber sap is collected. Mat's small rubber holding was a source of steady, if modest, income for himself and his wife. The sap is carried back in pails to a preparation shed where it is poured into flat pans and mixed with formic acid. Once it has set, it is pressed dry and then hung up in the rafters of the house to cure. The odor is strong, unpleasant, and pervasive.

punctuality or for other conflicts between the two cultures is emotionally very painful to traditional Malays. Thus climate helped to foment a classic example of ethnocentrism—a belief in the superiority of one's own practices—in which the British thoughtlessly extended their interpretations of behavior to the patterns manifest by Malays. The result of this misperception was hardly academic, as it helped to promote the importation of tens of thousands of Chinese and Tamil Indians to work in tin mines and on emerging rubber plantations.

By resting during midday, Kelantanese are able to maintain a daily schedule that I found very difficult to emulate, especially during the rice-growing season. They arise at dawn for *Suboh*, the first prayer of the day. A cold breakfast is eaten, and work is begun either in the rice fields or with cash crops, according to season. Later in the morning, when the sun is hot, people will work on small-scale rubber tapping or some other activity that permits access to shade. A meal is taken at midday, *berdiri* (literally, standing erect), after which *Zohor* is prayed. The period after Zohor is the hottest time of day, when most adults remain indoors napping or working on light handicrafts. When the shadow cast by a person's body exceeds the body's length, it is time for *Ashar*, after which people work in their gardens, return to rice fields, or carry out sundry chores. By dusk people return to their homes for what is generally regarded as the most important prayer of the day, *Magrib*, after which is the evening meal. Following the evening meal people will work on handicrafts, visit friends, drop by the local coffee shop, and generally pursue an active social agenda. Finally the day concludes with the prayer *Isha*, after which most people retire. Hardly a schedule for lazy people!

It took some time for Karen and I to adjust to this pattern, and neither of us ever became very skilled at napping, a contributor to our fatigue and an additional factor in our weight loss. Generally we would remain at home during the midday period, in no small part because visits to others were neither polite nor practical. However, we often ventured out on the motorcycle to run errands, to see friends in Kota Bharu, or to take in a film. On one occasion we foolishly took a morning drive to a beach some twelve miles distant, where we stayed until a bit past noon. This was a very un-Kelantanese thing to do, both because they have better sense and because they are very color conscious and prefer to avoid even the hint of a sun tan.

The next day, in a movie theater in Kota Bharu, Karen complained of feeling nauseous. We went out through a side exit to stand in the shade, while I worriedly inquired how she felt. She responded that she would be fine and immediately did a nose dive for the tarmac. I caught her just before she hit, picked her up, and was carrying her hurriedly toward a row of trishaws when she began to regain consciousness. Her first words were a testament to the power of cultural conditioning: "Put me down! My skirt's too short." In a foreign setting, feeling sick, and only semiconscious, she nevertheless managed to manifest a well-developed sense of modesty, reinforced by her awareness that Kelantanese are more sensitive about the public display of limbs than we are. I, on the other hand, on the two occasions when I lost consciousness, manifested little concern for my environs.

During the hot season, from May through September, we became used to measuring the temperature in terms of numbers of showers taken. Kelantanese, as most Malays, bathe several times a day. Nearly every house has a well before or beside it, sometimes partially screened by a low pandanus divider. To bathe, Kelantanese wrap themselves in an old sarong and considerable dignity and manage their ablutions quite modestly in full view of passersby. Neither Karen nor I were sufficiently skilled nor disposed to experiment with this procedure. I have mentioned that most houses are elevated on pilings to escape the flooding that accompanies the rainy season, but our modern house, while on stilts, had a kitchen at ground level with a poured concrete floor. This made possible the construction of a partitioned shower in one corner, where we could bathe in reasonable privacy excepting the occasional intrusions of neighbors. We quickly discovered what Malays had long known: showers are as cooling as they are cleansing. Thus our penchant for walking about the house wearing sarong and damp shoulders. A bad day was sometimes worth seven showers . . . and, yes, that meant seven interruptions of work.

The Insect Inventory

Cicak (pronounced chee-cha') are little wall geckos, small lizards that can walk up walls and across ceilings in search of assorted insect delicacies. They are common in all houses and are tolerated because they help to moderate the significant insect population. We also found them cute. As our house had electricity, it was particularly popular both with insects attracted by the light and with cicak drawn by the insects. The presence of cicak was both a boon and a bane. While they provided free entertainment and did succeed in eating their weight in insects each day, they also had remarkably poor toilet habits. Since there was a light in our study, cicak frequently situated themselves nearby on the ceiling, above the table we were using as a desk, the better to capture flying insects. As a result, my field notes carry speckled reminders of the exigencies of fieldwork. Further, my concentration was occasionally broken when a cicak, in pursuit of dinner, would overreach itself and fall to the table, stare briefly at me, and scurry away.

Unwittingly (and that is precisely the right word), one night in early May, Karen and I provided our little reptilian friends with an unexpected feast. It was after ten o'clock when we noticed that the lights were going out in our neighbors' houses. This was a departure from the norm and was shortly followed by another. Within fifteen minutes our living-room light had drawn hundreds of lovely flying insects with large white wings. Initially entranced by this spectacle of nature, we watched as they surrounded the light, landed upon walls, ceiling, and floors . . . and then began to lose their wings. Things go awry.

Too late, I extinguished the lights (as my better-informed neighbors had done earlier) and we made an unsuccessful effort to clean up the mess, then retired to bed. Emerging from our mosquito netting in the morning, we found the living area covered with light, fragile, pernicious wings, which stubbornly resisted the best effort of broom and dust rag. It took two days of determined labor to clear out the flutter clutter, and we soon learned that the wings were merely a harbinger of a greater infestation. It seems that the flying ants borne on the wings were a form of termite. Thereafter one of my maintenance tasks was to crawl under the house with my pickax handle and smash the surprisingly strong mud edifices these insects erected.

The termites were an occasional problem, and we learned to deal with them fairly effectively. The mosquitos, on the other hand, were a constant nuisance that one could only endure. Mosquitos ranged in size from those with which you are familiar to the size of horseflies. While not quite capable of flying off with young children, some (Anopheles) were known to carry malaria, and all were capable of irritating bites. Mosquito defenses consisted of a variety of mosquito coils that could be burned at night and that worked fitfully, citronella candles that worked not at all, and mosquito netting that was quite effective but tended to limit one's domain to the bed.

Mosquitos were a far greater trial for me than for Karen. Although indifferently attractive to members of my own species, I am beloved by a wide range of insects. Thus, when we sat together in the study, Karen was able to relax in comparative comfort and be entertained by my occasional contortion as I sought to swat an insect on the middle of my back. Her most peaceful times were at night when we both retired to the protection of the mosquito netting that surrounded our double bed. Sometimes we would find a few mosquitos nicely ensconced and awaiting our appearance. On such occasions Karen would cheerfully roll over, secure in the knowledge that either I would kill them or I, not she, would awaken in the morning with some new, itchy blemishes.

Mosquitos were a problem for our comfort, but one that could be endured without great difficulty. The ants, on the other hand, were an incessant challenge to our food larder and our piece of mind. Ants in the tropics come in assorted sizes, from large black-bodied ones capable of carrying off whole loaves of bread (well, slices at any rate) to tiny red ones that seem able to penetrate any container, perhaps passing directly through glass and metal in some mysterious sexapedlian fashion. We quickly learned to place our open edibles such as rice, flour, vegetables, and especially fruit on a single table for which we devised ant guards. Each table leg was in the center of a tin can filled with kerosene. This created a moat that effectively prevented these formidable Formicidae access to our goodies, assuming, of course, that no portion of the can touched the table leg, nor were there any dangling strings, projecting pieces of wood, or even stray hairs to provide a stepladder to heaven. We went on to learn that our definition of edible fell far short of the one employed by the ants, who were found cheerfully munching leather, items of clothing, books, and even some of my film negatives. They could get into anything and usually did. Karen even found an unopened jar of strawberry jam that had been penetrated by and infested with red ants. She did not take well to these incursions into our food stores and other belongings.

Ants quickly became Karen's bête noire, and she set about doing her best to reduce their population throughout our house and surroundings. She used poison, she baited traps, she struck them dead by the hundreds, she toyed with importing her own aardvark: in short, she became quite "ant agonistic." As an act of spousal support, I presented her with her own Flit gun and a quart of spray. Thereafter many of the entries in Karen's daily journal read as follows: "Washed, swept, killed ants, sewed," and "I washed clothes, killed ants and worked on getting the accounts into shape to send in." Her best days were those in which she located dense collections of the beasts: "Whee—killed a whole colony of ants living in a hole in the living room sink. Justice triumphs," and "Forgot best thing of whole day—found a whole huge nest of big black ants and decimated the population!!" As you might imagine, Karen's efforts to reduce the six-legged population were unremitting, if not Herculean. She sprayed, beat, boiled, and even burned thousands of the little devils, and after months of effort succeeded in making . . . not one whit of difference in the local ant population.

While ants were the most numerous of insect pests, they were not among the more formidable. There were spiders larger than my spread hand (I have pictures), centipedes, millipedes, and other multipedes. These latter, especially the millipedes, could inflict painful though not dangerous bites. However, scorpions, another element in the local insect array, could be quite problematic. There were tales of children and elderly who have died of scorpion stings, and our neighbor Hussein assured us that some reached five to six inches in length. The result of our encounters with a few such vermin was greatly increased caution. We would look under an object before moving it and, whenever possible, items that had to be moved were lifted at arm's length. Those of you who have friends recently returned from a stay in the tropics now have an explanation of why they are apt to approach their furniture in a paranoid fashion.

Rodentia and Fowls

Tropical climates such as Kelantan's provide a plentiful supply of rotting waste to please and attract the local rodent population. In Kelantan, rodents are divided into three classes: mice, rural rats, and urban rats. The distinction between rural and urban rats is less one of Linnaean morphology than it is one of simple mass: urban rats are bloody enormous! In cities rats can reach three feet in length (Yes, this includes the tail, but so what?) and weigh up to six pounds. They tend to live in the covered culverts and to scurry forth at night in search of edibles. Cats are far too sensible to take on such behemoths, and the only animals that threaten them are dogs. Despite whatever effects might be occasioned by going about in the midday sun, even individual dogs are reluctant to attack a large city rat, and on those occasions when these rodents are attacked, it is by a pack.

In the villages rats are usually no more than a foot in length, sometimes two. They abound in populated areas where garbage is often easily found, and they are quite willing to invade homes in search of sustenance. Village Kelantanese, who do not commonly have pets as Westerners do, do keep cats about to restrain the rodent population. The cats are not particularly well treated and are not generally welcome in the house proper. In contrast to smaller, urban cats sometimes kept as pets, a Kelantanese village cat is an imposing beast, characterized by a stocky body, large jaws, and a thick neck suggesting the possibility of steroids, or at least a weight-training program. For the most part, cats do their rat hunting at night. Lovely tropical evenings are sometimes punctuated by the squeal of unfortunate rats who have encountered foraging cats. The amount of sympathy generated by these unfortunate sounds is minimal.

Unlike most village houses, which have exposed beams and no ceilings, our "modern" house, mimicking Western fashion, had a false ceiling. This, as it eventuated, did not improve the quality of life. In most houses rats enter through holes in the floor or wall and, when not scuttling across the floor, run about on the rafters . . . quietly. Our false ceiling, however, provided a sheltered and secure area where, as nearly as we could determine, rats could hold their version of the NBA playoffs. Further, these unwanted visitors did not confine themselves to the ceiling but would, after we had retired, venture throughout the house in search of food. More than once we were awakened by scurrying visitors fighting over a discovered morsel, which could range from a bar of soap to the glued binding of one of our paperbacks. They were eclectic diners.

A relatively small rat captured in our kitchen and awaiting his terminal bath. Initially I was reluctant to drown these rodents, but practice and their pestiferous persistence altered my attitude.

If ants were Karen's special province, rats were mine, and I attacked them with slingshot, poison, and traps. The slingshot failed to daunt them, perhaps owing to my less-than-William-Tell-like marksmanship. The poison may have had some impact, but we were never able to witness any. Only the traps had a perceptible effect. One of my occasional morning tasks was to take a captured rat out and drown it in a pail of water. Initially, like a good American, I found this task distasteful and difficult. My first rat expired of sunstroke because I was reluctant to immerse it. However, as their nuisance value increased, I became inured to giving these animals a terminal baptism. Not only can one adapt to a new cultural setting, one can also change one's deeply ingrained attitudes about the treatment of animals. One of these changes involved a rooster owned by my neighbor Hussein.

Immediately outside our bedroom, only three feet from the house, was the stump of an old rubber tree. My neighbor's rooster was accustomed to use that stump as a forum from which he would loudly address the village at 4:30 each morning. To observe that Karen and I found this morning call to arms somewhat disconcerting is akin to noting that Californians find earthquakes discomfiting. We already had enough difficulty sleeping due to the heat and the rats. Quite frequently we would fall asleep in the early morning hours, only to be jolted awake a bit later by the crowing of this officious fowl. Further, our efforts to dislodge him by hollering and banging on the bedroom wall were callously disregarded. However, should one of us stealthily arise in an effort to do him physical harm, he would immediately retreat. (I would gladly have done him psychological harm, had I known how.) The rooster, whom we named after a rather noisy and obnoxious acquaintance, became an irritant of surprising proportion.

Over the ensuing months, in addition to calling him names, I threw sticks and stones at Sylvester. I also employed my slingshot in a vain effort to increase the distance between his perceived domain and ours. All of this was to little avail. It was apparent that Sly was both devious and fast. How fast? Faster than a speeding pullet. During the Chinese New Year I even resorted to shooting small rockets at him. These were made from a sliver of bamboo, to one end of which was taped an inch-and-a-half firecracker that gave up half its charge as thrust and terminated in a small but satisfying explosion. They were reasonably accurate and did serve to make Sly a bit more cautious, though they also alerted all our neighbors to my vermin vendetta. So much for the image of the dispassionate professional carefully avoiding controversial behaviors. Things go awry.

Hussein, ever the delicate politician and aware of our unhappiness with Sly, tried to explain to me that crowing is what cocks do and that cocks were necessary to freshen hens. I responded that, having tended some two hundred chickens in my New Hampshire village, I was aware of the behavior and services of cocks, but that Sly's preferred perch was nettlesome. Through a series of typically indirect conversations, we reached a compromise. I gave him money for another bird and Karen and I resolved the problem of what to do with a noxious rooster:

Rooster Curry, Malay Style

one 2-1/2–3 pound rooster or rooster parts, not boned,
chopped into smallish pieces (regular chicken may be sub-
stituted)
3–4 cups coconut milk (nonsweetened, from a can, OR make
by soaking nonsweetened grated coconut in warm water and
squeezing out milk, repeating until there is enough)
2 large onions, finely chopped
3 garlic cloves, finely chopped
2 Tb. ground coriander
1 Tb. ground anise
1 Tb. ground cumin
10 small dried red chilies, seeded and crushed, OR 1–2 Tb.
crushed pepper flakes
1 tsp. lemon grass powder
2 tsp. Turmeric
Salt to taste

Simmer chicken pieces in 2–3 cups of the coconut milk,
adding salt, until chicken is just tender and milk becomes
oily. Fry the onions and garlic in a little oil until tender, add
spices, and fry well. Add remaining coconut milk and simmer
about 30 minutes. Add to chicken and simmer, covered, until
gravy becomes thick. Serve with rice.

Cobras in the Kitchen

Snakes are a significant problem throughout the Malay Peninsula and particularly in Kelantan. To this day, despite the erratic
driving habits of many people, the leading cause of accidental death
in Kelantan is not traffic accidents but snakebite, especially that of
the King Cobra, which is both numerous and deadly. I have no clear
sense of how many species of snakes there are in Kelantan, but I
have been told repeatedly by villagers that the poisonous ones
outnumber the nonpoisonous. Whether or not this is true, Kelantanese have, with one exception, a common response to any snake
they come across: they kill it. The one exception is a large black
snake that subsists largely on mice and other small rodents.
Kelantanese actually encourage these snakes to take up residence

in their eaves or rafters, believing, with no small justification, that their presence means good luck (or at least a better night's sleep).

During the nine months we had been in the village, I had toured Wakaf Bharu and neighboring villages on motorcycle and on foot. I had been with Kelantanese when snakes were spotted and duly dispatched, and invariably my companions always saw the snake well before I did. The technical term for this ability is increased response salience and disposition. They knew where to look for snakes, and they had numerous past encounters to heighten their perceptions. Throughout this time, I never once encountered the dreaded King Cobra.

One afternoon in early October, I returned home on my Yamaha to find Karen standing on the front porch in a very composed, even formal fashion. She said in a perfectly controlled voice, "There is a snake in the kitchen, and I think it is a cobra." Being far more experienced with the local environment, I suggested that she had probably erred, as I had yet to encounter one of these venomous vipers during my travels. Full of masculine assurance, I entered the house and descended from the raised portions to the ground-floor kitchen. According to Karen, the snake had entered under the back door (lots of clearance) and then slithered into the shower stall. She had then blocked the run-off drain, placed a heavy chair against the shower stall door, and settled back to await my appearance. Having heard the fuller version of her tale, I reassured her about the snake, grabbed a nearby broom, moved the chair away from the door, and entered the shower stall. I approached the snake and poked at it with the broom. The snake responded by rising up, looking distinctly displeased with my presence, and flaring its hood. I shut the door to the shower stall, replaced the chair, put back the broom . . . and apologized most humbly to my wife. Things really can go awry.

I then went outside to get what I regarded as a reasonable length of wood with which to assault our unwanted visitor. I returned with an eight-foot-long hardwood staff that had been leaning against the back of the house. I placed another chair next to the shower stall, clambered atop it, swung the staff over the top and began doing my very best to smite the offending reptile, yea, verily. Unfortunately the ponderous length of wood moved slowly and gave the cobra plenty of time to evade my poorly aimed bashes. Further, if my blows, driven by considerable energy and fear, did little to damage the snake, they made a considerable ruckus as the corrugated sides of the stall were struck repeatedly. Within moments a worried Hussein burst through the side door, asked what was wrong, and sized up the situation.

There stood my diminutive friend in the center of the kitchen floor, staring up at the 6'4" anthropologist perched atop a chair and wielding a staff that would have done credit to Little John, himself. Hussein shook his head and grimaced in bemusement (an expression he frequently wore in my company). After I described the cobra, he informed me that I was going about the thing incorrectly and that I had chosen the wrong wood, as only bamboo is truly efficacious against poisonous snakes. He then went outside to locate what he regarded as a reasonable length of wood, returning shortly with a three-and-a-half-foot length of flexible bamboo, which I regarded as better suited to Charlie Chaplin than to the dangerous business of dispatching cobras. I watched from my elevated vantage point as Hussein then walked to the shower stall, removed the chair, entered the stall, and killed the cobra with several rapid and well-aimed blows. Properly chagrined, I descended from my eyrie to thank my 5'4" neighbor. He turned to me and suggested that we talk, as I had much to learn about snakes.

We sat on the kitchen steps leading up to the main part of the house, while he spoke and I took notes. He listed a series of rather deadly snakes and general precautions to take against them. He went into particular detail about cobras: "If you want to keep cobras away, sprinkle goose dung around the house. They don't like the smell." He then cautioned me that cobras marry and thereafter travel in pairs. I nodded noncommittally and entered this in my notes under the heading of "folk beliefs." Some ten days later I was forced to amend this heading.

Once again I was out, this time transporting our friend Clive Kessler to town, and Karen was in the kitchen trying to do some baking. When one of our cats began to hiss and back away from the door, Karen took note. Beneath the same back door and into the same shower stall came cobra number two. This time the snake, perhaps frightened by the fearsome cat, entered the shower stall and appeared to immediately exit through the drain hole. I returned home shortly afterward and seeking the snake, found it AWOL. This was a problem. A cobra in your shower is an unwelcome guest, but a cobra somewhere in the general

The first of our least welcome visitors. Intelligently, I took this with a telephoto from my perch on a kitchen chair *outside* the shower stall.

vicinity is a constant and deadly threat. The location of our outhouse, just behind our home and near the run-off drain, only compounded the problem. We were faced with dreadful (literally) visions of visits to the outhouse that might be interrupted in a most unseemly fashion. Thus I undertook what may be my greatest act of bravery: I grabbed Hussein's length of bamboo, which he had kindly left with me, and started stalking the cobra in the tall grass between the house and the privy. From a distance I would have appeared a fine imitation of a nervous flamingo, as my strategy involved taking the longest step I could, perching on one leg, and then examining my surroundings with minute, anxious attention.

After some ten minutes of this terrifying exercise, Karen called out from the house that she had located the snake, curled up midway down the run-off drain. I greeted this news somewhat like Fay Wray discovering that King Kong was a vegetarian. Although my danger had been illusionary, the terror was not, and my adrenaline level would have done credit to the entire defensive line of the New England Patriots.

Karen and I determined a relatively safe means of dispatching the snake. We first closed both ends of the drain while Karen heated water. I then removed the block from the outer end of the drain, grabbed my insufficiently long bamboo withe, arranged what I prayed would be an effective ambush, and called for her to pour the hot water in the other end. The cobra burst forth in irritated haste and I smote it, yea, verily. If I lacked Hussein's finesse, I made up for it with excessive enthusiasm. Powered by my excess of adrenaline, for approximately twenty seconds I did hit, strike, hammer, clout, ding, pop, slog, sock, pummel, swat, whack, beat, whop, cudgel, poke, punch, bang, bash, and thrash that unfortunate reptile. I then discarded what had once been a snake and climbed to our study, where I changed the entry of Hussein's advice from "folk beliefs" to "indigenous knowledge of nature."

Of Other Irritants

Not all pests are animals. Some are human, and they are apt to be the most tenacious and problematic of nuisances.

All cultures have marginal members, individuals who, for reasons ranging from a lack of resources to a checkered personal history, are not well integrated into their own societies. These people are usually unhappy with their personal circumstances, critical of the surrounding social environment, and at variance with the dominant goals and values. Anthropologists are familiar with this phenomenon, in part, because our discipline abounds with stories concerning the manner in which disaffected persons have tried to attach themselves to visiting anthropologists in hopes of improving their social situations. Not surprisingly, most anthropologists encounter one or several such individuals during the period of field research.

During the year and a half Karen and I were in the field, I dealt with a number of people who had the potential to be true pests. However, the Kelantanese sensibility is such that indirect allusions to work, to other involvements, to the need for travel flexibility, and so on, were generally sufficient to dissuade most hangers-on. There was one exception, however, a young man of mixed Malay-Thai ancestry who determined that I must become an integral part of his social network.

This fellow, whom I shall call Badi, lived with his mother at the edge of the village. Although bright, he seemed peculiarly insensitive to the nuances of Kelantanese communication, an important element of which was nonverbal. Where Kelantanese are characteristically indirect and deferential, he was forthright and even pushy. Kelantanese were not comfortable dealing with him and avoided him whenever possible. Badi had acquired a reputation for social obtuseness long before Karen and I had entered the area.

Badi found my presence a promising means of altering his own position in the village. He approached me during my first month and cheerfully offered to be helpful. Unaware of his lack of social graces and of his social standing in the community, I accepted his offer and encouraged him to accompany me on various forays about the village. I had thought that he might prove a suitable field assistant, for he did seem intelligent and quite familiar with the local area. I gradually became aware that Badi was trying to use his relationship with me to alter his status with others. One day I found him arguing with a Chinese shop owner who was an acquaintance of mine. When I inquired what the problem was, the shop owner explained that Badi was demanding a discount because he was my friend and field assistant. At this point he had yet to become either, and I soon resolved that these relationships would never mature.

Checking with my neighbor Hussein, with Yusof, and with others, I acquired information on Badi's history of difficulties within the village. I then resolved to terminate our relationship. Of course this resolution required action on my part, and therein lay the difficulty. I knew I lacked the social skills that Kelantanese would have called upon, and I feared giving such offense that I might become the target of the kind of gossip that Badi himself engendered. I tried my versions of indirect intimations, circuitous suggestions, and oblique hints, all of which had no perceptible effect on his determination to remain close to me.

The solution to this problem was ultimately Kelantanese and was provided by Badi himself. He had appeared in a number of color slides I had taken, and he requested color photographic copies. At first I demurred, citing the expense involved in the copying process. Shortly thereafter, having borrowed some Kelantanese wisdom, I agreed to make the copies if he would shoulder half of the expense. He agreed, the copies were made, and I began my Kelantanese-style campaign to separate myself from Badi. When he came by, I would make oblique allusions to the pictures, asking him how he liked them and generally inquiring after his satisfaction. This was, of course, also a reminder that he owed me money. After a couple of days of enduring such references, Badi came by less frequently. Within two weeks, I hardly saw him. The stratagem cost me M$7 (about U.S.$2.30) and was well worth it.

The CIA and Me

Not all my problems arose from the local environment. One owed its origin to behaviors undertaken by the U.S. government, specifically the Central Intelligence Agency in its unrelenting pursuit of Communism.

Shortly after the end of World War II, a group of discontented Chinese, who had fought against the Japanese during the war, identified themselves as Communists and attempted an armed insurrection. This precipitated the period termed the "Emergency," which lasted from 1946 until after Malaysia's independence in 1957. At its conclusion several hundred Chinese fled across the border to Thailand. Thereafter they would move back and forth across the border to create mischief and to seek supplies. When one government took decisive military action against them, they would cross to its neighbor. It seems that during the United States involvement in Vietnam, this roving band of Chinese Communists, which had probably never numbered more than a few hundred, drew the attention of our government. In any event, in 1968 there were village tales of CIA agents in southern Thailand, where they were reputed to be gathering information on the Communists.

One afternoon in November, I was visiting the village police post, a modest little structure containing two policemen and some records I wished to consult. Like all police in Malaysia, these men were posted from other states, Selangor and Perak. This meant, among other things, that their ability to understand Kelantanese dialect was limited and that villagers would view them as threatening outsiders. This arrangement was part of the government's effort to reduce the likelihood of bribery and corruption. They reasoned that police working in areas where they lacked relatives and acquaintances would be less likely to engage in questionable practices. Whether or not this was true, it was the case that the honesty and efficiency of Malaysia's police compared favorably with other countries in Southeast Asia.

The documents I was studying recorded births and deaths for the local administrative area. At least they were presumed to do so, but I gradually learned that what they lacked in accuracy they made up for in creativity. Villagers are quite indifferent to state rules such as these, and while deaths were usually reported, owing to the role of the Imam, birth reports were often omitted. Nonetheless I dutifully took down what information I could obtain on these two facets of life in hopes that I might be able to devise a use for it at some later time (I have yet to do so). I had been visiting the station regularly for several days and had become acquainted with the two police officers assigned to the post. That afternoon the senior officer (he may have been twenty-five years old) leaned over the little table where I was transcribing figures on birth and inquired in a conspiratorial fashion, "Tell me Cik Lah, how long have you been with the CIA?" Things go . . . well, you get the idea.

I immediately protested that I was not, never had been, and possessed no desire to be, a member of the CIA. In response the officer smiled, winked, and offered whatever assistance he could. I immediately returned to our house, grabbed my passport, letter of introduction from a dean at Cornell, and whatever other supporting papers I could find, and returned to the police station to demonstrate my independence of the CIA. The officer dutifully examined the documents, smiled, winked, and offered whatever assistance he could. Of course a CIA agent would possess a convincing set of false documents.

I later learned that much of the bureaucratic establishment had assumed I was connected with our government and was in Wakaf Bharu posing as an anthropologist in order to monitor the activities of Chinese Communists. After all, there I was, staying in a small village only fifteen miles from the Thai border and, for reasons I will discuss later, moving back and forth across that border on several occasions. Further, there had been detailed stories of CIA agents in southern Thailand posing as anthropologists!

This whole misperception could have greatly altered my relationship to the villagers, made my work difficult or impossible, and possibly even endangered Karen and me. Fortunately the governments of Malaysia and Kelantan, as well as the villagers, thought the CIA was a wonderful organization because it was opposed to Communism. For the Kelantanese in particular, Communism meant *Chinese* Communism and bore directly upon their fear of Chinese influence in Malaysia. Interethnic relations are complex and will be discussed later.

Concluding Comment

The preceding information has been included precisely because it is not a guide to good fieldwork technique. Indeed, this kind of material is not a part of what one encounters in most books on fieldwork. Hopefully, however, it provides the reader with some sense of the daily tribulations that absorb time and energy and that may have little or nothing to do with the field research proper. Finally, it also reveals that even trained and well-intentioned professionals can exhibit behavior that they know to be unwise. My misadventures with Sly are worth relating, but they hardly represent behavior of which I am proud. Still, fieldwork is an intensive learning experience, which means, among other things, that anthropologists learn a good deal about themselves.

6

Intimations of Sunburn

Communicating accurately across cultures and about them is one of the most intellectually challenging tasks possible. Anthropologists are aware that there is always some cultural content that will not readily translate across cultural boundaries. This may be because a term refers to a concept for which there is no ready referent in the second culture, or it may be because the two cultures segment reality in differing ways. Even with closely related cultures there can be distinct problems. Thus, to translate the German *gemütlich* as "comfortable" only approximates the meaning of the term and loses much of the culturally grounded nuance that would be present to any German.

This does not mean that a cultural element is wholly untranslatable, but it can mean that the translation process can be arduous and result only in a rough approximation. A Kelantanese wishing to reference the state of severe embarrassment and the complex social behaviors that can result in this state simply uses the term malu. In order for me to convey an approximation of the import of this expression I need several sentences that include both descriptors and examples, and I remain aware that I can still never capture the full meaning of the term. The only way to do so is to be born and enculturated in Kelantan. Thus any attempt to record for oneself, let alone to convey to others, the nature of a cultural reality is bound to be flawed. This does not signify that such efforts are failures or poor uses of our time. On the contrary, efforts to better understand others are quite useful and heuristic; it is simply that we should not regard the results of such investigations as truth with a capital *T*.

If concepts can be difficult to translate, it is also the case that there are whole domains that cultures may treat quite differently. This was brought home to me in a mundane fashion when I tried to assist Karen in purchasing bananas. The tropics abound with different varieties of bananas, and the problem is particularly acute in Malaysia, where bananas actually evolved. I recognized that there were many local terms for bananas, and I also rather foolishly thought that I understood my ignorance about them. The root word for banana is *pisang*, but there seemed to be an endless set of modifiers that distinguished one variety from another. Thus I asked lots of questions concerning the names of bananas in the tried-and-true fashion used by all travelers—point at the subject and ask what it is called. I compiled a lengthy list of names for little red bananas, for long yellow bananas, for fat yellow bananas, for large red bananas, for pink waxy bananas, etc. I then memorized these and returned to the market, determined to show off my banana acumen.

I started with a middle-aged woman seller whom I had frequented before, and noting that she had a stock of fat, yellow bananas, I asked for them by name . . . or what I thought was their name. She informed me that she didn't have the bananas before my eyes but that she did have another variety, at which she lifted up the bananas I thought I had referenced. I encountered several more failures in my efforts to buy bananas knowledgeably before I began to realize that Kelantanese do not simply employ our Linnaean classification for bananas. Instead, in addition to a concern with genus and species, they include such considerations as degree of ripeness and whether or not the fruit is bruised when they select appropriate references.

Ethnosemantics studies the manner in which cultures dissect (and define) reality, often employing different components of meaning in less elaborate fashions (Goodenough 1956). The kind of elaboration Kelantanese employ to distinguish among bananas points to an area of cultural importance, and much as we distinguish between sedan and coupe on the basis of the number of doors, Kelantanese make finer distinctions about bananas than we would find useful. Indeed, it was enough to drive me bananas.

Currently there is a schism between anthropologists who believe that we can never even approximate the reality of other cultures, and those who believe we can subject this reality to scientific investigation and "knowing." Like most dichotomies, this one produces more frustration and heat than it does utility and light. As in the case of most such divisions, the real work of investigation is carried out somewhere in the middle. Practical approaches to improving our understanding of other cultures can profit from both interpretive and quantitative approaches, recognizing that they are each suited for different tasks. Interpretive approaches are broad, sensitive to context, and good at generating ideas and hypotheses. However, they are also imprecise and notoriously difficult to replicate. In contrast, quantitative approaches are often quite precise and provide easily replicated data. Unfortunately, quantitative approaches achieve these strengths by omitting information and reducing complexities to quantifiable units. Thus they are less context sensitive, and while they provide fairly precise data, such data often doesn't convey much range of meaning. As it happens my dissertation research was directly related to this methodological issue.

As a psychological anthropologist, I was interested in the value structures that people use to guide their decision making and in their behavior as it reflects these values. I intended to study cultural and social values among the Kelantanese using both traditional anthropological methodologies and a quantitative approach borrowed from psycholinguistics and the work of Charles Osgood (1964, 1975, 1957). Typically, anthropology approached the subject of values in a highly interpretive "it seems to me" fashion. The best articulation of a model to study values was Clyde Kluckhohn's effort to establish a classification of values that would facilitate their study (1951). The procedure, however, remained much the same as it had ever been. Anthropologists would go into an area, remain for a considerable period of time, and emerge with an "impression" of the beliefs of the people studied. The result was often a sensitively written and fulsome account of another belief system. Unfortunately in those few instances where more than one anthropologist conducted such research, there were often significant discrepancies in their findings. They would usually agree upon the kinship structure, the nature of the economy, the political structure, etc. However, their descriptions of belief systems and values were often disparate, as these were very subject to personal bias and filters.

Aware of these difficulties, I had planned to study Kelantanese values, first using a Kluckhohnian analysis and then supplementing that with quantified data provided by a psycholinguistic research tool, the semantic differential, which, I hoped, would either support the more interpretive approach and increase my confidence in my insights or point me in more productive directions. I decided to wait until late in the fieldwork to initiate the semantic differential study, partly because I thought the methodology could adversely affect the initial impression I made on villagers and partly because I knew I would be more secure in both language and culture if I waited.

Belief Systems

My interest in values derived from my wider concerns with cognition and with how people construct meaning in their lives. Earlier images of culture treated it as though it were directive, and people were simply passively socialized into its patterns, like unthinking slaves receiving directions from an Egyptian overseer as they labor to construct a pyramid of meaning. My own orientation holds that people are meaningful participants in their cultures, aware of their circumstances and capable of taking steps to affect patterns both of significant symbols and of mores. However, this does not mean that people are perfectly aware of all the social and cultural forces that act on them.

While the values are fascinating and important, they are also elusive. It is difficult to study those beliefs that are closest to people, in no small part because people often do not consciously introspect about those values that are most dear to them. Anthropologists term such significant influences on worldview and behavior "core values," and they are seldom verbalized (Kluckhohn 1951).

Belief systems are also structured in discoverable ways; that is, they are not simply a hodgepodge of ideas, attitudes, and perceptions. Instead major values are integrated and have established interrelationships among their various components (Hutterer et al. 1985: 1149; Raybeck 1975; Rokeach 1973). This should not be taken as an argument that belief systems are perfectly integrated and thus free of friction and conflicts. On the contrary it is often the tension between competing beliefs that allows individuals a range of choice in determining appropriate behaviors, and that also provides the impetus for change in an existing system. Individualism is arguably a core value for U.S. society, perhaps *the* core value (Bellah et al. 1985). Nonetheless many of us value and are concerned about issues of conformity, striving to be similar to those about us. This is particularly true of secondary school, where the pressures for conformity can be particularly intense, and in the business world, where the dark suit, striped tie, and polished dark shoes approximate a uniform.

Belief systems do not dictate behavior, but they do influence the choice of behavioral alternatives, and they can make some behaviors very unlikely indeed. Thus while Kelantanese are not required to be quiet and indirect in their dealings with others, they usually are so, and breaches of this behavior are noted and dealt with by others (Raybeck 1986a). It would be exceptional for a Kelantanese villager to lose his temper with a coresident and to engage in a shouting match. It happens, but when it does, it is treated as an aberration that must be addressed. The test of a value's durability is its congruence with major core values and with patterns of behavior in which people are already steeped.

It was because of the difficulty of accurately assessing values, and because of their importance and often charged nature, that I had decided to approach them utilizing both "soft"—participant observation—methods and "hard"—quantifiable empirical—methods. The sensitivity of the subject matter suggested that I would have to approach the task of information through a variety of means. With my key informants, who knew and trusted me, I could be forthright in my questions and solicitations of assistance. However, with many villagers I would need to engage in typically Kelantanese indirect inquiries, something like a hunter circling around to approach quarry from upwind.

Qualitative Methods

There are a variety of approaches in anthropology that could supply both direct and indirect information on cultural values. Even my frustrating attempts to collect genealogical data provided insights into some of the elements of valued Kelantanese character and behavior. People with whom I worked would often speak glowingly of an individual and give me reasons for their approbation. Similarly, though less commonly and less obviously, they would also indicate disapproval concerning certain individuals and/or their actions.

The use of life histories, in which individuals relate their recollections of their lives, often emphasizing aspects they deem important, also worked as a promising means of gaining insights into village values. One old man detailed the steps he had taken when he first moved to Wakaf Bharu. During our conversations he provided some key comments concerning the importance of maintaining good ties to others and of securing harmony among others in the village. Another woman, discussing some of the gossip that had bothered her in the past, gave evidence of the importance of village membership and of the wealth of knowledge people acquire about one another's past behavior.

Case studies, sometimes called extended case studies, focus upon a particular event or upon a linked series of events and examine both the individuals involved and the reasons behind their behaviors. I found that those events that were most prominent in the village gossip network often involved village-defined deviance; that is, departures from the established values. Examining these instances and collecting information on them gave me an improved sense of how values actually work in daily life and the ploys that people can utilize to circumvent unwanted, yet valued, strictures. By focusing on a question of disputed inheritance, I discovered a disparity between the role of women as defined by highly valued Islam, and the role of women as it actually existed in village society (Raybeck 1980–81; Raybeck 1991c; Raybeck 1992b). Some of this material is discussed in chapter 8.

Nonetheless the best method for obtaining information on values and other aspects of the Kelantanese belief system seemed to be continued curiosity coupled with a modicum of sensitivity. Simply observing what went on about me proved to be an effective way to gain a better sense of the cultural reasons behind the behavioral patterns I witnessed. However, lest you think this means I immediately understood and appreciated the behavior I witnessed, the following anecdote should prove instructive.

During my initial fieldwork period, an excellent example of a subtle behavioral exchange was provided by the village Imam and a local Malay merchant. I had been sitting with two Kelantanese friends on their porch, engaging in the common afternoon entertainment—watching passersby. I saw the local Imam and another villager greet one another traditionally with clasped hands, a bow, and hands brought back to breast, and then move on, at which point my two friends chuckled and began whispering. They had clearly seen more than I and were delighted to explain matters to me.

It seems there had been some friction between the Imam and this villager for months owing to difficulties between their children. The Imam's son had been acting roughly toward other children, notably the son of the merchant. In the judgment of many villagers, including the merchant, the Imam was partly responsible, since he had not remonstrated with his son; indeed, he had a reputation for spoiling the child. My friends were aware of this situation as a backdrop to the meeting we witnessed.

According to their report, when the Imam and the merchant met, the merchant displayed his displeasure with the current state of affairs by bending less than he should have in deference to the Imam. Apparently the Imam recognized the slight immediately, for he proceeded to bend much lower than usual in a fashion that parodied the relationship, and then drew both hands back to his chest, where he held them for what my friends reported to be an extended period. In this fashion the Imam not only refused to offer an apology to the merchant, he increased the degree of offense, yet he did so in a nonverbal fashion that others could attend to or not, as they chose. My friends were amused by this interchange, but they also predicted that relations between the Imam and the merchant would become a more serious problem. Later events proved them correct, and before the matter was finished, the village head, a man related to the Imam, had to act as a mediator in repairing the relationship.

The behavior I had witnessed was an indication of how subtly and indirectly Kelantanese can communicate with one another, and it also demonstrated that the language of character (budi bahasa), on which I was gathering information, was composed of significant nonverbal elements. As well as noting what people said to each other, I began paying a great deal of attention to the forms of behavior around me. As a result I am certain that I discovered more than I would have otherwise. Probably my most useful means of obtaining insights into the way Kelantanese conceive of their social world involved the coffee shops (kedai kopi), where men and sometimes women would lounge, exchange information, and gossip about the behavior of others. My favorite strategy was to begin a discussion with a friend about an aspect of Kelantanese values. Shortly after I would begin such an endeavor, it was common for other villagers to join in the conversation, either to elaborate on what my friend was saying or to disagree with it. One afternoon at my favorite kedai kopi, in the company of four Kelantanese friends, I began an open discussion of which values were deemed more important:

> In discussing village values and what makes a person better than another, Yusof quickly responded that one person was better and had a better *perangai* [character, temperament] primarily due to his *asohan* [his training, or the way he was raised]. Although there was some disagreement about the order of importance, the others agreed upon three central values for kampong life and these were as follows: *masharakat* or *pergaulan kampong*—meaning by this simply the society in which they live or the people about them; budi bahasa—which essentially means courtesy but can also be translated by such personal characteristics as generosity, thoughtfulness, kindness, etc.; and finally *ilmu*—meaning also *pelajaran hidup* or the finding and following of a life way that is fitting and pleasant to the individual [sesuai]. Concerning masharakat kampong all agreed that people should like to give one another help and advice and to generally form a solidarity group that can be depended upon for material and emotional sustenance. Under this idea of the kampong as an integrated, functioning whole is the concept that between kampongs that are geographically removed from one another there may very well be different lifestyles and values. [This is epitomized in the saying, "*Lain padang, lain belalang*" (Different fields, different grasshoppers).]

Despite the rather ragged writing style of this partial excerpt from my field notes, it is apparent that I obtained some very useful information from an afternoon's recreation. It also underscores the importance of language proficiency. This approach would never work through an interpreter, nor would it even have been very successful had the people involved been able to speak English. The object is to begin the discussion of a subject and then retire to the background, while those who best know pursue the issue.

Occasionally this approach can result in significant surprises. I had always been impressed by some of the detailed analyses of kinship systems, particularly those that characterize British social anthropology. I had the impression that a great deal of anthropological time and thought was necessary to produce the subtle analyses of marriage patterns, residence rules, and associated concerns. However, one afternoon my coffee shop conversation revealed another possibility, reflected in the following field note excerpt:

According to the five men, as recently as thirty years ago it was most common for first cousins to marry so that each kampong would usually consist of no more than four or five sets of *waris* [relatives]. The reason for this was to keep the *pusaka* [inheritance], primarily the rice lands, in the waris. Back in those days, the preferred husband was a farmer and the degree to which he was preferred was proportional to his industry and to the amount of land. With the introduction of wage jobs or wage labor, people found that they preferred having as a *menantu* [an in-law] a person who worked in an office, as opposed to a farmer. Hussein Hassan put this quite bluntly when he said that a farmer's work is dirty (*kotor*), while the professional work is more halus ["refined, courteous," an important value contrasted with *kasar*, meaning rough, uncouth, and poorly socialized], and in addition the professional will probably make more and will have a *pandangan lebeh tinggi* [his outlook will be higher and broader]. As a result of these changing preferences in choice of menantu, people began to marry out more and more. Nowadays, according to the men, it is understood that marrying out not only brings in attractive spouses but also extends the waris. And it is thought that this is preferable to the old way of keeping the waris inbred. An additional factor has been the increasing participation of young people in the choice of their own spouses. Yusof Daut gave a rough estimate that 80 percent of the young people now largely determine who they will marry. This is directly attributable to the school system wherein the kids are given an opportunity to get to know and mix with each other. As a matter of fact HH is opposed to this integrated schooling, which began just after the war. He is worried about the sexual looseness that may result from such unsupervised social contact. YD and HH then gave me the order of the criteria for marriageability, as it is today. First, the type of work that he does. Second, his perangai [character], and his *latar belakang* [background]. Third, his upah [or how much he makes]. And only fourth, whether or not he is waris.

Please note that the preceding sensitive and complex analysis of changing marriage patterns owes absolutely nothing to my anthropological percipience. Indeed the topic arose by chance. I can take credit only for having the good sense to write it down.

The preceding methods were extremely useful for developing ideas about the nature of the Kelantanese value system and for helping me to refine the questions I would ask my key informants. I found that one rough check on their reliability could be obtained by looking for concordances among patterns of belief. Thus if a value is central, it should be supported by additional secondary beliefs concerning behavior that are congruent with the value. There are of course limits to this approach, as value systems are imperfectly integrated, but generally I found I was able to develop an increasingly coherent and well-structured image of Kelantanese values. Of course there was always the nagging question: were the structure and coherence actually part of the whole, or had I developed them in an effort to create a consistent representation of their belief system? This is why I had also determined to employ a quantitative methodology that would be less subject to personal interpretation.

Quantitative Methods

I have already discussed one of the major shortcomings of quantitative approaches, the need to omit information and to reduce cultural complexities to categories that can be numerically manipulated. There is, however, a greater problem with such methods when employed across cultures. Methods tend to embody the assumptions of the culture in which they are devised. Thus a technique, test, or system that is created in one culture may be poorly adapted to collect data in a different culture. This is particularly true in the realms of intelligence testing and investigations of cognition (Cole and Scribner 1974; Munroe and Munroe 1994).

Imagine for a moment that you are in a room, sitting at a desk. A Japanese individual speaking imperfect English enters, wearing traditional robes and carrying several objects that he places before you along with instructions in English. The instructions tell you to take the brush you have been given, dip it in the ink, and copy as many of the Japanese characters as possible within five minutes. Would you fare as well as the average Japanese eight-year-old? While this example may seem artificial, I assure you it represents a number of the difficulties involved in utilizing research instruments for cross-cultural comparison. Either the instrument is more appropriate for a given culture than others and introduces corresponding biases, or the instrument is altered to fit each culture, which then raises issues of comparability. If you had been given a pen and asked to copy letters of the alphabet, could your results then be compared to Japanese working with brush, ink, and characters?

I was aware of the difficulties described above and spent some time seeking a quantitative research instrument that would minimize these problems. My choice was the semantic differential, a psycholinguistic instrument for objectively assessing the connotative meanings of concepts.[11] I will not burden you with the details of its construction (you may, of course, read the endnotes), but I do wish to assure you that the methods employed in the formation of the semantic differential include a number of safeguards to insure that the resulting instrument is a product of the culture in which it is constructed, and that it is not simply a transposition of the American version with its associated cultural assumptions.[12]

Essentially the semantic differential must be created in the cultural setting in which it is to be used. This involves a great deal of preliminary work, ranging from translation to the collection of data for factor analysis, etc. At one point Karen and I had to process 120,000 bits of information to prepare it for appropriate computer analysis. The information was then mailed to Illinois for factor analysis on a mainframe computer, a task that I can now accomplish in the field with my Macintosh Powerbook. The set-up work takes months, but once the instrument is in place, it can be used easily and with little time investment.

I was conscious of the importance of selecting a sample in fieldwork. Even those anthropologists who rely exclusively on impressionistic methods take care to gather their information from a variety of different sources to reduce the likelihood of bias. Consider what would transpire if you asked Newt Gingrich, Strom Thurmond, and Robert Dole to comment upon the policies of President Roosevelt's administration. Arguably one might receive a somewhat skewed perspective on American politics. Similarly anthropologists in the field wish to be sure that they obtain as many different perspectives as are well represented among the population with which they are living (they can't get them all). Toward this end, anthropologists often select a representative sample rather than a random or other probabilistic sample.[13] Random samples require population sizes and procedures that are often incompatible with the small communities in which anthropologists carry out most of their research. Representative samples are intended to represent the salient aspects of the population under study, but this approach relies heavily on the perspicacity of the anthropologists and their familiarity with their social milieu.

The semantic differential also permits individual responses and group responses to be analyzed separately, which could facilitate a comparison of beliefs and attitudes held by the members of identifiable subcultures. I was interested in comparing the values perspectives of four different subcultures. As Kelantan is overwhelmingly rural in population, my baseline would naturally be the villagers whom I could use as exemplars of Kelantanese culture. However, I was also interested in groups of people whom I thought would diverge from this standard: high school students, who were being exposed to Western-style education and ideas; taxi drivers, who for reasons mentioned earlier were associated with modernization; and prostitutes, who formed a deviant subgroup already at odds with some major Kelantanese values.

Clearly I made my research choices based on a strategy, but equally clearly, except for the villagers, the subcultures could not be regarded as representative of the wider society. Instead I hoped to obtain participants who would represent their subculture accurately and fairly fully.

One of the strengths of the semantic differential is that, in its finished form, it can be employed among both the literate and the illiterate. Thus while the high school students and some taxi drivers received a written version to which they were asked to respond, most other participants participated orally.[14] This required considerable time, as I had to work individually with each respondent. From the members of each group I collected semantic differential responses to twenty-five concepts relating to values and other aspects of Kelantanese culture.[15] For each concept, the participant had to make a judgment against twelve pairs of adjectival opposites. Thus the administration of a single semantic differential with attendant instructions, examples, and clarifications could take a couple of hours.

Initially I had dreaded the data collection aspect of the field project, as collecting such information is often routine and dull. I discovered, however, that the process of orally administering the semantic differential often resulted in unanticipated benefits. One afternoon I was administering the semantic differential to Pak Awang Kecil, an elderly man who had proved an invaluable source of information on Kelantanese culture prior to World War II. His response to the concept "I, myself" was very positive, even more so than those of most villagers with whom I had worked. After we were done, I asked why he had been so positive in his assessment of his self-concept. He relied, "If I don't think well of myself, who will?" and then launched into a very insightful discussion of the relationship between the group and the individual. The information I obtained that afternoon assaulted one of anthropology's common stereotypes; that peasants are almost exclusively group-oriented and that the individual is of comparatively little moment. I am confident that I owe my awareness of this material to the efforts involved in collecting quantitative data.

This example makes clear another lesson about fieldwork. One is exposed to useful information all the time, even when collecting narrow quantitative data. Often the trick lies in recognizing that the information is there and that it warrants pursuit. Of course there are times an anthropologist would have to be exceptionally opaque not to perceive the importance of unfolding events, as the following excerpt from my field notes indicates:

> Went down to Isahak's where I had arranged to administer the sd to Cik Ismail b. Haji Mat. (He is about fifty-five, a great chess player but a lousy subject). At any rate it became apparent early in the evening that Ismail was not understanding the task and that repeated explanations, while illuminating everyone else in the room, did nothing to clarify the matter for him. The second concept we tackled was the concept of *orang Melayu* [Malay person]. Ismail repeatedly stuck to the middle of the scale even when asked whether Malays were *benchi* [hateful] or *sayang* [loving] and so forth. He put on a great show of making a tough decision—rubbing his chin and looking very thoughtful. After this show of great

penetration he would say—*sederhana, tengah-tengah* [average, in the middle]. This finally elicited from a number of men in the room, including Isahak and some men who were markedly younger (twenty to twenty-five years), comments of skepticism and some said at one point that Ismail wasn't very brave about answering. The idea being that they didn't agree that Malays were equally placed between hatred and love. They felt strongly enough about this to overcome their traditional reticence in front of an old man.

As you may imagine, it takes a strong rationale for young men to publicly disagree with, and even to criticize, a respected elder. You may also imagine that I paid more attention to how Malays perceived themselves, particularly in relation to other ethnic groups, such as the Chinese (Raybeck 1980).

As I continued to employ the semantic differential, I was gratified to find that it did a fine job of supporting my earlier and more impressionistic study of Kelantanese values (Raybeck 1975) and that it also provided useful insights into the differences between my four samples. Administering the device to the literate population of a nearby high school was easy. All I needed to do was to copy the forms with appropriate instructions in Malay and pass these out during a school period.[16] The written version took only some twenty minutes to complete and the high school officials were quite cooperative—once I had invested some months in obtaining the necessary permissions.

The high value that Kelantanese place on education led many parents to encourage their children to attend primary school, which was free except for a small charge for books and materials. Most children managed to achieve basic literacy in romanized Malay as well as some proficiency in mathematics. Despite the proportionately large number of children who acquired some primary education, relatively few went on to secondary school, largely for economic reasons. Poor families found it difficult to spare the presence of an adolescent who would otherwise be contributing to the family income. Not only was there a substantial fee for attending secondary school, which varied with the size and quality of the school, there were few secondary schools in the state, and nearly all were located in distant urban areas, such as Kota Bharu. Due to these financial considerations and to the Islamic bias regarding women, somewhat less than one-third of the secondary school students in Kelantan were female.

Like primary schools, secondary schools were modeled after the British educational system. They were strongly oriented to a continuing educational pattern and did not instruct students in particular skills. The bias was toward a Western-oriented curriculum containing algebra, geography, literature, etc. This bias was reinforced by teachers who were mostly from the west coast, and who were significantly more Westernized than the teachers in primary schools. Consequently students in secondary schools were exposed to a variety of nontraditional beliefs, and increased exposure to modernizing influences characterized much of secondary school education.

The students who responded to the semantic differential were all between the ages of fifteen and eighteen and were attending two of the largest secondary schools in Kota Bharu. Both schools, one for boys and one for girls, were considered to be among the best in the state and had well-qualified faculties.

As in many developing countries, students attended secondary school in anticipation of acquiring a respected white-collar job, and that expectation was demonstrated in their occupational goals. For the boys, these included being army officers, teachers, various professionals, and entering government service. A minority expressed a desire to continue their studies at the university level. Significantly none expressed a desire to enter the business sphere, nor was there any interest in returning home to be a farmer. This was a reflection in microcosm of the national situation where Malays controlled the civil service and the army but were poorly represented in the business world, which was dominated by the Chinese. Among the girls, some anticipated entering teaching, medicine, and the creative arts. Again only a small minority wanted to continue their education beyond secondary school.

Working with these students was quite easy, as all were literate, clearly understood the task, and filled out the semantic differential forms with little need for assistance or additional clarification beyond that included with the instructions. Interestingly the responses of secondary school students deviated most from traditional villagers. This was particularly true of their response to *Custom*, the all-important traditional adat that villagers view as linked to their social and cultural identities (Raybeck 1980,

1992a). These students were subject to nontraditional educational experiences and were being encouraged to pursue careers in a modernizing economy that owed nothing to adat.

The semantic differential responses helped to support a perspective I had been developing from my conversations with Yusof, the son of my neighbor Hussein, and with other young people. They were notably disaffected with traditional values but also did not fully understand the new patterns that were emerging from the process of modernization. The result was the emergence of an ominous tendency to reject the old in favor of new goals for which they lacked appropriate means.

The literature on modernization abounds with examples of youths who, caught between the old and the new, become disheartened and engage in deviant activities such as alcohol, petty crimes, etc. (Bodley 1982; Nash 1974; Peacock 1968; Scott 1985). What is particularly poignant is that the youths in jeopardy are often among the brightest and most motivated members of their generations. What I encountered in Kelantan through my interviews, interactions, and the semantic differential was the emergence of a similar pattern in which Kelantanese youths were becoming estranged from their own culture. Without question their responses to the semantic differential indicated a greater degree of cultural deviance than any of the other groups, including the prostitutes (Raybeck 1975).

While student responses to the semantic differential provided a worrisome look at the future, I still needed a sense of the variability of Kelantanese culture among adults who had been socialized in the traditional culture. Hence my interests in taxi drivers and in prostitutes.

Taxi Drivers

As I mentioned earlier, taxi drivers were selected because they appeared well disposed toward modernization, yet usually had been reared in accord with the dictates of traditional culture. Anthropologists refer to individuals who bestride two or more cultures as marginal people, people who may be at the periphery of their own culture owing either to a disaffection with its values and goals, or to an inability to accommodate change. Badi, the pest described earlier, found himself in a situation resulting from the circumstances of his birth. Choice had nothing to do with it. In contrast taxi drivers follow a profession they actively choose, and they are often motivated to do so because of the attractions of modernization.

In the late sixties driving a taxi was romantic; it was also a means of obtaining wages, still not a common opportunity. The average driver made three to four Malay dollars a day, if his was not a long-distance run, and most aren't.[17] In an urban center, taxi drivers could generally be found in or near the market area, waiting for the young boys they hired to collect a full complement of passengers while they frequented coffee shops and gossiped among themselves. Their demeanor and joking behavior reflected an adventurous masculine ethic that was seldom encountered in the kampong. They were usually perceived as one of the few modern romantic figures in Malay society, and this image was reinforced by a shiny Mercedes over which they had full control while on the road. On the negative side, their image also involved a degree of sexual notoriety. It was widely believed that taxi drivers frequented urban prostitutes, and villagers sometimes referred to them as *ayam jantan*, roosters.

Taxi drivers enjoyed several economic and cultural advantages, yet little was required to enter this profession beyond a license and some driving skill. This occupation provided an avenue of upward mobility for individuals who were unlikely to advance due to poverty and/or a lack of formal education. The elements of glamour and modernization that this employment offered also made this an attractive alternative to traditional rural village life.

In Kelantan most taxis that traveled interstate were based in Kota Bharu, although a large village occasionally boasted a single taxi that offered local service. The Kota Bharu taxis were owned largely by Chinese merchants, and only infrequently did a driver own the taxi he drove. The owner of the taxi paid for the state license, the insurance, and maintenance as well as for the vehicle itself. In return the owner received eight of every ten dollars that the taxi earned. Over a year a taxi driver would average four to six times the income of a Kelantan farmer. However, the expenses for a taxi driver exceeded those of farmers, who grew much of their own food.

Only half of the drivers with whom I worked had fathers who were engaged in traditional occupations such as farming. The other fathers were involved in more modern pursuits such as bus driver, policeman, etc. That their sons also chose nontraditional occupations is partly accounted for by the fact that the fathers less often owned agricultural land. Nonetheless the majority of the sample resided in villages and professed little interest in living in the city. Several complained, however, that their relatives and even other villagers often pestered them for money in a fashion that breached the understandings of *gotong royong*, mutual assistance.

The majority of the drivers acquired their driving skills while serving in the army. When questioned about why they had chosen taxi driving as a career, there were three common answers: for the money; for the romance; and more generally, to improve their circumstances. Surprisingly, although their current profession had often led to a very good income, only two of the sample desired to remain taxi drivers. Most wanted to become more independent in the future, usually by opening a small shop.

Taxi drivers were, and remain, an interesting group of people. They were usually quite intelligent but lacked much education. Most taxi drivers were quite conscious of the choices they were making in their profession, as the following excerpt from my field notes demonstrates:

> Cik Lah is a typical driver of the older generation. He is thirty-eight and has been driving for eight years. He has six children and has been married for ten years. His father was a teacher, and he used to work on a rubber estate near Tanah Merah. (He now lives in KB). He felt that his opportunities as a rubber worker were limited and determined to learn how to drive in order to become a taxi driver. He took lessons from one of the other men on the estate and qualified for his license. The lessons cost him nothing. He gives his reasons for wanting to become a taxi driver as the following: "I wanted to improve my situation and to make more money. I thought that I could do this by becoming a taxi driver, but I have found that there is much less money in it than I thought. Now I would like to stop driving and try something else, perhaps a small kedai selling general merchandise. Unfortunately I have been unable to save up any money and so this remains just a desire."

> Other drivers confirmed that they had made conscious decisions to become taxi drivers and then set out to get a license, etc. It was not a job that they stumbled across. A normal

working period for Cik Lah is from 6 A.M. to 10 P.M. each and every day. If he wants a few days off he must try to arrange this in advance with his T[aukeh]. Sometimes he works till midnight. However, all the time spent on the job is not laborious. Much time is spent at either end of his run waiting to get a full taxi, and during these periods he has plenty of time to drink coffee and chat with other drivers.

And from another section of notes:

The esprit surrounding the typical clique of drivers is one of the most notable aspects of the profession. As a group the drivers are rather close knit and present a good example of a functioning peer group. The only divisions I have noticed so far appear to be between the younger and older drivers, but it is possible that one also exists between the long and close haulers. Drivers speak of themselves forming a society [pergaulan] and recognize this fact. They speak of feeling sayang [loving] toward one another, and a great deal of joking goes on between them. The waiting periods provide ample time to cement their natural interest bonds as well as to gossip and swap stories.

While the older drivers seem to usually have joined the profession to improve their living circumstances, they state that many of the younger men have joined just because they like driving a big car. They comment that more and more people are becoming drivers lately. Saturday is their busiest period due to people coming into the big towns. Midweek—slow.

The taxi drivers received my invitation to participate in the semantic differential research project with considerable enthusiasm. It appeared that I would have few problems collecting information, especially since a number of the drivers were literate and could complete the written forms, thereby saving me hours of work administering the oral version. Unfortunately I encountered two unanticipated problems that were directly related to the social positions of the taxi drivers. First, the forms had to be administered where the taxi drivers were waiting for fares, usually a coffee shop. There were always a number of cohorts in the area, and they delighted in interfering with any given respondent. Someone filling out a form could expect that others would look over his shoulder and comment upon his choices, sometimes in colorful language.

This cheerful badinage threatened both the honesty of the responses and their independence from one another. Having monitored the responses of another, a driver might be inclined to emulate or react to the other's choices. I found I had to discard most of the initial responses in order to avoid these problems. I solved this particular difficulty by offering to buy lunch for each respondent at "my" favorite kedai. This enabled me to collect the information apart from other drivers and improved the integrity of the data collection process.

The second problem was one I should have anticipated. Several of the drivers had claimed literacy, but I discovered this often meant they could read street signs and little more. This difficulty was a bit more intractable than the first, since I would make a driver malu if I questioned the degree of his literacy. Rather than risk alienating the drivers (for word would surely spread if my behavior were discourteous), I collected a number of responses that I knew to be unusable. The process of collecting semantic differential responses was integral to the empirical, quantitative research I wanted to complete, but the methods I employed also exemplified the importance of the impressionistic fieldwork that had preceded it.[18]

Prostitutes

For various reasons, some of them rather obvious, working with prostitutes presented some challenges. Knowing that villagers would be aware of my presence in houses of prostitution, I took pains to explain my research purposes and my need to obtain information from these women. Most villagers seemed to accept my justifications for this research, but I remained uneasy that they might harbor negative views of my activities. I feared they might not share their honest impressions of my work with me but would likely gossip about me among themselves. I later discovered that my fears of making a bad impression were unnecessary, not because the gossip network was too inactive but because it was highly active. It seems that people not only knew which house of prostitution I had been in on a given day, they usually knew whom I had interviewed and what had transpired. Although I found the absence of privacy nettlesome, I was pleased that my rather controversial research was not endangering my position in the village. On the contrary I was again engaged in providing a major source of entertainment and amusement.

In conservative Islamic Kelantan feminine chastity and fidelity are highly valued. Likewise, premarital and extramarital sex are strongly repudiated, and people who engage in such behaviors are often censured. Although there is no reliable data, the frequency of such sexual misconduct in Kelantan is probably very low (Raybeck 1986a). The close-knit nature of villages, coupled with an active gossip network, mitigates against such occurrences. So too does the young age at which a girl marries, and the attention her parents and later her husband pay to her behavior.

In those rare instances when a young girl did become involved in a premarital affair, her behavior would result in shame (malu) for her and her relatives. Nonetheless her parents and her waris are expected to support her and to try to find her a husband. It occasionally happened that a particularly rigid family would seek to disown such a daughter or would make life so difficult for her that she would flee. When a girl in these circumstances left her village she had few options. She might seek menial employment in an urban center, which was very difficult to obtain, or she might become a prostitute (perempuan pelacor). The latter was often a somewhat gradual process beginning with a waitressing job in a coffee shop, an occupation that was barely respectable. After a few casual affairs a girl might gravitate to a full-time house of prostitution.

A more common source of prostitutes than unwed girls was the population of divorcées (bujang). The reasons for this were various and ranged from an inability to contract a satisfactory second or third marriage, to actual sexual delinquency. The fact that the majority of Kelantan prostitutes were divorcées is reflected in the term "bujang," which was used colloquially to mean prostitute as well as divorcée.

When a girl or woman became a prostitute it was likely that traditional support mechanisms had broken down. Her welfare and support were the responsibility of her family, her relatives, and her village, in that order. Consequently although a divorcée turned prostitute might occasionally remain in her natal village, it was more likely that she would take up residence in an urban area.

The greatest concentration of prostitutes in Kelantan was found in Kota Bharu. Within the city, houses of prostitution tended to be grouped in small clusters. The houses were usually inconspicuously located in an alley or other area well back from the main road. The condition of these houses ranged from very run-down and smelly to large and well-kept houses, such as might belong to a well-to-do landowner in any village. The poorer houses were generally inhabited by from three to seven older and less-attractive prostitutes. These paid M$30 to M$40 a month in rent and usually charged three dollars for their services. Such a prostitute would clear from M$40 to M$100 a month, much of which is invested in gold jewelry. At that time gold was only about US$36 an ounce, yet I observed some of the older prostitutes wearing as much as M$800 worth of bracelets and necklaces while waiting for a customer. Younger, attractive prostitutes were found in the better houses. They usually charged M$10, retaining M$8 and giving M$2 to the owner of the house. Such girls were more popular, and their income averaged between M$200 and M$300 a month. Unlike the older prostitutes, most of the girls bought only a small amount of gold jewelry and instead placed most of their savings in a Post Office Savings Account where they collected 4 percent interest.

I learned that my research was best pursued in the late morning and early afternoon. In the morning the women, unlike most Kelantanese, usually slept late. By late afternoon they were either at work or being visited by boyfriends. I offered each woman a modest sum (M$3–M$10) to complete a semantic differential form.

Interviews with twenty prostitutes selected from both the poorer and better houses revealed some generalities concerning them and their circumstances. The majority had no formal education, and the few who had attended school rarely went more than two years. With two exceptions, all prostitutes came from a rural background. The fathers of most of these girls were either farmers or fishermen who themselves had little or no education. Thus most prostitutes were illiterate and from a rather traditional village background.

Questions concerning the prostitutes' motives for moving to Kota Bharu elicited a wide range of responses and varying degrees of frankness. The most common answers listed the greater amount of personal freedom in the city and the exciting pace of life there. However, a few women did state that remaining in their village would have been too difficult in view of their profession and their relatives. One girl in particular detailed the problem stemming from her father's anger and the rejection of her waris because a love affair of hers had become a topic of village gossip. Only four women stated that they would prefer to live in a village setting if they had their choice. This preference probably reflected a good deal of rationalizing, but it contrasted markedly with the typical attitude of most Kelantanese.

Not surprisingly the great majority of the interviewees looked upon their present profession as a temporary one. Most had hopes of marrying again and having a stable family life. Most were also saving money in hopes of opening a small coffee shop or selling stand. I was unable to get a reliable estimate of the number of prostitutes who did manage to leave the profession, but perhaps as many as half of the younger women accomplished this goal. There were numerous accounts of friends who through savings had set themselves up in a small business and later had married.

Two problems arose in my attempts to gather information. The first involved my relationship to the women. Initially they were intent in defining me as a customer, as someone for whom they had a set performance. My initial efforts to explain my intentions were often laughingly discounted, while serious efforts were made to get me into a compromising posture (prone). As I made it clear that my intentions involved only verbal intercourse, many of the prostitutes, especially the younger ones, became disquieted. They were not used to dealing with men socially, except for customers and their boyfriends. They replaced their initial displays of brashness with bashfulness. They seemed flattered at my interest in their lives but were understandably ambivalent about discussing their current situations.

Gradually they came to trust me and to understand that I would not make any untoward use of the knowledge they supplied me. I discovered later that my acceptance was facilitated by information they obtained from some of their customers, who included two of my village friends. I was also aided by the prostitutes' own gossip network. My work and dealings in one house seemed to rapidly become known to other houses, and since I was paying my participants, I had numerous volunteers.

My other difficulty was one I had anticipated but hoped to overcome. Of the twenty-five concepts to which I was asking each participant to respond, one was perempuan pelacor, or prostitute. I realized that asking prostitutes to respond to this category was problematic, but I had hoped that the women would be able to respond fairly objectively. After the first two responded by selecting all middle values and the third became flustered, I dropped the concept from their semantic differential.

Due to their illiteracy, I had to administer each semantic differential individually to each prostitute. This again gave me an opportunity, after the material was collected, to use their responses to gather more information. The situation of prostitutes in Kelantan is much more ambiguous than one might expect, given the strictures of Islam and traditional morality.

While the majority of women labeled as prostitutes leave the village, some remain, and they generally do so for good reason. All but one of seven prostitutes who were living in a village setting were involved in caring for and supporting families, which sometimes included aged relatives. The exception was an outspoken, middle-aged woman who had inherited her mother's house and who steadfastly ignored the disapprobation of relatives and neighbors.

All of these prostitutes commuted to the state capital three or four times a week for business purposes, and none entertained clients within the village. Such a practice reduces the visibility of the prostitute's occupation and allows other villagers to be more accepting of the individual than they would otherwise be. Residents of two villages in which a prostitute resided displayed a complex regard. One woman, the sole support of three children and an elderly mother, was acknowledged to be a prostitute, but villagers, emphasizing that she was a dutiful daughter and caring mother, also termed her a good person. The other prostitute was also engaged in supporting a family, but her reputation for a short temper and a sharp tongue elicited a more ambiguous response from other villagers. They approved of the manner in which she cared for her children, emphasizing that these were well behaved and skilled in courteous behavior, but they termed the mother a weak and undesirable person. Significantly they discriminated between her sexual behavior and her irascibility in making this judgment. It is apparent that a known prostitute who limits the visibility of her professional activity and who exhibits other behaviors congruent with village values can be reasonably well integrated into village society. Villagers tend to compartmentalize her behavior and to discriminate rather carefully in assessing her social persona.

If my research with prostitutes took up quite a bit of bandwidth in the village gossip broadcasts, it also provided me with some insights into how well accepted I had become.

One afternoon as I was preparing to go into the state capital to continue my research with prostitutes, a middle-aged, married acquaintance asked for a ride on my motorcycle. I cheerfully accommodated him and asked where he wished to be taken. He cited a barber shop near the center of Kota Bharu, which is where I left him. I went on to a kedai kopi where I spent half an hour sipping iced coffee and preparing my interview schedules. I then walked two blocks to the house of prostitution in which I was currently working, and as people were already accustomed to my afternoon visits, I entered the foyer unannounced. I found my acquaintance sitting in a rattan chair with a young woman on his lap. He immediately engaged in several behaviors that would reduce the likelihood that I would relay his transgression to others. First, he thanked me for the lift and noted humorously that the barbershop was only his first stop. Then he tried to establish that my purpose for being there was similar to his. This would have made my silence much more likely. When I declined this gambit, waving my clipboard about as I did so, he became increasingly nervous and left the establishment without pursuing matters further. For the next few months, he avoided me whenever possible, and when we did encounter one another, he was polite to the point of obsequiousness, a quality that he had not displayed earlier in our interaction. It took months to reestablish a semblance of our earlier relationship as he gradually became convinced of my discretion. In fieldwork discretion is not simply nice, it is necessary.

What is gratifying concerning the example above is that my acquaintance had treated me very much as he would have a Kelantanese covillager. First, he had not openly lied to me but instead dissembled. He took pains to point out that he had indeed stopped at the barbershop. Finally, he endeavored to create a shared backstage of the sort that villagers engaged in deviance will employ with one another. While I have no illusions that I was regarded as a villager (*orang sini*) and entitled to all the prerogatives such status implies, it was also clear that I was not being viewed as an outsider (*orang luar*). I will discuss the significance of this distinction in the next chapter.

7

Shady Activities and Ethical Concerns

The process of doing fieldwork necessarily involves ethical issues. Anthropologists intrude into the lives of others, and despite the best of intentions, the possibilities for doing harm are very real. We have long argued that the interests and welfare of the people studied should be one's first concern. Currently there is little disagreement about this issue among practicing anthropologists, but what *is* disputed is the best means to ensure the well-being of the people with whom one works. Like the "Prime Directive" of *Star Trek*, the general policy is noninterference—or, at the least, minimal interference—in the lives of those with whom the anthropologist works. However, anthropologists live among and interact with people who generally pay close attention to the researchers' behavior. Thus it is all too easy to influence others in ways that may not be immediately apparent.

As noted earlier, anthropologists, like long-distance hikers, carry their own cultural baggage. The influence of this baggage, both on us and on those with whom we come in contact, ranges from subtle to obvious and is highly variable. While one can often avoid giving intentional affront and causing intentional harm, the unintended consequences of the anthropologist's behavior may prove quite detrimental. Problems may involve both omissions and commissions and range from an insensitivity to local issues of concern, to an inability to adjust to normative expectations, to outright bad behavior. While I have a high regard for the ethical sensibilities of most of my colleagues, I would be foolish to argue that all anthropologists are enlightened individuals who care deeply about the well-being of others.[19]

Extremes of black and white abound in religious sermons and political treatises, but seldom in the real world. The complexities of any social setting compound the difficulty of making ethical choices. Even in one's own culture and society there are often conflicts concerning the "proper" course of action. Do you report Uncle Bob for cheating on his income tax? Do you keep a secret because you were asked to, even though you know that doing so will harm someone else? Imagine the increased complexities that occur in a field setting.

It is very easy for an anthropologist to become torn by competing interests, to be caught between conflicting loyalties, and to be asked to choose among contending factions. At such times the right course of action is seldom discovered by reference to a list of rules for ethical behavior.[20] Generally, ethical decisions in the field depend both on the inherent morality of the anthropologist and upon the degree of understanding of the local situation. Like the examples above, many ethical decisions require a degree of compromise. It is rare that an anthropologist, faced with an ethical question, can choose a path that pleases all constituents. The following examples involve my participation in situations that had clear ethical import. Sometimes my choices were easy, and I retain confidence that I chose wisely in many of these. At other times, however, the judgments were difficult, the situations complex, and my position ambiguous. While I hope to have done "right" in each of these instances, I lack full confidence that this was always the case. As you will find, several of my decisions involved obfuscations, some concerned temporizing, and still others included outright lies (honesty is *not* always the best policy).

Insiders and Outsiders

The distinction between insiders (orang sini) and outsiders (orang luar) is a strong one for villages. Insiders are people who have been born and reared in the village, or they have resided there for quite some time. Insiders are entitled to an automatic measure of respect. They are viewed as a part of village society with whom one strives to maintain sesuai and toward whom one displays courteous behavior. One may omit, conceal, and otherwise obscure information, but arrant lying is an affront and is engaged in only rarely and with considerable cause.

Outsiders, however, represent the world beyond the village. They are unknown and are often seen as potentially threatening. This perspective extends to the local police imported from other states, and to various officials who visit the villages in an attempt to gather information. On several occasions I was present when a collection of villagers cheerfully and quite skillfully lied to outside officials. These unwitting victims seriously recorded the information they were given and then departed, thus accomplishing the villagers' objective: keep outsiders out of village affairs.

The villagers' attitude toward the machinery and representatives of the wider state of Kelantan is a wary one. For historical reasons (Chan 1965), villagers have had as little to do with external authority as possible. In olden times requesting help from the sultan invited the intrusion of his army, a group of toughs whose cure was often worse than the complaint. The current attitude toward police and government representatives ranges from mildly distrustful to openly suspicious and sometimes even hostile (Raybeck 1986a). It is generally believed that outside authorities are unlikely to understand or appreciate the nuances of village social life and that they are more apt to prove harmful than helpful. As you will see shortly, there are good grounds for these concerns.

If government officials are outsiders, lacking social standing and respect, so too are other villagers who lack ties of kinship or friendship to local villagers. Should such individuals offend a villager or engage in behavior that puts village interests at risk, the response can be severe and in our eyes extreme. On one occasion four young men entered the periphery of the village early one morning and attempted to steal a water buffalo. The buffalo protested loudly and several villagers, including the owner of the tattling beast, were awakened. They ran out, captured the would-be rustlers, and proceeded to administer a lengthy and thorough beating. The local police somehow learned of the event and appeared on the scene, where they proceeded to administer their own beatings to the four thieves. Shortly afterward the police paraded the youths through the village, where they were jeered by villagers who had already learned of the morning's occur-

rences. The culprits were in visible pain. One clutched his
stomach and limped, while the others all showed signs of physical
abuse.

The villagers' response to these young men indicated that
they were not seen as possessing human rights. One woman, a
midwife known both for her helpfulness and for her strong
character, called out to the police, "I hope you didn't hurt your
hands!" Clearly, outsiders should walk softly when entering a new
village. As Hussein had told me sometime earlier, one should
"behave like a hen, not like a rooster." Strangers who transgress
against village interests can be treated as much like animals as
humans.

After Karen and I had been in the village for more than a
year, it became apparent that we were no longer viewed as simply
outsiders. I don't mean that we were accepted as full members
of the village, but rather that we occupied some vaguely defined
interstitial status that reflected a degree of acceptance and membership. This was heartening and helped my research; however,
all privileges entail responsibilities. Karen discovered she was
expected to participate in several of the women's activities, and I
found that I was counted upon to promote the interests of fellow
villagers when challenged by others. These expectations reached
an apex of awkwardness one evening as the result of actions taken
by a friend.

Along with a number of other villagers, my friend from the
guard unit, Yusof Ismail, had loaned money to a young man from
a neighboring village. Despite several hints and even some open
requests, the young man had declined to pay back the monies
owed. This occasioned some gossip and ill feelings toward the
young man, but Kelantanese villagers dislike direct confronta-
tions and little was done to make him pay his debts.

During this period, there were several performances of an
intervillage competition occurring in Wakaf Bharu. Yusof became
aware that the young man was attending these, and one afternoon
he sent around word that he would confront the man at the end
of the show. Later that same afternoon, he dropped by our house
to visit and raised the issue of friendship in typically indirect
Kelantanese fashion. He wondered whether friends should support one another in times of adversity, and professed that he
would come to my assistance if I were in need. (Unlike my
neighbor Hussein, Yusof was never very subtle in his hints.) It

seems that Yusof was in the process of rounding up support for his intended actions that night, and he noted that some of his other friends would be there.

This situation was delicate and a source of potential trouble. Yusof had already had something of an "adventurous" youth. His grandparents, with whom he lived in Wakaf Bharu, had arranged an early marriage for him in hopes that the responsibilities of a family would help to moderate his behavior. He had a reputation as a "brave person" (*orang berani*), which was not entirely a compliment. In the delicate balance of village life, people who are headstrong and emotional are apt to create problems in maintaining sesuai. A good citizen is one who retains emotional control and whose behavior is always predictable. Yusof was both admired and feared for his penchant for direct confrontation. His declaration that he would confront the debtor in a public setting made the village a party to his actions.

Yusof was clearly conscious of the implications his actions held for the village. He noted that it was less important that he be paid back than that others receive the money due them. In stating this, Yusof was placing himself as a champion of the insiders against the actions of an outsider. This also gave him a rationale to seek assistance from his friends in the village. Nonetheless there was a genuine risk that Yusof's intended actions would result in violence that could jeopardize village harmony and the relation of Wakaf Bharu to its neighbor, Kampong Sarong Burong, the village from which the debtor came.

My dilemma was clear. The social customs with which I was becoming increasingly familiar obligated me to support a friend in need. At the same time, I, like any other villager, should not be found to be courting violence or even physical confrontation. Finally, I also feared that my involvement could estrange me from those members of the village who disapproved of Yusof's challenging behavior. My resolution of this contradictory set of expectations rested squarely, or perhaps rectangularly, on my ability to temporize. I told Yusof that I would be there in any event, as I was collecting data on the number of people who attended such performances. I said that, should he need my assistance, he would have it, but that I hoped the situation could be resolved peacefully. He seemed satisfied and left to encourage others to attend what I increasingly began to think of as the "showdown."

That evening, a Saturday, near midnight, the competition broke up and audience members began to leave the field that had been the scene of the competition. Yusof and approximately twenty assembled villagers were waiting beside the path watching for the young man. Most of these villagers were spectators rather than supporters, and I sidled over near them, where I tried to be as inconspicuous as my skinny 6'4" frame would allow.

The young man appeared, wearing a bright yellow shirt and in the company of three friends.[21] When he entered the dirt road that led toward his own village, Yusof stepped forward from the group and confronted him, demanding in a rather loud voice that he repay the monies he owed various villagers. The young man, visibly nervous, didn't answer. At this, Yusof, demonstrating his fine grasp of the nuances of Kelantanese subtlety, grabbed him by the shirt and slapped his face twice. This was a major offense. The head of any Malay is considered the most sacred and significant part of the body. It is a matter of etiquette to keep your head lower than one to whom you wish to display deference. Even on those rare occasions when children are physically punished, they are never struck in the face. To do so is to risk the emotional stability of the person being struck. It is also enormously disrespectful.

Everyone present became very quiet and waited to see what would unfold. Happily the result was anticlimactic. The young man and his friends, taking in the assembly present, quite sensibly did nothing. He mumbled something about repayment, upon which Yusof released him and watched as he and his companions walked slowly and steadily down the dirt road. For the next two days, I listened to stories concerning Yusof's behavior. Some found him brave, others foolish, but it was generally agreed that he had acted in the interests of the village. When I inquired about the sums of money involved, I was informed that, as far as people knew, the young man had owed a grand total of M$8, two of which he had borrowed from Yusof.

I had not expected Yusof to act in such an intemperate fashion, but even if I had known his intent, ny problem would only have been reduced, not eliminated. Kelantanese are not blindly loyal to one another. There is strong pressure to support fellow villagers and especially members of one's kindred, but a person who persistently and aggressively acts wrongly will eventually lose the support of friends and relatives. Traditionally such offenders were banished from their villages and found few opportunities for employment beyond the village. Women were usually forced into prostitution or a life of servitude, while men often chose between joining a group of robbers or the sultan's army. Yusof's reputation and offense placed him in a liminal category but not beyond the social pale. Had I refused to acknowledge his claim on my support, many villagers would have questioned my character. As it eventuated, I was, quite simply, lucky.

Although the preceding example did not constitute a major social event, it posed a difficult ethical question because I was caught between conflicting expectations that were shared by those with whom I lived. In another situation of much greater magnitude, where the issues at question involved outsiders, I found the ethical problem occasioned by my presence far easier to resolve.

The Kelewang Incident

One of the major sources of village entertainment and gossip involved a pair of brothers-in-law who lived just down the road from us, and who had been on bad terms for three years.[22] Ali was a well-liked villager, born and raised in Wakaf Bharu, who worked hard and who supplemented his farming income by working as a carpenter. He was known to be honest, dependable, and possessed of a strong temper. Despite the last, he also had a reputation as a "good hearted person" (*orang baik hati*), a person who acts from genuinely good motives as opposed to someone who behaves well out of a concern with form.[23] In contrast Ismail was a village ne'er-do-well with a reputation for being lazy, unreliable, and spiteful.

Years before, Ali had married Khadija, Ismail's sister. Khadija was also well thought of and had spent several years caring for her ailing father. During this time Ismail only infrequently visited their father and never brought him medicine. Villagers viewed his behavior as inappropriate and unfilial. Before the old man died, he made a premortem bequest of most of his land to his dutiful daughter, leaving only a small plot near the road for Ismail.[24] This inequity rankled Ismail, especially when he found that he got little sympathy from other villagers.

After Ali and Khadija married, Ali built them a nice house at the verge of a major village path on a portion of the property that Khadija had inherited. Shortly afterward Ismail asked Ali to build a house for him on the small plot of land that was adjacent to Khadija's property. He and Ali bargained about the price, and Ali gave him a particularly low rate because he was a brother-in-law. Ali then proceeded to build the house, and when it was completed, he asked for payment. Ismail gave Ali only half the sum agreed upon, citing their family relationship and his poverty as mitigating reasons. This was the origin of their ongoing quarrel. Most villagers backed Ali, but they did so subtly. People treated this as a delicate relationship, as they would any situation where there was bad feeling. The problem was compounded, however, because the two men shared relatives in common, who were obligated to be supportive to both.

After three years of bickering and poorly veiled hostility, a major altercation occurred that was to challenge the harmony of most of the village. Shortly after midday one afternoon in early June, the hot season, both men were reacting to the heat in appropriate fashion. Ali was in his house napping, and Ismail was next door in front of his house taking a bath. Two of Ali's children were running about and making a bit of noise. Ismail chastened the children, and when the older child didn't obey, Ismail was reported to have grabbed him, slapped him several times, and threatened him.[25] This is a major departure from accepted behavior. Children are rarely struck, and only parents have the right to administer physical punishment. In any event, Ali reported being awakened by the troubles and immediately losing his temper.

Witnesses describe how he emerged from the house looking enraged and carrying a *kelewang*, a three-foot-long cross between a short sword and a machete. He ran over to Ismail and immediately attacked, striking him once on the outside of the left thigh and once high on the left shoulder, a blow that may have been intended as lethal. Ismail, screaming loudly, had raised his hands in a futile effort to wrest the blade away from Ali. Neighbors immediately ran out to find Ismail shouting for help while blood streamed from cuts on his hands, shoulder, and leg. They grabbed Ali, sat him down on his porch stairs, and started trying to cool him down. While everyone was focused on Ali and the kelewang, Ismail limped down the path to the local police shack, where he reported the assault and asked to be taken to the hospital.

This created an immediate problem for the village, which wished to avoid police interference in its affairs. Thus Ali, at the advice of his relatives and others, went down to the police post and turned himself in. He was taken to Tumpat, the "county seat," and placed in jail. He was kept in jail for three days, until his relatives and friends were able to raise the three-hundred-dollar bail, a large sum for poor peasants. It is worth noting that several of the relatives who helped supply the bail were related to both men. It is an indication of Ali's social standing that the Imam, a man not related to him, brought in the registration of one of his own parcels of land to use as security for Ali's release. A very chastened Ali returned to the village to await the outcome of his actions.

Ismail was taken to the main hospital in Kota Bharu, where he spent nearly two weeks recuperating from his wounds. When one of his relatives and I visited him, he loudly declaimed his intent to prosecute Ali and to see him jailed for a long time. Later, when he had returned to the village, Ismail would sit on the steps healing and telling each passerby how unjustly he had been treated and how he would get even through the courts. As Ismail informed all who would listen, the date for the first hearing was set for late June.

In the interim, police canvassed the village, interrogating anyone they thought might have information on the assault. Virtually all villagers, disliking the presence of the police and the threat that they represented, avoided any substantive answers. One afternoon as I was passing the police post, the young sergeant called to me to come in for a moment. He wanted to know what I knew of the events surrounding Ismail's injuries. I never hesitated, and like a good villager, I said that I had heard there had been a fight, that I had been out of the village at the time (true), and that I knew little of the details (false). In actuality I had been working hard to stay abreast of events, but I realized that, should I betray (this is the right word) village interests to the police, I would be altering my status in the village, jeopardizing future research, and not incidentally, disadvantaging friends. I allied myself with village interests rather than those of the state and engaged in what I still regard as an ethical lie.

It is perhaps because I was clearly supportive of village attempts to keep the police at some remove that I was made privy to some classically traditional, behind-the-scenes maneuvers designed to solve the problem without outside intervention. One evening in late June, Ismail received a visit from three villagers: the Imam, the village headman, and a well-regarded individual who was related to both Ismail and Ali. They suggested to Ismail that he might consider dropping the court charges if Ali were to make a public apology and pay him two hundred dollars compensation (*sagu hati*). Ismail is reported to have rejected the offer initially, at which point it was gently explained that he was not behaving as a good villager should, and that he was jeopardizing his position in the community. I have no doubt that this message was conveyed in a far more refined and indirect fashion than I have done here, but the effect was still obvious. In a small peasant community, no one person can easily subsist without the support and occasional assistance of others. This gives community sentiment considerable weight, and coresidents can bring considerable pressure to bear on an offending member (Raybeck 1991a). Ismail agreed to the deal.

The three men then left Ismail and went next door where they made a similar argument to Ali concerning his payment of compensation to Ismail. For reasons very similar to those described above, and because he seemed genuinely contrite, Ali agreed to both the apology and the payment. In return the three men agreed to help him raise the gift money.

Three days later both Ali and Ismail were taken to Tumpat where they hired a letter writer to petition the court to dismiss the case. The letter was then given to the magistrate, who said he wanted to see the full report before dismissing the case, and he asked the police to continue their investigation. That afternoon Ali, the Imam, and I rested at the house of one of Ali's Tumpat relatives and discussed the case. The concern, which was now being manifest by Ismail as well, was that the court would ignore the wishes of the plaintiff and interfere in village affairs. As we discussed the dangers of the way in which the court was apt to reason, Ali showed me a copy of the letter that he had submitted to the court.

The letter began by admitting he had done the deed, by observing that he had never been involved in violence before, and by claiming that he and Ismail were, after all, brothers (*adik-beradik*). Technically this was not true, as they were related as in-laws (*ipar*), but in adat, the sibling relationship is supposed to be the model for all close kin relations. The argument was that brothers forgive one another and keep their difficulties within the family. Finally, Ali argued that he was not solely to blame for the unfortunate attack. When he awoke from sleep and heard his child cry out, in what he believed to be jeopardy, his soul became startled (*terkejut*) and was weakened. At this point he was attacked and entered by the spirit of *Shaitan*. The devil made him do it.

As you might imagine, the court was not taken with this argument, and after two weeks it fined Ali five hundred dollars for his offense against public order. The fine was paid only when the relatives of both men pooled their resources. Villagers were very unhappy with this outcome. They had already solved the problem to their own satisfaction, and the court's action merely confirmed their prejudice regarding the undesirability of outside interference in village affairs. Many people blamed Ismail more than Ali for the ensuing difficulties, as he was the one who had carried the problem to the authorities before there had been any possibility of village mediation.

Although the court was not impressed with Ali's defense, villagers accepted his claim of supernatural possession. Beliefs in supernatural intervention are well established in Kelantanese culture (Kessler 1977; Laderman 1991; Raybeck 1974). It is well known that children, ill adults, and those asleep are particularly susceptible to mischievous spirits. Ali's claim of possession provided a means for villagers to rationalize his behavior and to deflect to the supernatural some of the responsibility for his deviant act. This was important as Ali's behavior had been literally "inhuman." He had lost emotional control and behaved in an animal-like fashion. Without recourse to preternatural agencies, it would be very difficult for villagers to reconcile themselves to such an extreme departure from the accepted.

During the next few months, the villagers mounted a coordinated effort to ensure that Ali and Ismail would no longer threaten village solidarity. When a feast was held, both men would be invited and usually seated in the same circle of five or six diners. Generally, an influential villager, even the headman or Imam, would be included in the group. In typically indirect Kelantanese, these two were being told that their behavior was under scrutiny. During the ensuing months, relations between these two never became cordial, but they did behave correctly and there were no further outbreaks of animosity. Of course both continued trying to attract public opinion to their side and gossiping about the shortcomings of the other.

Ali later furthered his acceptance by the village when he completed a voluntary fast as an act of contrition. This was in December at the end of Ramadan, the month when Muslims fast from dawn to dusk. People who wish to exhibit religious merit can do so by fasting for an additional six days. At the conclusion of his fast, Ali held a feast to which he invited villagers who had supported him, including Karen and me and, not incidentally, Ismail. The feast served both as a demonstration of his regret over the event and as a marker, by and large, concluding that particular act in the ongoing drama of village life.

Murder Unincorporated

All societies must contend with deviance, behavior that challenges the social order and poses social problems for others. Deviance refers to any human attribute (behavior, appearance, belief) that departs sufficiently from the norm to elicit a sanction. Sanctions are actions taken by individuals or representatives of society that are intended to promote conformity. Deviance can range from essentially trivial acts that are generally tolerated by most members of society, to behaviors that are viewed as a serious threat to social order. Similarly sanctions can be informal and found in the spontaneous displays of approval or reproval manifested by members of society acting on their own accord.

Deviance in small social units, such as villages, is generally judged on a continuum. Responses to deviant acts are not strictly conditioned by formal rules and culturally prescribed standards for behavior, but are instead a reflection of complex social judgments that take into account the nature of the offender as well as the nature of the offense. In Kelantan a major concern is always whether or not the offender is a covillager or someone with close ties to the village. If the person is an outsider, there are a range of possible sanctions that would rarely even be contemplated for an insider.

Within Kelantanese villages, informal sanctions of the sort I have described earlier suffice to deal with most problems, including some of considerable magnitude. Between villages, however, there are few mechanisms to enact sanctions. As I have noted, Kelantanese are reluctant to involve external authorities in village affairs, and this leaves little recourse to legitimate sanctions. Well before the arrival of the British, Kelantanese traditions included what might be termed deviant sanctions.

During the initial fieldwork period, there were individuals who made a good portion of their livelihood as "enforcers," or even as assassins. Most of these men were known to live in an interior region of Kelantan in the vicinity of Tanah Merah. A villager who wished to sanction a member of another village could hire one of these people to address the problem. There were several levels of deviant sanctions available. The enforcer could be hired to wait beside a path and to strike the offending passerby in the forehead with an *enam-sembilan* (literally, six-nine). This is stout stick about three and half feet long. The ends are bound with cord in a distinctive over-and-under pattern that resembles a line of sixes and nines—696969 [26] A blow to the forehead with such an instrument generally leaves a distinctive welt that marks the individual as someone who has been sanctioned. While the enforcer's employer is hardly ever revealed, most people, including the offender, usually have a good idea of who was responsible and why the action was taken. This measure serves as a strong warning to the offender to desist from a course of activity.

If the offense was very serious or a prior warning went unheeded, it was possible to increase the severity of the sanction. An enforcer could be hired to use a *kapok kecil*, a small axe or hatchet. Normally, the blunt end is used to give a penultimate warning: "Heed this, or the next time it will be the sharp end." Again the object is to leave the malefactor with a warning, in this case, a distinctive right-angled scar on his forehead.

Assassinations using the kapok kecil, while hardly common, were known to occur throughout Kelantan. It was reportedly possible to hire an assassin in Tanah Merah for a fee ranging from M$50 to M$100. Such murders were sufficiently prominent to attract the attention of the police. A state law was passed making it illegal to carry a kapok kecil, and efforts, largely futile, were made to apprehend assassins in Tanah Merah. Such murders were not restricted to rural villages. The month we arrived in Kelantan, a state representative was killed with a kapok kecil in the central market area of Kota Bharu by a hired assassin.

As might be imagined, when such murders occurred, they fueled the gossip machinery for quite some time. Although most villagers refused to condone such acts, there seemed a clear understanding that outsiders who give offense to villagers are taking serious risks.

During the period Karen and I were in the field, we were never apprised of an assassination. However, during the tumultuous pre-election period, I did learn of an enam-sembilan assault on a Wakaf Bharu villager that had purportedly been arranged by a covillager. Such occurrences are rare, and because of their potential for fracturing village harmony, they create a great deal of nervousness and ambivalence on the part of villagers. While I was not involved with either of the principals, and while I could not be certain of what had actually transpired, I was under pressure from a number of people to participate in the gossip.

The difficulty I faced once again involved factions within the village. The person attacked was a supporter of party PAS, the Malay-rights party that ruled Kelantan. The person rumored to have hired the enforcer was an Alliance supporter. Thus in addition to the usual divisions that followed kinship lines, people also tended to choose sides based on political affiliation. This was during a period in which political actions were becoming increasingly extreme and political rhetoric ever more heated. Again my preferred course of action was as little action as possible. My position was made more complex, however, by the villagers' knowledge that I was interested in, and tried to follow, village gossip. My resolution of this difficulty was, when asked, to repeat only those generalities that were already part of the gossip network. On those few occasions when I garnered new information, including some evidence that the rumors were accurate, I did not divulge it.

My ploy seemed to work well with most people, but those villagers who were closest to me, both Yusof and Hussein, hinted that they understood my strategy and also indicated that they thought I had chosen a prudent path. Hussein went so far as to quote a proverb to the effect that noisy hunters seldom encounter game.

Smuggling and Other Illegal Acts

My interest in values led quite logically to an interest in those deviant acts people engaged in that were contrary to law or custom. The behavior of Kelantanese in this regard does not particularly distinguish them from the rest of us. When was the last time you did 65 mph on an Interstate? However, the Kelantanese had a relationship to the state and nation that was distinctive, and that helped to color their attitudes toward behavior that violated external laws. As elsewhere, judgments of deviance depend heavily upon who is judging.

From a village perspective, outsiders comprise anyone who is not tied directly to coresidents. This includes the state and national political structures. Villagers are aware that they are subject to state and national taxes and to laws that emanate from elsewhere; they also have some awareness that other elements of the nation may judge their behavior negatively.

The cultural and linguistic distinctiveness that characterizes Kelantan often leads non-Kelantanese Malays to be quite ambivalent about the state (Raybeck 1980). They regard it as a valuable repository of traditional culture, but they also view it as we might once have regarded the Ozarks—a backward, unpredictable, and occasionally threatening area in which one might travel but not reside. Members of other ethnic groups and functionaries of the national government are very chary of Kelantan, considering it a bastion of rabid Malay rightists and religious zealots. West coast women whose husbands are employed in the school system or in the police force have been known to express concern about the posting to Kelantan of their spouses, because Kelantanese women are reported to be both attractive and skilled in love magic.

Kelantanese are reminded of their state membership by encounters with the state bureaucracy, including the collection of annual taxes, and by the celebration of the sultan's birthday, one of the more important annual holidays in the state. Most Kelantanese are conscious of the differences between their state and others, but they are more apt to characterize these differences in cultural rather than in political terms, save for the role of the Pan-Malayan Islamic Party (Nash 1974; Salleh 1974).

The Kelantanese are aware that they are the center of the conservative, Malay-rights-oriented PMIP, and they know, through news media and through coffee-house gossip, that the national government, dominated by the Alliance Party, is in opposition. Occasional political conflicts and speeches within the state also serve to emphasize the role of the state in contradistinction to the national government. The PMIP, in turn, draws upon valued Kelantanese images of Islam, ethnicity, and traditional values in a largely successful effort to be seen as an integral part of the culture (Downs 1967; Kessler 1978).

Not surprisingly, Kelantanese are least cognizant of their membership in the nation of Malaysia, the most inclusive and most distant community in which they participate. The average Kelantanese is aware of the nation but not keenly so. There are the ubiquitous portable radios and the rare television that carry national news. However, villagers crowd into the house of a neighbor with a television to watch not national news but a traditional Malay movie or performance. To the extent that the nation is considered, Kelantanese are rather ambivalent about it. Kelantanese take pride in Malaysia, its Islamic orientation and its comparative political stability. However, Kelantanese also see the nation as somewhat threatening because it contains many non-Malays, especially Chinese, who seem bent on pursuing their own self-interests.

Traditional Kelantanese culture possesses several elements that, while valued by villagers, are opposed by state and national law, and even by Islam. Kelantanese may actually take pride in those behaviors that violate state and national statutes. Indeed I have argued elsewhere that Kelantanese can affirm their cultural identity through participation in behaviors regarded as deviant by the wider society (Raybeck 1986a). These activities include smuggling, bullfighting, a variety of gambling activities, and others.

Smuggling is a fairly common phenomenon, especially in those areas of Kelantan adjacent to the border with Thailand. While there is some traffic in drugs and other controversial items, most village Malays who participate in smuggling move more innocuous contraband—long-grain Thai rice. Smuggling has been undertaken for years because Thai rice commands good prices in Malay markets and because Kelantanese wish to avoid government import duties, which they view as an unnecessary and undesirable intrusion into their entrepreneurial activities. A wide range of villagers can and do participate in such smuggling, but many of the more established smugglers are middle-aged women with extensive trading networks (Raybeck 1992b). Although most smuggling tends to be small scale, villagers derive considerable satisfaction from eluding or preferably outwitting government customs officials.

By late August, 1968, I was trying to study the deviant activities that transpired in Sungai Golok. Sungai Golok then was a midsized town of approximately ten thousand people. The town is in Thailand, just across the river of the same name, immediately opposite the Kelantanese town of Rantau Panjang. It is famed throughout the peninsula as a center for illicit activities. One could (and still can) purchase everything from companionship, to drugs, stolen goods, pornography, pharmaceuticals, and even black market electronics of considerable complexity.

I wanted to know the extent to which Kelantanese visited the area and what their purposes there might be. I was also interested in the cross-border smuggling that was reputed to be quite common. I also knew that I would have difficulty getting the desired information, partly because I was not known to the people of Sungai Golok and partly because of the sensitivity of the issues involved. As usual my success hinged far more on the trust of friends than it did upon my intelligence.

I had some sense of the frequency of illicit activities in Sungai Golok from my village friends, one of whom was an older woman, Cik Minah, who had a reputation for being among the most skillful of smugglers. Minah was a large, ebullient woman with a strong personality and a score of grandchildren. That my principle source of information should be a grandmother was not surprising. That she was willing to reveal to me her techniques was both surprising and gratifying. People from Wakaf Bharu go down on the 6:00 A.M. train or on the 11:20 A.M. train, taking with them goods such as coconuts, bananas, small mollusks, vegetables, and prepared food to sell at Sungai Golok. The train trip takes about one and a half hours; the price of a one-way fare, third class is M95 cents, and the necessary pass is M$1.50. This pass is good for six months and must be renewed after that. Each trader spends about M$2 a day on transportation, and this must be recouped before they can show profit.

At her suggestion we left together one morning on the 6:00 A.M. train from Wakaf Bharu to Rantau Panjang. She cautioned me not sit too close to her lest I draw attention to her or to us. (Clearly my pale, lanky form generally drew attention, and my friends were used to this.) We arrived at Rantau Panjang, where we went through customs together. Having explained that she was there to sell some batik, she took the train across the river to Sungai Golok. I, instead, walked across the causeway that spanned sixty yards of river between Rantau Panjang and Sungai Golok, looking down at the numerous boats moving back and forth from shore to shore. I knew from Minah that many of these were operating as illegal ferries for both people and merchandise. They charged M15 cents, about a nickel US, and their existence was well known to authorities.

A few yards from the railroad in Sungai Golok is the "Thai Railway Market," a scene of bustling activity that seems to defy any principle of organization. Items for sale in the market range from clothing and food to machinery and medicines. Nonetheless much of the important business of the market goes on inside neighboring warehouses, rather than out in the open. Minah approached a man she had dealt with for years and arranged to buy three hundred pounds of long-grain Thai rice. Included in the price was a fee for initial transportation costs. He would smuggle the material into Malaysia to a point where she could claim it.

While moving about the market and asking questions of the few Wakaf Bharu villagers I recognized, I was told by several young men that almost all the houses lining the Sungai Golok side of the river were engaged in smuggling (only a slight exaggeration, as I later discovered) and that runners would usually clear M$10–15 a day. Big operators, of course, cleared much more, and they lived in better circumstances. However, the majority engaged in smuggling were strictly small-scale operators like my friend Minah.

While immigration officials would probably be concerned if Chinese and Europeans slipped back and forth across the border without passports, they apparently were not concerned with Malays. A case in point: one of the young men of the group with whom I was talking was in Sungai Golok without a passport, and he had to go back via the smugglers' ferry in order to catch the train from Rantau Panjang back to Kota Bharu. Since immigration officers know the times of these trains, they can pretty well estimate when the ferry will be in heavy use. In this case an immigration official rode up to within fifteen yards of the ferry landing on the Sungai Golok side, sat, and watched our friend depart on the illegal ferry. I was told by my friends that if I had tried to go, he probably would have stopped me, although he was wearing neither a gun nor a hat. The latter is significant, as hats were an informal indication that an officer was on active duty.

Later that afternoon Minah had me walk with her to the causeway, where we paused and watched the boats below. She pointed out one boat that was being loaded by young boys who were taking bags of rice from the backs of bicycles where they had been balanced for the trip to the river. She said the skiff carried her goods. I expect she recognized the boys rather than the bags of rice, but I neglected to ask. We watched as they poled the boat across the shallow river to a point on the Malaysian side of the bank. There three waiting boys immediately loaded the rice bags on the backs of the bicycles, walked them up the bank and disappeared among the alleys of Rantau Panjang.

Half an hour later we boarded the train in Sungai Golok and then passed through Malaysian customs at Rantau Panjang, where we declared we had nothing to declare. At the end of the transit of the town, the customs officials disembarked, leaving a sole policeman to wander up and down the car corridors on patrol. Some short time later, the train stopped at a small village. (Kelantanese trains stop at all villages.) Three boys quickly appeared outside the windows of our third-class coach with their bicycles and bulky cargo. Several passengers, obviously familiar with Minah, set to work forcing the windows all the way open. At this point I learned another field lesson. I had been given assistance by Minah, and now under a custom involving a cooperative work ethic (*gotong-royong*), I owed her my active assistance. Thus when one of the windows became stuck, she looked to me to free the recalcitrant aperture. I managed to do so without spraining my wrists and found the young boys were quite happy to pass the sixty-pound bags of rice up to me to be pulled through the window and passed to another who stacked them on the floor. It was here that I learned just how resourceful (and well connected) Minah was.

After first looking for the remaining policeman, Minah reached into a small cloth bag and drew forth a key that just happened to fit the toilet doors on the train. The door to our car's john was opened, the rice was stacked in the small room, and then safely secured with the key. Minah sat back to wait comfortably until we reached Wakaf Bharu about an hour later. At the station the door to the toilet was unlocked, and the bags of rice were passed through the windows to waiting helpers and neatly stacked on the rear of a waiting trishaw. Minah then exited the train in a leisurely fashion and took her somewhat regal place in the seat of the trishaw. She rode with the contraband rice to Kota Bharu, where she would store the rice until the opening of the central market the next day.

Minah told me that she cleared between M$10 and M$15 per transaction. Her only real expenses were the young men in Sungai Golok who moved the rice across the border. All other assistance was free. Indeed I discovered that villagers took pleasure and even some pride in helping Minah thwart the authorities. The village attitude toward customs and duties is that they represent needless interference in the affairs of village members. Those who helped with Minah's well-crafted smuggling operations often cheerfully bragged of their activities at the coffee shops. When it became known that I too had been involved in one of Minah's forays, I discovered that my status in the eyes of most villagers had once again improved. Again none of this could be attributed to my careful calculations concerning Kelantanese culture.

Cock and Bull Stories

Like many peasants, Kelantanese strongly believe in fate. Peasants committed to a fatalistic worldview believe that much of life is foreordained, destined to be, by powers beyond one's control (Wolf 1966). The Kelantanese version of fate is *takdir*, an Arabic word that references the power of Allah to control human existence. Kelantanese often excuse their poverty or misfortune by references to takdir. Similarly they will explain the wealth of others by the same means. Interestingly, however, they explain their own good fortune and profits as the result of hard work and cleverness.

One of the common foibles of many who believe in fate is a willingness to gamble. Peasants, perhaps because their opportunities for advancement are so circumscribed, tend to view gambling both as entertainment and as an avenue to improving their circumstances. In Kelantan the gambling problem became so bad in the 1940s that the sultan took an active role in limiting the possibilities for wagering. Laws were passed outlawing the two most popular forms of gambling, on which Kelantanese had been known to wager their entire land holdings: cockfighting and bullfighting. I soon discovered, however, that while the sultan commands a great deal of respect, he is still viewed as an outsider and that villagers were quite capable of making their own determinations of what was desirable and permissible.

Peasant societies consist largely of rural populations often little differentiated in terms of wealth or other distinctions. Kelantanese add texture to their social lives by developing reputations for cleverness or skill in a particular area of endeavor. There are a variety of respected skills (*kepandaian*) that villagers may emphasize, such as Koranic chanting, the weaving of traditional mats (*tikar*), songbird training, cooking, and of course, the training of fighting cocks and bulls. Thus cockfighting remained an extremely popular activity among males, and a villager could

One of my neighbors grooming his fighting cock prior to a practice match. Both birds' spurs are left dull or are covered so they will not harm one another.

gain a reputation as a clever trainer with only one or two successful birds. The popularity of fowl fighting and its cocksure place
in Kelantanese culture are indicated by the specialized vocabulary that has grown up about it. There are terms for the various
types of fighting cocks, for their body parts, for their trainers, for
aspects of the actual matches, and for the areas in which these
fights transpire.

Cocks were trained in backyards and generally matched
against other birds in a comparatively harmless fashion. That is,
there were no metal spurs attached to the cocks' legs, nor were
their own spurs sharpened by their trainers. Matches to the
death, with metal spurs, were known to occur, but they were rare,
happened mainly in urban areas, and were viewed by villagers as
a foolish waste of a well-trained bird.

Cockfighting requires little in the way of space or special
preparation. Cockfights could be announced days ahead of time,
but more frequently they were held during afternoons with little
by way of publicity. The usual locale was someone's backyard
and the number of spectators, many of whom would wager,
seldom exceeded twenty. Trainers displayed little fear of discovery, knowing that other villagers would warn them if police were
in the area. One of my neighbors trained his birds in full view of
passersby, often calling out to them to watch when they sparred
with each other.

Villagers can take a proprietary interest in a good fighting
cock and will sometimes organize and support intervillage matches.
These are very well attended but are usually held in the outskirts of
the village, off the path and even in the edge of the jungle. The amount
of money wagered by individuals at such times is often quite large,
sometimes more than M$1,000.

The police are well aware that cockfighting is endemic to
most villages, but there is little they can do. No villager would
report another for such activities, partly because there is no
offense to village harmony and partly because anyone who did so
would receive strongly negative, if informal, sanctions. These
might range from gossip, to exclusion from certain village activities, including the all-important area of mutual assistance (gotong
royong). Any police officer who ventures down a village path can
be confident of being preceded by gossip detailing his location
and surmising his intent.

If training fighting cocks is a common and popular means of gaining a reputation for a valued skill, training fighting bulls is both less common and more highly regarded. Part of the regard stems from the expenses involved. The owner of a fighting bull will likely have paid a considerable amount for the animal when it was only a calf. Calves sired by fighting bulls with strong reputations could command as much as M$10,000, though that was rare.[27] Add to these costs the expense of feeding the animal, caring for it, and training it, and you have a pastime that only a few are willing to support.

Unlike Western bullfighting, which is hard on the bulls and sometimes on the human participants, Kelantanese bullfighting involves comparatively little physical damage. Two bulls are brought face-to-face in an arena via thin cords that are passed through their tender nostrils. When they approach each other within about three feet, dominance instincts take over, and like competing lawyers, each bull endeavors to push the other back and out of the way. Eventually one bull decides it has had enough of this strange pastime, turns, and runs. This is usually the end of the contest, but if the retreating bull has made a good fight of it, they may be brought together one more time. Generally the losing bull will immediately retreat, but if he makes a stand of it, the contest continues. In most cases injuries, when they occur, aren't too bad. Bulls' horns are never sharpened, and the greatest danger is an eye injury.

Unlike cockfighting, the spatial demands of bullfighting are considerable. There must be a large, fenced arena in which the bulls can contest, and there should also be sections for spectators that are covered by thatch roofing as protection from the sun. For these reasons bullfighting seldom occurs in Kelantan. The semipermanent structure would be too likely to draw the attention of the authorities, so the arenas are constructed elsewhere . . . in Thailand. Kelantanese villagers who wish to organize a bullfighting contest contact bull owners and arrange to rent one of the arenas that can be found just across the border in several of the small villages. Word circulates through the villages that are involved, and on the appointed day several hundred Kelantanese traverse the Sungai Golok River via ferry to watch and to wager at a scheduled bullfight.

My friend Yusof Daud, the village clerk, knew of my interest in deviant behaviors and, more importantly, understood the reasons for my curiosity. One day he informed me that there was to be a bullfighting contest just across the border and that one of the Wakaf Bharu villagers would be entering his bull. In his generous fashion, he offered to take the day off and to show me the location of the contest. I immediately accepted, and three days later we were on my Yamaha, bound for a remote little village at the edge of the Sungai Golok River. The village was nearly opposite one of the more popular bullfighting arenas, and at that point the Sungai Golok was only some seventy yards wide. It seems the village was quite used to accommodating contest-goers, as there were, in addition to the usual coffee shops, a large number of food stalls and an assortment of illegal ferries.

I had come to this enterprise suitably encumbered with notebook and some newly purchased, *expensive* photographic equipment. Yusof arranged passage for us on one of the unnecessarily tiny skiffs. I paid for both our fares (a total of M30 cents) and rather tremulously clambered aboard our designated boat, followed by Yusof. We settled ourselves while I tried to protect the US$1,000 worth of equipment I had dangling from my person. I then watched in consternation as another four people came aboard. The boat owner, rather than establishing a maximum number of passengers, gauged his acceptable complement by watching the gunnels. When they were within two inches of the river, he reluctantly concluded that he couldn't accept more fares. He pushed off and poled steadily for the opposite shore, while I kept a close eye on the gunnels and contemplated the virtues of a strong belief in takdir and of waterproof containers, both of which I lacked. The trip probably did not take three hours, but the experience of time is notoriously subjective.

The path at the other side led directly to the bullfighting arena at the edge of the village of Wat Not (clearly a pseudonym). The arena was approximately eighty yards across and surrounded by a stout fence, just beyond which was a circle of stands most of which were covered with thatch. General admission was M$1.30 with another dollar charged for seating in the shade. Quite sensibly, being neither British nor anthropologists, virtually everyone chose to spend the additional dollar.

That afternoon there were perhaps seven hundred to eight hundred people present when the bulls were brought forward. All bulls due to contest on a given day must appear together in the arena. The trainers then move about examining other bulls and seeking to establish among which bulls the contests will occur. Once two owners agree that their bulls will fight, they must then decide whether it will be an even match or whether odds will be given. The odds are then announced to the assemblage and the bargaining and betting gets underway. According to Yusof, the trainer of a victorious bull could win anywhere from M$50 to M$500 depending on how the betting went.

That afternoon, there were only four matched pairs, thus the small crowd. A major contest can often draw nearly fifteen hundred people, and I have seen one where my estimate of the crowd was eighteen hundred. The first match occasioned a great deal of shouting and betting as both bulls were known to be brave and had winning records. After the shoving was over, the only damage I could perceive was small cuts about the faces and necks, and those were uncommon. It is likely, however, that there was also a good deal of bruising. All bulls appeared to be well groomed and well fed.

The third pair to fight included a smallish tan bull owned by a Wakaf Bharu villager who lived behind the Imam. Demonstrating how village residence can take precedence over ethnicity, the trainer was a Chinese who had been born and reared in Wakaf Bharu and who was strongly supported by Malay covillagers, even though his adversary was Malay. The trainer had swum the Sungai Golok River three weeks earlier with his bull and was keeping him at the arena in a rented stall. The small Wakaf Bharu bull was not well known, and since he lacked imposing size, his owner was able to get two-to-one odds for him. The wagering was heavy among Wakaf Bharu villagers, and at the invitation of several friends, I ventured M$10 on the contest. I was encouraged to bet a great deal more, but I demurred, citing a shortage of funds, which was all too accurate.

The contest was surprising. Initially both bulls strove for dominance, snorting, pushing, and raising clouds of dust from the arena floor. Finally, after it appeared the tan bull would lose, he steadily forced his larger opponent into the protective railing. Partly because the larger bull had fought well and partly because it was a contest with odds, the two were rematched in the center of the ring. This time, however, the larger bull bolted from the mark and fled even before the cord had been pulled from his nose.

Two bulls contesting for dominance in a Kelantan bullfight. The light-colored bull is from Wakaf Bharu and is about to win its first match by pushing the larger, dark bull back to the fence.

The victory was noisily celebrated by Wakaf Bharu villagers who moved about collecting their winnings and complimenting themselves on their knowledge of fighting bulls. After the last match, everyone left the arena and headed for the ferries, resulting in boats that were even more crowded returning than they had been going out. Yusof and I returned to Wakaf Bharu, and that evening I had the pleasure of sitting in a coffee shop and hearing a reconstruction of the day's events. Once again my participation in marginal activities seemed to have brought me closer to the villagers. There were several stories featuring my participation in bullfighting that spread well beyond the village, and that helped to give me a reputation as a person of discretion.

Concluding Comment

In retrospect it is not surprising that my participation in a variety of liminal activities improved my standing in the village. Most people in most societies engage in what might be termed "soft" deviance, behavior that departs from norms but that does not actively threaten the interests or well being of others (Raybeck 1991b). People who hold themselves aloof from such involvements are, like the occasional driver doing 55 mph on the Interstate, apt to be viewed as strange and, perversely enough, somewhat deviant. On the other hand those who join in the enjoyment of a disapproved activity, such as gambling, can form mutually supportive bonds based on both shared experience and, to a degree, shared vulnerability.

Social situations are always complex, and deciphering the nuances of a strange social context can be particularly challenging. There are instances of my above-described behavior where I remain uncertain of the wisdom of my choices. While my actions were well intended, I cannot be sure that they were always appropriate or that they had the effects I desired. To return to my earlier arguments: the only reasonable guide to moral behavior is comprised both of ethical intentions and a sensitivity to the surrounding cultural conditions. Even then, compromises are inevitable, and a degree of doubt is a common companion to any anthropological sojourner.

8

Sunrise to Sunset

The Seasons

Like early explorers who were often away from home for extended periods, many anthropologists conduct their fieldwork over lengthy stretches of often more than a year. While relatives and friends sometimes view these sojourns as unnecessarily protracted, there are good reasons for spending more, rather than less, time in the field. As I have been trying to demonstrate, fieldwork is difficult. The task of developing a good understanding of a culture in which one was not raised is very demanding, though also very enjoyable. Further, I have been clear about the need to develop rapport and about the gradual manner in which mutual trust is inculcated. Then too, part of what slows the research process is that things go awry, and it is difficult to follow a preplanned and efficient schedule.

There are, however, additional grounds that argue for an extended period of field research. Every society has an annual cycle, a yearly period that is defined, not simply by dates on the calendar, but also by natural events and by such important social markers as religious holiday and birthdays of significant figures. Any fieldwork of less than a year misses at least part of the annual pattern and runs a consequent risk of losing important information. While there are some narrowly circumscribed kinds of field research that can profitably be accomplished in a brief period, most research dealing with significant cultural questions benefits from a research time of at least a year.

There is yet another, more subtle, reason for desiring at least a full year in a cultural setting, and this has to do with the experience of time itself. Time is one of those cultural constructs that is highly susceptible to varying interpretation. We are the culture of the digital watch. When asked what time it is, instead of answering "About a quarter to ten," as we would have done even fifteen years ago, we now say "It's 9:47." We live in a culture that segments time in small, precise units, and whose members are becoming increasingly concerned with how these ever smaller units are expended. Even within our own culture, one can encounter very different approaches to, and definitions of, time (Levine 1988). Consider the difference between the definition and use of time as it exists in New York City versus a small Kansas farming community. In the former instance the pace of life is rapid, the concern with punctuality considerable, and time is defined largely through mechanical means of measurement, such as clocks. In the latter case, the pace of life is more leisurely, the concern with punctuality moderate, and time is defined through natural events, such as planting periods, as much as by mechanical means.

If these distinctions can be found within a culture, imagine the differences that can occur across cultures. Since time is something that is subjectively apprehended fully as much as it is objectively measured, differences in the experience of time are hardly surprising. The uses of, the approaches to, and the very definitions of time can vary significantly from culture to culture (Hägerstrand 1988; Jones 1988; Rutz 1992).

Like other aspects of culture, conceptions of time are learned and are embedded in sociocultural contexts (Hägerstrand 1988:35). All cultures provide their members with adequate information for judging time. Several researchers have suggested that the conceptions of time that characterize cultures derive largely from natural and social rhythms (Jones 1988; Latif and Spencer 1981; Levine 1988; Zerubavel 1981). Concepts of time are tied clearly to environmental as well as to cultural components. Through a process of entrainment where "one cyclic process becomes captured by, and set to oscillate in rhythm with, another process" (McGrath and Kelly 1986:80), time can interrelate sociocultural, psychological, and physiological elements. For such reasons it is well for anthropologists to be familiar with the local understanding and appreciation of time.

Like many peasants (Foster 1965; Kluckhohn and Strodtbeck 1961), Kelantanese traditionally appear to be present-, not future-oriented (Latif and Spencer 1981). The future looms as an unpredictable and uncontrollable element that may create problems beyond the meager coping mechanisms of the typical villager. An appreciation of this perspective helps one to understand why Kelantanese are often far more concerned with current circumstance than with a vague and somewhat troubling future. This view has significant ramifications for political behavior, as we will see later.

Kelantanese customarily recognize five seasons, though there is considerable uncertainty about how these relate to the calendar. The season which elicits greatest agreement is the rainy season (*musim hujan*), which is generally regarded as lasting from October through February. This is followed or even overlapped by the season of winds (*musim tenggara* or *musim angin*), which extends from February through April. The flower season (*musim bunga*), when trees, shrubs, and flowers bloom, occurs during May, but several of my friends, while recognizing this season, neglected to volunteer it when asked to list the seasons. The hot season (*musim panas*) extends generally from May through September, and following the harvest, is a period for traditional activities and entertainments. Finally, the period usually spanning August through October, when fruits ripen, is appropriately termed the fruit season (*musim buah*).

It is clear that Kelantanese seasons are tied not to the calendar, but rather to experiential circumstance. Seasons can easily overlap and are subject to varying interpretation. The fruit season has been variously reported as beginning in July or in October and as ending in August or in November. Part of this variation stems from the absence of any strict intersection with calendrical conventions, but an equally important determinant of these differing judgments tends to be the kinds of fruits favored by the person estimating the season.

In addition to such unmistakable natural markers as the rainy season, the annual cycle is further defined by the Muslim calendar, which, because it is lunar, lacks the periodic precision of the Gregorian model. Although many Kelantanese only hesitatingly identify the months of the Muslim year, all are familiar with the major Islamic markers, especially the fasting month, Ramadan (*bulan puasa*). Religious celebrations, such as those marking the end of the fasting month, the prophet's birthday, and the prophet's pilgrimage to Mecca have significant social implications at once binding villagers together and connecting them to a wider international community. For the most part such holidays provide a means of increasing the solidary bonds of villagers and kinsmen, not only through shared experience but also through expected patterns of visitation (Raybeck 1986).

Divisions of the day also reflect both ecological and religious influence. Although the Kelantanese day is formally ordered by the cycle of five Islamic prayers, it is informally ordered by the work routine, which in turn reflects the influence of the sun and changes in temperature throughout the day. Midday is termed "standing erect," berdiri, a reference to the sun when it is directly overhead.

Social-historical time is designated by both natural and social markers. Natural markers consist of events and phenomena of sufficient significance to be remembered by most people. In Kelantan these include the major floods of 1926 and 1967, both of which anchor the past, especially for older illiterate villagers. Since Kelantanese traditionally had no means to record birth dates nor much interest in doing so, age among older villagers was estimated by reference to the kinds of activities they could undertake at the time. A middle-aged man approximated his age by noting that he could tie his own sarong by the flood of 1926, which would have made him approximately five to eight years old at the time. At the village level, major fires and other notable events serve a similar purpose, but usually only for coresidents. Two exceptions in Wakaf Bharu were the coming of the narrow-gauge railroad in 1914 and the building of the bridge crossing the Kelantan River in the mid-1960s, which gave the village much easier access to Kota Bharu.

Social markers, while useful, are not relied upon as greatly as are natural markers, probably because the former represent less immediate forms of experience. One exception to this generalization is the marker involving the World War II period of Japanese occupation. The occupation was a period of turmoil and difficulties that deeply affected many Kelantanese, and that generally serves as a generation marker for the elderly even today. There are those who were born before the coming of the Japanese and those born after. At the village level, time markers can include the deaths of prominent persons and noteworthy violent crimes.

People who violate the pace of village life come into conflict with basic village values concerning time, the importance of interpersonal relations, and village solidarity. Kelantanese, as mentioned earlier, strive diligently to maintain harmonious interpersonal relations and to display appropriate signs of respect to fellow villagers. People are expected to avoid making one another embarrassed (malu) and to observe a set of rules for proper behavior termed the "language of character" (budi bahasa). Part of this language involves an unhurried pace of life wherein there is always sufficient time to realize social obligations, to visit and pay respects to relatives, friends, and neighbors. The casual and flexible treatment of time that characterizes the pace of village life integrates well with village social concerns (see Latif and Spencer 1981).

The elasticity of time is apparent in the scheduling of events, whether personal or public. Family meals occur before or after the appropriate Islamic prayer, but not at what Westerners would regard as fixed times. Except for the evening meal, it is not uncommon for members of the family to eat separately, depending on their needs and activities. Events such as weddings or feasts are usually scheduled with reference to a prayer time or sometimes simply to a half-day period so that guests will be arriving and leaving over a span that may extend for five to six hours. Behind such temporal latitude is a belief that neither dinners nor diners should be rushed and that attendance at an affair is what matters, not the time of arrival.

An excellent example of the Kelantanese attitude toward time and punctuality is provided by that most favored form of village entertainment, the shadow play or *wayang kulit*. The shadow play is so named because the puppeteer sits behind a screen, holding puppets between the screen and a lamp so that the audience on the outside views only the shadow of the puppet itself (see figure 2). The puppets are usually constructed of goat or sheep hide and are of a solid piece, save for an articulated arm. Puppets are carefully shaped and then decorated with a large number of apertures of assorted sizes and designs. These make the shadows that much more distinctive and visually interesting. The puppeteer can greatly increase the drama of the puppet's

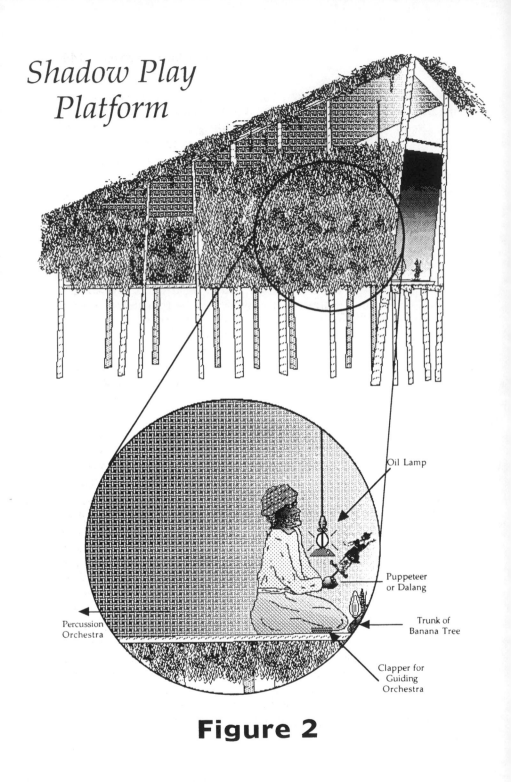

Shadow Play Platform

Oil Lamp

Puppeteer or Dalang

Percussion Orchestra

Trunk of Banana Tree

Clapper for Guiding Orchestra

Figure 2

A Shadow Play platform erected in the main area of Wakaf Bharu. Inside are over a thousand dollars worth of puppets and musical instruments that are unsecured save for the formidable reputation of the puppeteer, a man feared for his knowledge of of the supernatural.

The same platform in the evening. The scene is from an episode of the *Ramayana,* a favored epic originating in India. The tale is named for Sri Rama and describes his efforts to regain his throne and to rescue his wife from a demon king.

A closeup of shadows of several of the charactgers in the Ramayana. The two dark figures to the left are clowns who frequently make ribald comments on village life as well as on the unfolding story. The tallest figure is Laksamana, royal brother of Sri Rama; the one on the far right is a demon.

movements by bringing it closer either to the screen, where detail is apparent, or to the lamp, where it appears to loom menacingly.

Wayang kulit performances are held during the evening, usually during the post-harvest season from May through September, except for special events, as when a wealthy villager may support a performance to celebrate an event such as a wedding. The story line portrayed through the wayang kulit is most commonly drawn from the great Hindu epic, the *Ramayana*, the whole of which takes months to fully unfold.

Wayang kulit performances generally begin around nine o'clock and end at one or even three o'clock the next morning. Starting and ending times are approximate, and villagers are made aware of an impending performance by music from the orchestra (*gamelan*) that accompanies the puppeteer. Gradually villagers drift into the cleared area where the wayang kulit platform has been erected, and when the puppeteer judges that a sufficient number are present the performance begins. Thus the starting time is determined by the actions of both puppeteer and audience and reflects the interactive nature of village social life. The wayang kulit ends when the puppeteer decides. Moreover while the termination of the evening's performance generally coincides with a shift in the story line, it seldom represents a conclusion.

Except for religious holidays, the distinction between work time and leisure time so characteristic of the West is seldom recognized in village life. Instead time is defined by daily, monthly, or annual social and religious activities during which pleasure and work often intermingle. Following Magrib and the evening meal, villagers often visit with one another, but they frequently take with them handicraft items on which they will work as they talk. The idea of scheduling various kinds of activities at differing times is not one with which most villagers are either familiar or comfortable. Instead time tends to be defined by the activities undertaken, and estimates of duration frequently refer to such enterprises (e.g., the time required to plant three bundles of padi; see Ong 1987:108). In several important senses, time, its reckoning, and its treatment, reflect and reinforce valued aspects of Kelantan village social life.

While all cultural systems reflect a balance between experiential and abstract forms of time reckoning, the Kelantanese approach to time clearly derives more from experience than from the abstract, formal models for calculation that are more significant in most Western societies. As such, time is deeply embedded in the social and cultural life of the Kelantanese to the point where it can reinforce, as well as reflect, distinctive cultural patterns. Had I not been in Kelantan for more than a year, it would have been very difficult for me to have become sensitive to these issues.

The manner in which seasons impact upon the patterns of social life can be striking, and an anthropologist must be present to appreciate them. Joel Savishinsky, having spent more than a year with the hunting and gathering Hare Indians of the Yukon Territory, found marked differences between the summer and winter months (Savishinsky 1974). In the summer, Hare camps come together for social purposes, to trade, and to maintain a network of interdependence. In the winter months, the Hare disperse to separate family camps throughout the bush, where they hunt and enjoy comparative solitude. These cycles of ingathering and outgathering related to a variety of important social concerns, from marriage patterns to stress relief, and the mechanisms for dealing with these would not have been apparent had Savishinsky only lived among the Hare for a few months.[28]

The influence of the seasons on Kelantan village life, while not quite as dramatic as among the Hare, is significant and serves to establish both social tempos and social activities. Let me touch briefly on three of the major seasons and their consequences for villagers.

The rainy season begins with the rain, not in accordance with abstract measures of cyclicity. The prominence of this marker is apparent to anyone who has ever experienced a Kelantanese rainstorm. First you see an imposing wall of dark cloud moving toward you. This is followed by sound, initially a distant susurration, as of a water tap left open. This quickly becomes louder, and as you look in the direction from which the sound emanates, you can see a surprisingly solid, gray veil of water being drawn across the landscape. The drops are big enough to kick up little spouts of dust in the road before transforming them into mud. When the wall of water washes over you, it is as though you have stepped under a waterfall. You are immediately soaking wet, and your sandals begin to sink ever deeper in the mire of the trail.

When such experiences become daily occurrences, the rainy season has begun and all are aware of it. The downpour causes most people to cease whatever activities in which they are involved and to seek whatever shelter, however poor, they can find. On more than one occasion, when I was caught abroad in a bad storm, strangers welcomed me (and others) to share their shelter. An anthropologist's store of memories is stocked with such experiential recollections, some of which are quite pleasant and some of which. . . .

On one evening, coming home late from Kota Bharu, I was hit by a rainstorm featuring thunder, lightning, high winds, and remarkably heavy rains. My little Yamaha was so cowed by the dramatic nature of the activity that it ceased to function. Things go awry. I was only three miles from home, and happily (?) the lightning provided plenty of illumination for the long walk. An hour later I was puffing hard, pushing the cycle through the deepening mud, and cursing the loss of my flip-flops, which had disappeared in the sucking quagmire. I arrived home drenched, shoeless, tired, and late. Karen, who is less than fond of lightning, greeted me with relief and once again questioned the sanity of fieldwork.

In addition to their being occasionally hazardous, Kelantan rains also provided beneficial for my research. During the heaviest part of the rainy season, flooding invariably occurs. In most years, the flooding is local, amounts to only a couple of feet at most, and quickly runs off. This is a period that most people, especially children, actively enjoy. Many houses have old, narrow, wooden boats lying behind or under them. These are dusted off and used in visiting friends and relatives in the area. It is bemusing to watch these craft being poled up and down village paths normally reserved for foot traffic and motorcycles.

Some years the inundation goes well beyond the temporary. Flooding can occur throughout much of the state, especially in the low regions along the Kelantan River. Unfortunately these are also the areas that have the densest populations and that raise the bulk of Kelantan's rice. Such floods are seldom confined to Kelantan, and a prolonged flood can seriously impair the ability of Malaysia's people to feed themselves, often necessitating the importation of rice. The attitude of children toward these trials contrasts markedly with that of adults. School is called off, leaving children free to gambol in water and to invent a variety of aquatic pastimes.

Children playing in the rain and temporary flood waters in the midst of the rainy season. The rainy season brings free time to both children and adults and is often a time for working on crafts and relaxing at the local coffee shops.

During the peak of the rainy season, when rains fall for much of the day, people travel and work far less. There is less visiting between houses and less access to social engagement. In the afternoons it is possible to find whole families at home working on various crafts and chatting. I discovered it was far easier to enter a house where people were a bit bored and happy to have something to talk about than it was to intrude myself into someone's work schedule. Much of my more time-consuming work, such as recording genealogies, was conducted during this season, leading Karen to refer to me as the soggy anthropologist.

The rainy season is followed by the planting season.[29] Please do not assume that this means the rains have ended. Rather, they have merely dissipated to the point where roads reappear and outdoor activities can be contemplated. The planting season can start as early as January and is the period that makes most demands on males. It is during this time that the rice fields are turned, dykes are repaired, and new shoots started in seed beds. The actual planting of the rice can be carried out by either gender, but generally the males do the bulk of the work. Planting consists of hiking up your kain between your legs, taking a bunch of ripening shoots in your left arm, and then bending over to shove the roots of the shoots into the rich, flooded soil of the rice field. The actual process is bend, shove, take a shuffling step to the side, and repeat. Endlessly.

In response to some of my questions about farming, young Mat from the jaga determined he would teach me the techniques of padi planting. I spent a perfectly miserable morning trying to emulate Mat as he bent, shoved, and shuffled. Not only did my height and unfamiliarity with the task account for my slowness, I discovered that my description of the planting procedure had omitted a relevant step. Every twenty minutes or so we would take a short break, climbing out of the rice field to light a cigarette. You lighted a cigarette whether or not you smoked, since it was used to burn off the leeches that had collected on your ankles and calves. I quickly became persuaded that rice planting was among the more difficult and less pleasant tasks I had ever undertaken, and I recalled the British epithets about "lazy Malays" with wonderment and some bitterness.

The planting season and the subsequent harvest are also periods that underscore village solidarity and the role of mutual assistance (gotong royong) in village life. Farmers pledge one

Mat, introducing me to the "joys" of rice planting. The bundle of shoots in the foreground was mine. Not surprisingly, Mat did three bundles in the space of time that I did one. The clouds behind him suggest another rainstorm which arrived later that morning.

another assistance with labor-intensive tasks, and the rule of reciprocity is strongly enforced. If one person works for another for three days, that individual is owed three days' labor in the future. Anyone who flaunts this convention risks being excluded from future assistance. During the height of the harvest, every able-bodied, or nearly able-bodied, person works to get in the harvest. I have seen amputees and people with significant mental problems actively engaged in one or another aspect of harvesting, from the actual cutting of the rice stalks to the winnowing of the grains.

For much of Kelantan, where there was single-cropping, the harvest was finished in May. In irrigated areas planting could actually occur as late as June and a second planting was often undertaken in the fall. In all areas, however, when the harvest was completed, social life changed dramatically. This was the period of the hot season; the period of free time, the period for weddings and of celebrations tied to Islam. This was also the time of entertainments.

During the post-harvest hot season there are a variety of entertainments and competitions that occur within and between villages. Kelantanese attitudes toward competition are ambiguous at best. They like the excitement provided by such affairs but are concerned about the potential for interpersonal embarrassment (malu). For every winner there must also be a loser, who experiences the emotional costs of failure and who may, because of envy or ill temper, threaten the equanimity of village social relations. Thus contests among Kelantanese seldom involve head-to-head competition. Instead they are structured in such a fashion as to minimize the likelihood of provoking interpersonal friction.

The structure of most contests places some sort of behavioral or environmental buffer between the contestants. Bird singing contests, one of the most popular forms of competition in Kelantan, pit birds, not people, against one another. Similarly more direct contests such as top spinning or kite flying involve environmental constituents, such as the compaction of sand or the strength of the wind, which cannot easily be held constant (Raybeck 1989). Thus losers can always excuse their performance, while winners are encouraged not to become boastful about an event that they only partially controlled.

The particularly social nature of Kelantanese time is manifest in some of the hot season competitions. Several contests such as kite flying or those between songbirds involve a timed interval during which the competition is judged. Kite-flying contests nicely illustrate the problems of competitions, their resolutions, and the role of time in such traditional events. Kite-flying competitions generally occur between villages and represent an opportunity for individuals to be recognized for their competence in kite building, a traditional skill, and for their aesthetic abilities at decoration. Kites are made of layers of colored waxed paper cut out to create superimposed patterns, then stretched between a light wooden frame constructed in accord with several traditional patterns. The more attractive and better decorated a kite is, the less likely it is to do well in flight competition, though there are separate events where kites are judged strictly on appearance. The object of the flight contests is to fly as near to vertical as possible during a timed interval without manual assistance, and lighter (less decorated kites) do better than heavier ones. Nonetheless many of the kites entered in flight contests are beautifully decorated with layers of brightly colored paper that create images resembling stained-glass windows. This emphasis on aesthetics tempers the importance of the competition itself, since a kite may garner a good deal of admiration for the maker without being a strong competitor.

Competitions are usually held in a cleared rice field, beginning in the morning and continuing on through late afternoon. The actual competition involves the behavior of a kite over a timed interval rather than its behavior with respect to any other particular kite. Once a kite is lofted, it is tied to a short vertical stake protruding from the baked pan of the rice field, and after this the owner can no longer influence the kite's behavior. To the top of the stake is affixed an ordinary wooden ruler, which can revolve around a nail driven through the one-inch mark and which can be used to measure how close to the vertical a kite ascends. As the kites approach a common altitude, a timer is started and the degree to which a kite achieves verticality during the measured interval determines how well it has done. There are a series of flights consisting of approximately half a dozen kites each time, leading to a process of elimination that results in a single winner by the end of the day.

The judge responsible for timing the five to seven kites in a flight is generally a respected and prominent member of a village not represented in the competition. Commonly judges are Islamic priests or village leaders, who are well-off by village standards and who frequently own and wear wristwatches. Nonetheless I never witnessed a judge using a wristwatch to time the interval for a flight of kites. Instead the timer commonly employed for such a task is a coconut clock. This is a simple construction consisting of a pail of water in which is floated a half coconut shell with a small hole bored through the center. The measured interval is simply the amount of time it takes for the shell to fill with water and sink, usually three to five minutes.

Clearly the coconut clock provides a measurement of an interval that is significantly less precise and far more variable than that which could be obtained by utilizing the wristwatch that many judges possess. When I asked different judges why they employed the former rather than the latter, I always received the same reply. The coconut clock, despite its imprecision, was highly visible and protected the judges from claims that they might have favored a particular contestant by shading the amount of time available for the kite flight. This example, simple as it is, makes an important statement about Kelantanese culture and the willingness of Kelantanese to subordinate temporal exactitude to social concerns.

Ties That Bind

The hot season is also a period of increased visiting among friends and relatives. Social bonds, especially ones that have been strained, are often re-cemented at this time. Patterns of invitations and visits are sources of interest to villagers at large, who monitor the health of family relationships throughout the village. One of the more significant invitations involves a religious celebration that occurs early in the hot season in the first Muslim month of *Sura*. To be invited to a Sura is a mark of regard and acceptance.

The tradition is named for Sura or "ashura" and commemorates Noah's ark. Purportedly when Noah's passengers were all crowded aboard his boat, there was not much food to be had. Each person volunteered some food to go into a communal pot from which all would eat. The contemporary Sura consists of a great melange of foods, including beef, chicken, rice, assorted vegetables, coconut milk, potatoes, and numerous spices. This is all placed in a large *kuali* (a cooking pot shaped like a large wok) over a ground-level outdoor fire and cooked slowly for five to twelve hours. The longer you cook it the better it is supposed to be. A *Makan Sura* (feast) may be presented either by one person, or by a number of people who join together and contribute various foods in the traditional fashion. Usually anywhere from fifty to sixty people are fed, and the cost may be anywhere from M$18 to M$25.

Karen and I were pleased to be invited to a Makan Sura produced by a neighbor. We arrived garbed in our Malay finery, which is to say that Karen looked splendid while one might charitably say I appeared "well intentioned." When we arrived the Sura was still cooking in a very large kuali that had been set into a hole in the ground that contained hot coals. I was told the Sura had cooked throughout the evening, with some of the sponsor's relatives taking turns to stir it.

It is common for both men and women to be invited to a Sura, but as on other occasions, the sexes eat separately. The men eat seated in small circles in the front room, while the women eat in informal clusters in the kitchen, often making fun of the men. As with other Kelantanese gatherings, there was no set time for either starting or concluding the affair. People arrived over a period of some three hours, chatted, ate, and departed, often carrying a piece of the Sura with them for those at home. Each person received a plate containing a portion of Sura, cut into twelve pieces and covered with grated coconut that had apparently been cooked in turmeric (as it was orange), and palm sugar. The Sura itself had the consistency of a hard tapioca pudding and was colored an inauspicious grey-blue-black. The taste could only be described as "curious." There was an underlying flavor of chicken and santan, but occasionally other flavors were also encountered. I later discovered that some of these other flavors were provided by toads and insects that had, perhaps with misplaced religious fervor, leapt or fallen into the kuali during the night-long cooking of the ingredients.

Both Karen and I dutifully ate most of our Sura and were rewarded with the bundled leftovers to carry home. Unlike our experiences of some earlier house-visits during Hari Raya Haji, the atmosphere we encountered at this feast was more nonchalant and more accepting of us. We were treated more as familiar eccentrics than exotic oddities. A number of people inquired about my progress with my research, centered at that time on adoption, and made helpful suggestions concerning sources of information.

Increasing acceptance is an enormous asset to fieldwork, but it also involves some risks. As villagers became more adapted to and understanding of our presence, we felt ever greater pressure both to conform to local mores, which was understandable and even desirable, and to become fuller participants in village social life. I found that friends who had spent time with me in answering questions expected some reciprocity. I encountered requests to help with a variety of tasks, most of which were small and served largely to solemnize my recognition of the social debt I owed a particular individual.

One of my more prominent engagements involved helping a number of friends erect food stalls near the village *padang* (open field), the area where various performances, including wayang kulit, were conducted. Such stalls are small, approximately six-foot, square structures, that are anchored by four large bamboo posts to which is attached a platform on which the food is displayed and a pandanus leaf roof that serves as protection from occasional showers. The roofs are approximately seven feet off the ground and are difficult for Malays to secure. My Kelantanese friends suggested that, with my height, I should be able to hoist the roof up and secure it without either shinnying up a support post or using any of the flimsy jury-rigged supports employed in such endeavors. I became a specialist in roofing small structures, a task that took little time and effort, but which garnered both gratitude and some good humored jibes about my ability to tie down the roof. I am one of those who finds a square knot appropriate for virtually any task involving rope or string. Unfortunately the material commonly used to secure roofs was rattan, and I can assert that it is but poorly adapted to square knots.

On another occasion a villager who had been of considerable assistance with some of my genealogical efforts asked me to participate in a "house moving" (*pindah rumah*). I should mention that this term is meant quite literally. Traditional Kelantanese houses are constructed of local materials. As described earlier, walls are generally of woven pandanus, as is the roof. Flooring consists of planks or split bamboo, and what partitions exist are either hanging pandanus mats or cloth dividers. Kelantanese houses do not weigh a great deal, and moving them does not require the use of winches, large trucks, or anything more complex than a lever. Power is provided by relatives, friends, and neighbors. The move occurred in August, a common time for such ventures. The hot season may seem a perverse time for activities that require a great deal of energy, but the choice is dictated by the need to avoid mud and soft ground. During the hot season, virtually all land takes on the character of a baked, rough, ceramic surface. No mud.

When I arrived at the house on the appointed date, it was apparent from the state of things that a good bit of work had already been accomplished. However, in typical Kelantanese fashion, most of it seemed to be going on without any form of centralized direction. Two-by-fours and large pieces of bamboo had been lashed lengthwise and breadthwise to the supports of the house several feet above the ground. (Remember that Kelantanese houses are raised on stilts.) Brush had been cleared and people were busy lopping off the limbs of trees that would obstruct our progress. Some of the preliminary work was done by the owner and his relatives, although by the afternoon other people were also lending a hand. Before many people had shown up one of the young boys blew several times on a trumpet made of water buffalo horn. This made a rather penetrating noise resembling the romantic sound of bull elephant seal in rut. (I confess to watching the Discovery Channel.) Within forty-five minutes or so about thirty people had arrived. Each person cut a long, stout stick, about two inches or better in diameter and about five feet long, which would be used as a lever against the cross-lashed beams connecting the house supports. Once the moving started, the supporting beams rode atop flat boards or logs that had been placed in position for this purpose.

The actual moving of the house didn't begin until about 4:00 P.M. and during this time one break had to be taken because, despite being in the middle of the dry season, there was a heavy rain shower. Of the thirty people present, approximately ten were young men or youths and only three were old men. However, when the seniors made suggestions, their comments were usually heeded, even though the old men did not appear to assume leadership. Actually, out of the thirty people present, I received the impression that there were twenty-five leaders.

Once the work started, it progressed smoothly, although with everyone shouting suggestions and directions, the general image was one of near total disorder. The house was moved with levers, each time on the count of three with everyone lending their voice. The count was given by the owner who sat cross-legged on the front porch of the house we were striving to move. Although I found his position somewhat curious, I was informed by others of the belief that his presence actually made the house lighter.

My task had initially been to join a group of young men who bent beneath the lashed cross-pieces and lifted up in an effort to make the load lighter to move. This time, however, my height proved more bane than boon, as I was unable to straighten up enough to get much power into the lift. Thus I took my place with a sturdy lever and joined the majority of grunting, sweaty, surprisingly happy males who labored to move the structure in three-inch increments.

A Kelantan house which we had just finished moving a total of 30 feet. The men at the side are piling up poles that were used to lever the house to its new location three inches at a time.

A number of young children hung about on the outskirts watching our progress and making comments on how much more I sweated than did my companions. We completed the move about 5:30 P.M. The house had been moved approximately twenty feet to the side and ten feet toward the village path. The move was because the owner was constructing a new house that needed some of the space occupied by the old. Just before we completed the move, in an uncommon display of timeliness, a number of female relatives of the owner, including his wife, his mother, and several of his sisters, arrived with a trishaw loaded with a great pot of *bubur*. Bubur is a rice porridge that has been cooked for some time and to which is added a variety of foods ranging from peas to sago palm sugar. It is highly digestible and represents the Kelantanese answer to energy bars. After the work was completed all the men climbed up into the shell of the new house, where we were served large bowls of bubur. Like good males, we spent the remainder of the late afternoon in exaggerated recollection of difficulties encountered and energy expended.

Day-to-Day

Despite the colorfulness of some of the experiences I have related, much of field research involves following a daily schedule that can be somewhat humdrum. In a period as prolonged as a year and a half, anthropologists may develop a bit of complacency and may even establish a daily pattern that, especially during the long days of the rainy season, can verge on ennui.

Each morning Karen and I "seized the day." Typically we arose, chased the rooster, killed some ants, disposed of whatever rodents had ventured into one of the traps we maintained, and made breakfast. I determined that the literal meaning of *carpe diem* was "complain about the day." Often Karen trudged dutifully to the market to purchase the day's supplies, while I worked on notes, read, or traveled about in search of information. I regret to report that on a distressingly large number of days my research plans were not wholly realized.

I frequently began the day with my notebook and a schedule of activities. However, by 10:30 A.M. or so, especially during the hot season, the temperature became sufficiently oppressive that I often found excuses to return home to shower and to work on some project in the study. Things go awry. Often, during the middle of the day, both Karen and I simply sat and read. We read newspapers, the international version of *Newsweek*, classic literature, mysteries, science fiction, histories, travel tales, practically anything we could find in English. So desperate were we for reading material that in Kota Bharu I actually purchased *Playboy* magazines for the literary rather than the pictorial content.

Our other means of dealing with the midday doldrums was to escape to Kota Bharu to take in one of the several matinees playing there. Theaters in Kota Bharu ranged from the recently constructed, comparatively posh, and comfortable Odeon to the Rani, a crumbling, poorly ventilated structure that, unfortunately, frequently ran old American and English films. I say unfortunately because watching a film at the Rani necessitated a degree of fortitude not called for in the other theaters. Watching a movie at the Rani meant propping your knees firmly on the seat in front of you so that your feet would be well off the floor. The reason for this slightly odd posture was quite simple and known to all patrons. In addition to the odd assortment of paying customers, the Rani supported numerous freeloaders, the most prominent of which were city rats. These spent most of each movie playing soccer up, down, and across the aisles. I remember appreciating the irony one afternoon when Karen and I went to the Rani to watch *King Rat* with George Segal. A fine film, but it did remind us of our ecological plight.

We were occasionally distracted from our concern with athletically gifted rats by the highly visible aerial antics of bats. The bats apparently perched in the rafters of the Rani and were fond of sweeping across the movie screen during a film, preferably in one of the more suspenseful moments. Admittedly these events did add an element of drama to film viewing. One afternoon, they were even able to enliven a Doris Day film. (I told you we got desperate.)

Normally Karen and I enjoy a range of films from foreign and classic to Westerns and comedies. Kelantan, nonetheless, managed to enlarge our film horizons in unexpected ways. Not only did we watch the few contemporary films that came to Kota Bharu, we saw films of every vintage. At one point the Odeon ran a series of Tarzan films—the early ones, the very early ones—the ones done near the dawn of photography. We saw them all. During one of the finer films, *Tarzan Finds a Son*, the chief villain turns to a native bearer and asks something in a presumed African language. The audience around me immediately began debating the significance of the utterance. The villain as it turned out was a Dutch actor who had clearly spent time in Indonesia. The director must have instructed him to "say something African" and he responded in perfectly serviceable Indonesian, a language very similar to Malay: "*Manalah jalan kecil?*" [Where is the path?] This was the sole Indonesian/Malay interjection in a film utilizing English and some Dutch, and the Kelantanese in the audience were bemused, to say the least.

In addition to such Western epics, we saw Malay films, Indonesian films, Japanese films, and those curious Chinese sword-and-frolic epics directed by Run Run Shaw. (Who could make up a name like that?) The latter featured mediocre acting, predictable plotting, but impressive athletic activity, particularly balletic leaps of several stories' height. Nonetheless the most memorable of the non-Western films were those referred to as Hindustani. These are made in India and exported throughout much of the world, where they are often extremely popular. Virtually all of my Kelantanese friends who frequented the theaters told me that Hindustani films were their favorites and that I should be certain to see them.

I was curious about the appeal of these films and determined to take in several until I could identify why they were so attractive to Kelantanese. Karen went with me—once. (Her curiosity was more easily satisfied than mine.) I went several more times, each time buying an extra ticket for a Kelantanese friend with whom I could discuss the film afterward. The attraction of Hindustani films quickly became apparent. There is only one film, but it has numerous incarnations that, like faulty clones, greatly resemble the original without quite being the original. The basic cast always features a somewhat plump hero and heroine who are prone to burst into song, especially when crossing large expanses of lawn or garden. There is also a best friend/ clown of the hero who interferes with progress until redeeming himself at the end by an act of often accidental usefulness. Finally, there is the villain, often an older man, sporting a mustache, with a propensity to frown. The plot involves unexpressed love—misunderstanding—love thwarted—vanquishing of the problem/villain—resurgence of love—song and dancing, especially when crossing large expanses of lawn or garden.

It seems the Kelantanese affection for this genre is similar to our own penchant for watching "B" Westerns, wherein the plot and the cast, from horse to heroine, display the same pattern of predictability. Indeed the predictability is the major appeal of Hindustani films. Those films were judged best that stayed closest to the formula described above. Those films that displayed a degree of innovation in either plot or character were disparaged as being less enjoyable and as having departed from the ideal. In a world of change such as Kelantan was starting to experience in the late sixties or such as we are currently enjoying, predictable outcomes are comforting, and they can ease one's suspicion that the universe may be a more stochastic entity than we have been led to believe.

Happily the routine of daily life can interfere with research in ways that are ultimately constructive. I became close with Hussein, my next-door neighbor, in a variety of informal contexts where what we both sought was simply conversation and companionship. Usually I neglected to carry my notebook and abandoned thoughts of a structured research agenda. Instead he and Zainab would occasionally simply drop in to chat, often bringing some food with them. When they adopted a lovely daughter, Ruslinah, they would bring her over so that both of us could appreciate her and hold her.

Karen and I tried to reciprocate as best we could. Karen introduced Nab to bread baking and quickly gained fame for her home-baked banana bread. Kelantanese do a lot with bananas, but baking them in bread was a novel concept; one that quickly spread as Karen responded to requests for the recipe.

Our visits next door were influenced by Hussein's purchase of a small black and white television set, one of three in the village. At that time, there were only a couple of government-run stations, and these selected their fare from Japan, England, Indonesia, and the United States. They also showed some rather elementary local productions and some older Malay films. There were two shows featuring Malay films that were very popular with villagers. On appropriate evenings, scores of villagers would visit next door, where they were welcomed by my neighbors. Hussein and Nab, not unlike the puppeteers described earlier, announced that a film was about to begin by turning up the volume of the set so that the distinctive theme music could be heard in neighboring houses. People would appear and fill the front room, while late arrivals balanced on the porch and peered through the windows. Upon completion of the film, near midnight, everyone left quickly and peace reclaimed our section of the village.

Starting in May, on Friday evenings we—usually just I— found reason to visit Hussein and Nab. It seems that one of the networks had begun running *Star Trek*, a show of which I was/ am quite fond. I now had an opportunity to reciprocate some of the kindness Hussein had shown me when he explained the backgrounds to some of the Malay films I had seen. It was, however, somewhat disjunctive to sit on a wooden floor surrounded by villagers, most of whom were illiterate, and to explain the nature of a show devoted to a future characterized by complex technological developments and a variety of social experiments.

In a similar fashion we became close to Yusof Daud and his family. We would drop in simply because we were glad for their company. Yusof and his wife, Gayah, were always warm and welcoming. More than any other person in the village, Yusof understood and sympathized with my research tasks. I have already indicated some of the many ways in which he was helpful, but I may not have stressed how important his friendship became to me. He and his family were a constant source of support to whom both Karen and I could turn with our questions and problems. Their numerous children were also a great source of pleasure, as they were bright, outgoing, and cheerful. Two years ago I was reminded by one of Yusof's sons that, when he was a young teenager, I had helped him with his mathematics and English homework. Today he is Dr. Mohd Suria Affandi bin Haji Yusof with a Ph.D. in chemistry. Times change.

While fieldwork manuals say nothing about such needs, the desire for elements of familiarity in the midst of field research can be quite powerful. Abandon the image of the stoic anthropologist always standing aside from others in a constant attitude of watchfulness. Like most human beings, excepting perhaps some lawyers and hermits, anthropologists appreciate social contacts. They also often find familiar surroundings more congenial than strange ones. Consequently Karen and I sought out friends beyond the village, especially ones who spoke English and with whom we shared some common culture. In the early stages of fieldwork, we visited Amin and Zainab so frequently that I feared we were becoming genuine pests. We discovered a Peace Corps couple, George and Sally Sanders, who were both congenial and helpful. Later, we encountered a British schoolteacher and his wife, Len and Jean Crossfield, who were similarly helpful and friendly. It became apparent that there was a fairly tight network among English and Americans in Kelantan and a great deal of visiting between them. I wish I could name and acknowledge all those from whom we received hospitality. While, with the exception of Amin and Nab, these people did not directly contribute to my field research, they were very important sources of comfort and aid during some stressful times.

Our work and daily responsibilities made demands on both of us, but Karen's situation was more isolated than my own. Not only did she have more difficulty with the language, she frequently remained alone at home when I was traveling about. Partly to provide company we decided to adopt a kitten. Our first kitten arrived in July and was generously supplied by the Sanderses, who brought her out in a paper bag. "Squirt," as most cats will, soon began directing the household. Our second kitten arrived at the back door, filthy and partly starved. I admired his style, named him Studs (after Lonigan), and watched as he transformed from a gray to a white cat and a healthy, irascible hunter of cicak and mice. We now had twice the number of pets we had envisioned and were determined to hold at this level. Kelantanese attitudes toward animals, as I have mentioned, differ from our own, and they did not readily understand our willingness to lavish attention and resources on cats that were far too small to be useful in controlling the local rat population.

A month later, despite our good resolves, Karen pulled off her great cat-napping caper. It seems that villagers were aware of our fondness for these animals, and someone acted on that knowledge. One August morning on her way to the market, Karen found the following bundle that she described in her journal:

> Across the road and down from the house a short way I spotted a ball of fur with six eyes peeping out—three adorable (healthy!) kittens someone had obviously left, in hopes, perhaps, the softies would take them in. To kedai and back. Cik Nab not feeling well, lying down. Bought langsat—tastes sort of like grapefruit, quite good. Kittens still there. I take Doug to see, we begin to weaken. Breakfast, dishes, clothes, work on words. D read and worked on the semantic differential. Check kittens several times. Around noon two of them

up to the house mewling, third one apparently picked up by
someone; have to take them in; healthy and really cute—a
boy and a girl. Studs and Squirt ambivalent; Squirt looks
like she'll be OK. Studs a bit more intractable.

What Karen omits from this account is that each time she
"checked" the kittens, they took a few faltering steps after her
when she returned to the house. Three checks later, they were
virtually on our doorstep. After we were unsuccessful in seeking
homes for them, we adopted the two new kittens and named them
Bronislaw and Lucy, after two very prominent social anthropologists. Karen now had plenty of company during my absence and
a reputation among neighbors as being a soft-hearted person
(*hati lembut*). However, our fondness for cats had an unexpected
benefit, for it was Studs who alerted Karen to the presence of the
second cobra, which might otherwise have surprised her in a far
more formidable fashion.

The Paper Wars

Anthropologists who conduct their fieldwork in remote field
settings are in a poor position to deal with whatever bureaucracies
may be involved in monitoring or supporting the research. Instead
we must depend upon the kindness of strangers to be of assistance.
Due to the slowness and unevenness of the mails, and to differing
understandings of needs, this dependence can prove problematic.
Anthropologists who are about to leave for distant locales would be
well advised to appoint a surrogate to monitor the mail, look after
recalcitrant bureaucrats, and assemble needed information and
research tools. This person should also be well acquainted with
the proposed research and its schedule. This advice is the result
of a somewhat painful experience.

During the period of initial fieldwork, it took approximately
fourteen to seventeen days for a letter to move from Malaysia to
the United States. Assuming that the party on the other end
answered promptly (a rash assumption), it would take another
ten days to receive a reply. This unavoidable aspect of communication had significant impact both on research and on the little
day-to-day tasks involved in staying alive, to whit receiving money
for such amenities as medicine and food.

On January 17, shortly after arriving in the field, we were pleased to learn that I had been awarded a Special Research Fellowship from NIMH of five thousand dollars to support research for one and half years.[30] In March Karen and I learned that NIMH had cleared the money for my award. Now all that remained was transferring installments from that sum to us. Two letters informed us of the somewhat labyrinthine maneuvers that we would need to undertake in order to obtain the money. With the assistance of the secretary at Cornell's anthropology department and of a friend, we began the exchange of forms and paperwork that was to result in obtaining the money. Sure.

We dutifully filled out forms that called for everything from social security numbers to our mothers' maiden names. We wrote out a more detailed schedule of anticipated financial expenditures. In return we received a description of procedures to follow in order to get the funds transferred to Cornell, from whence they would (presumably) be transferred to us. We filled out another set of forms and sent them off airmail. In the interim we were subsisting (accurate word) on funds remaining from a small award from the London-Cornell Program. We watched the mails with the same attention a hungry cheetah might devote to a nearby antelope, but nothing arrived. Bearing in mind the difficulties of the mail, we resolved to be, somewhat uneasily, patient. By late April our patience had not been rewarded and our funds were nearly exhausted. We sent out another set of rather plaintive letters requesting assistance.

Our friend in Ithaca checked with several Cornell Offices and discovered that NIMH had indeed transferred the funds, but no one had taken the trouble to inform us or to begin the procedures necessary to get the money to us. When we learned of this, we sent a letter of thanks to our friend, a letter of inquiry to the Grants Office, and several structured prods designed to get funds released. In return we learned that, as in the case of any business venture, the preferred procedure was for us first to spend our money, and then to supply receipts for which we would be reimbursed. This is a fine, businesslike set of expectations that should be quite at home in a fine, businesslike environment, but *not* in the field. First, we had practically no money to spend. Second, many of our daily expenditures involved numerous small sums, and accounting for them would have involved a considerable drain on time available for field research. Finally, many of our economic transactions were with people who were illiterate and who could not supply receipts even if they wished to.

By the time we had convinced Cornell to transfer part of the money to a bank in Kota Bharu, it was mid-May and we had less than M$60. I had to approach our landlord, a man who was persuaded that we were, like most Americans, quite wealthy, and ask him for an extension on our rent. Not only was Mat Kadir kind and understanding, he offered to loan us money. By late May, Amin, Nab, and other friends aware of our increasingly difficult straits offered to lend us money. It seemed that everyone was willing to give us money, save the source that was supposed to.

Finally, on May 26, money arrived. Mind you, this was not the anticipated money from Cornell, but was instead a tax refund of US$181. Once again solvent, we paid our rent, bought two remarkably delicious Australian steaks, and contemplated erecting a tent near the post office. Two weeks later the first installment of US$1,000 arrived, and we relaxed our vigil. As you may imagine, we initiated other transfers far in advance of the dates they were needed.

In addition to the pressing issue of funds for the field, we also had to attend to Stateside expenses. My undergraduate alma mater was dunning me for interest payments on my educational loans, and Cornell, despite my remote location, was charging me for the pleasure of remaining registered at the university. In August, as part of Cornell's record-keeping procedures, we were sent a form and instructed to forward it to the registrar's office. Thus the form traveled twenty thousand miles in order to arrive at an office in the same building from which it had originated. It was then that we realized just how deeply embedded was the bureaucrat's creed: Never let efficiency get in the way of procedure.

In the midst of the ongoing field research, we received another massive missive from NIMH, informing us that the living stipend (now our sole source of income in the field) was only good for twelve months and that any extension would require a reapplication procedure. Unlike the initial application, which took the efforts of my full doctoral committee and Cornell's Grants Office to complete, this one was simpler. Perhaps out of sympathy for the plight of anthropologists, the reapplication procedure only required the signatures of three people: me, a representative from the Grants Office, and the chair of my doctoral committee. Since we planned to be in the field for at least an additional six months, it was imperative to make application for the extension. We asked for and received the appropriate forms and then sent them on to Art Wolf, my dissertation chair, who, as anthropologists will, was conducting field research . . . in Taiwan. His location was as remote as our own, but we anticipated postal impediments and left a good margin for delay, or so we thought. It seems that shortly after we had mailed the cumbersome and complex forms to Taiwan, he had left to return to the States. Things go awry.

I could continue to document the difficulties of trying to make financial arrangements from the field, but I think the point has been made. Most procedures used by banks and other commercial concerns are appropriate for businesses with access to complex communication resources, not for anthropologists in the field. Even with the electronic communication possible today, there is no easy way to get a signature from a remote field site to a financial institution. Thus the advice: arrange as much in advance as possible, and have a good, resourceful friend ready to assist in times of need.

Sun Block

Fieldwork makes two significant and continuous demands on anthropologists. First, we must always attend to the sociocultural context in which we work, for we never know what element of behavior will prove important or yield a major new insight. If we always knew what we were looking for, there would be little need for fieldwork. While I would not argue that anthropologists maintain a constantly heightened state of awareness, neither would I suggest that we can afford to relax fully. Anthropologists need to be mindful that we are continually at work and always observing. I have tried to indicate some of the indirect means by which I stumbled across some of the insights described above. Some of my best information owed more to serendipity than to sagacity.

Second, and perhaps the most draining demand of fieldwork, anthropologists must always be conscious of their public performance. Erving Goffman (1959) has argued that people perform for each other and that we are all, to a greater or lesser degree, aware of our performances and those of others. It takes a good deal of effort to monitor one's performance in a familiar setting where one is relatively unobtrusive. Imagine a setting where you are unfamiliar with the sociocultural nuances known to others, yet are also a constant and highly visible source of interest and entertainment. As I suggested in chapter 2, the absence of privacy and the high visibility of all aspects of one's behavior are very difficult to endure for extended periods. There is, however, a palliative for this difficulty—take a break.

During the field period of eighteen months, Karen and I took several small trips to other locales for the sole purpose of relaxation. We traveled to the neighboring state of Trengganu to watch the leatherback turtles come ashore and lay eggs. We journeyed to a distant village to admire a Buddhist temple. We went to the Perhentians—handsome, tropical islands off the coast of Trengganu—in order to get a blistering sunburn. Well, that wasn't the precise purpose, but it was one of the major results. However, we only took two extended holidays, and in the perverse manner of field research, we paid for both in unanticipated ways.

Our first real break from fieldwork came at the end of May, after five months of research. Don and Carrie Brown, close friends from graduate school, were conducting research in Brunei, just across the Malacca Strait. We had agreed to meet in Kuala Lumpur, the national capital. Karen and I arose early one morning to take the 6:00 A.M. train to Kuala Lipis. We traveled third class, less because that was anthropologically appropriate than because we were broke. This trip was taking place near our economic nadir. The Browns had sent us US$50 just to make the journey possible.

Third-class passage on a narrow-gauge railroad that stops at virtually every kampong is a time-consuming undertaking. Add to that a great deal of heat and humidity and numerous fellow passengers and you have an experience that, while memorable, is a poor means of promoting relaxation. The other travelers were largely middle-aged women bent on entrepreneurial activities. Almost all had some goods they were transporting to market at Pasir Mas or Kuala Lipis, and the majority of these hawked their wares out of open windows each of the many times we stopped in a village. Villagers—in a futile effort to maintain a favorable balance of payments and to offset imports with exports—hawked a variety of foods, clothing, and beverages from the station platforms. Actually, in most cases there were no platforms, and they simply walked along the train bed shouting their wares and conducting the occasional transaction. To this bedlam add the smell of warm fish and the scuttling of a covey of crabs that kept escaping from their tub, and you have a somewhat less than auspicious start for a pleasant holiday.

We arrived in Kuala Lipis only an hour late and tremulously sought out the locale of long-distance taxi drivers. We joined with two young women and a girl to complete the passenger complement for our driver, whom I soon nicknamed Captain Quick. Possessed of considerable driving skill and an unwonted belief in his own immortality, Captain Quick was one of those drivers we had come to fear when riding the Yamaha. Captain Quick seemed convinced that he possessed a lien on whatever section of the roadway he preferred. This, of course, made it much easier for him to take corners at high rates of speed, since he was under no obligation to keep to one side. After several hours careening about the curves that make up much of the coastal highway, Karen and I began to think that his intimations of immortality might be better founded than we initially supposed. In any event, we arrived in Kuala Lumpur in a timely if not a relaxed fashion about 8:30 that evening, a full ten hours earlier than the train.

We met the Browns; selected the Hotel New Zealand, a clean inexpensive establishment; and settled in to enjoy the holiday. The first activities were foreordained; we took hot showers, used the sit-down, flush toilet, and set off in search of Western food . . . and beer. The Browns had been in the field longer than we and were at least as interested in becoming reacquainted with Western-style amenities. We ate first at an Italian restaurant, where Don and I boggled the waiter's mind by ordering two entrees each and a number of beers. We then retired to the hotel and luxuriated in the comfort of a bed with a firm foam-rubber mattress.

The next two days were filled with shopping, eating, beer drinking, and socializing. I did make one stop to wrestle with the immigration authorities and obtain a passport stamp that would simplify my travels to Thailand. (This was, of course, before I discovered just how simple such trips could be.) Later the first evening, we engaged in activities designed to enhance our development as professional anthropologists. We went to a small amusement park, where we clambered into the bumper cars and proceeded to smash against one another until closing time.

Our culinary explorations were broad enough to embrace Chinese and Indian restaurants as well as Western ones. At several of these establishments, Karen and I reveled in pork dishes. I suspect we did so only partly because we like pork, but also because it had been forbidden to us for an extended period and eating it seemed somehow to make our vacation even more removed from the field. Or so I thought. I discovered when we returned to Wakaf Bharu that we had been seen by a policeman, a nephew of a Wakaf Bharu villager. He had recognized us leaving a Chinese restaurant where pork was known to be served and took pains to relay this bit of vital information back to the village. My respect for the efficiency of Kelantan's gossip network increased apace.

As vacationers will, we had saved a portion of our money for the final meal. The four of us went to the Malaysia Hotel, one of the finer establishments in the city. There I distressed our waiter by ordering two steak dinners. Actually, distressed isn't quite the term. The waiter literally refused to believe the second order and assumed that we were having language difficulties. He called for the manager, who, once assured of my ravenous nature, approved what must have seemed a rather Visigothic request. Apparently they seldom served anthropologists.

Having determined that time was not quite as precious as we had thought prior to our memorable taxi flight, we left that night on the train. We had reserved sleeping berths but discovered that these must have been designed by Keebler's for its employees. They were too small for Karen and wholly impossible for me. We found seats in second class and decided that we would sit up for the duration of the journey. The return trip was, in its fashion, as memorable as the trip to Kuala Lumpur. It was hot, slow, and tiring. We arrived in Wakaf Bharu late the next afternoon. It had taken us twenty-two hours to travel approximately two hundred miles, during which Karen had refused to use the questionable toilet facilities. She was very happy to get home.

The cost for this venture turned out to be more than the hundred dollars we spent. We were only absent from Wakaf Bharu for four days, but it was during this period that the "kelewang incident" happened. I returned to discover that the most significant act of deviance to occur in the village in years had transpired while we were on vacation. I had to work particularly diligently to reconstruct the actual event and then to acquire information from witnesses several days after their experiences. Things go awry.

If the first vacation was enriched by friends, the second was enlivened by relatives. We took our second vacation in mid-December at the height (or depth) of the rainy season. We had waited this long partly because we had been busy and partly because we had been expecting a visit from my brother, Bruce. During 1968 Bruce, a captain of artillery with the Americal Division, I Corps, was stationed in Vietnam, where he was busy risking his life and impairing his hearing. He was with a mobile artillery unit, a jump battery, that was dropped off on various hilltops by Chinook helicopters to support ground operations. His presence in the midst of the war caused us great concern, which was not alleviated by continuing reports of the conflict carried by armed forces radio broadcasting from Saigon, only some 450 miles across the South China Sea.

Bruce had written in October that he was trying to get a leave to visit us. In late November he sent us a letter stating that, given the intricacies of the army bureaucracy, it was less certain that he would be able to get away before returning Stateside. Two weeks later, Bruce wrote to inform us that he couldn't make it and was going to be sent home ahead of schedule. Though sorry to have missed him, we were quite happy that he was well out of harm's way. Since Bruce was no longer expected, and since we would soon face another series of social obligations related to the end of the fasting month of Ramadan, we decided the time was propitious for a break and left in mid-December.

This vacation we decided to spend five days, partly because I had a number of work-related tasks to complete involving bookstores and government offices. We arrived in Kuala Lumpur via the same means used before, save that this time our taxi driver was safe and slow, very slow. Seasons changed and governments rose and fell before we arrived at our destination.

For the next few days, we enjoyed a sybaritic round of hot showers, assorted beverages, good food, and a comfortable bed. Two days into this idyll, while Karen was out shopping, I was relaxing in our hotel room at the New Zealand, when I received a phone call: "Hello, Mr. Raybeck. I'm afraid I've got bad news for you. Do you have a brother in Vietnam? [Long pause, during which horrific thoughts filled my mind.] Well, this is he." On occasion, my brother possesses a truly vile sense of humor.

It seems the army, like an indecisive Procrustes, could not decide the appropriate length of Bruce's in-country time. It had, yet again, changed his orders and scheduled him for a later departure. With the additional time, Bruce planned a surprise visit to us in Wakaf Bharu. He flew into Kota Bharu and took a taxi to Wakaf Bharu where he was greeted by knee-deep waters, but not by us. The next day, acting from equal parts frustration and resourcefulness, he returned and talked with Yusof, Hussein's son, who spoke some English. Bruce made it clear that he wished to enter the house and search for clues to our whereabouts. Hussein, like a good neighbor, let him into our house—and kept him company throughout his search. In our bedroom Bruce found Karen's journal, which detailed the places we had stayed in our earlier visit to Kuala Lumpur.

Suitably equipped with a list of hostels, Bruce flew to Kuala Lumpur and began making phone calls. He reached us on his third attempt. The next few days were spent talking interminably and introducing Bruce to some of our favorite ingredients of Kuala Lumpur's social stew. Karen and I also labored, largely in vain, to keep him from paying for everything we did. We spent an entire day engaged in vital activities such as playing pool; revisiting the bumper cars; and shopping for ourselves, for relatives, and for Bruce's attractive, clever, and patient—very patient—wife, Judy. Numerous good meals and a number of beers later, Bruce left for Penang and we returned to Wakaf Bharu.

At home we were immediately visited by Hussein and by a number of villagers who asked after Bruce and inquired how successful he had been in reaching us. We got a detailed description of his behavior while in the village and, especially, while in our house. The typical everyday alertness of Kelantanese villagers exceeds that of most Neighborhood Watch programs. Part of the security for all villagers is the knowledge that others will take an interest in their affairs.

We made two additional discoveries of a less pleasant nature. In Karen's absence, the ants, abetted by the abundance of rain and the dearth of insect spray, had reestablished dominion over our household, providing Karen with hours of meaningful activity. In a far more grievous event, a Chinese acquaintance, Cho Bee, a man well liked by virtually all villagers, had had a traffic accident and had died. The villagers' responses to his death were to prove important elements in my efforts to understand interethnic relations in village Kelantan. Once again I had to reconstruct what had occurred from a variety of sources, largely after the fact. The next chapter will describe some of the utility of this effort.

Concluding Comment

I have tried to demonstrate that the process of fieldwork is a gradual one during which the anthropologist is continually revising impressions and beliefs about the people with whom he or she resides. Part of that process involves an increasing refinement of understanding, but part also requires expanded exposure to the differing elements that comprise the local social system. The opportunity to participate in the variety of activities that constitutes village social life quite simply requires at least a year, since many of these activities are seasonal in nature. More important to the anthropologist, the seasons generally constitute a whole that needs to be experienced rather than heard about. I believe I would have missed important insights into Kelantanese culture if I had been in the area for a briefer period.

I have made five simple arguments in this chapter: most fieldwork should last at least a year; a respect for reciprocity is essential for maintaining viable social relationships; the daily round of life in the field is often as wearing as it is rewarding; while in the field, there is great utility in arranging for a surrogate to manage one's affairs; and anthropologists, for their own mental well-being, must occasionally take a respite from their research, even at the risk of missing important events. I cheerfully admit that these observations are neither profound nor novel. However, they are significant, and an awareness of them can help an anthropologist deal with some of the myriad complexities that are involved in an extended period of study in another culture.

9

Sundries

Anthropologists must confront a number of problems in fieldwork, and one of these involves access to different social components of the village. I indicated in chapter 2 that factionalism can provide obstacles, especially if the anthropologist becomes identified with one particular clique. However, there are also other differences that can divide communities and influence fieldwork. Ethnic differences are among the more basic means by which people segregate themselves, but perhaps the most fundamental is gender.

The problem facing any anthropologist is that one's sex is both entrée and obstacle. It provides an advantage when dealing with one's own sex and sharing elements of behavior that often transcend cultural borders. However, it can reduce, or, depending on the society, even eliminate access to members of the other sex. Anthropologists recognize that, unlike sex, which is a physiological given, gender is culturally constructed and quite variable (Bonvillain 1995; Brettell and Sargent 1993; Rosaldo and Lamphere 1974). One constant in the construction of gender is that men and women are defined in opposition to one another (Brown 1991; Ortner 1974; Ortner and Whitehead 1981). To be a woman is to not be a man, and vice versa. Not surprisingly, many cultures establish a significant degree of social separation between the sexes, sometimes from concern about their interaction, and sometimes from a well-ingrained belief in propriety.

In Kelantan the situation was quite complex, as there were rules about gender that could be flouted and conventions that had to be respected. In general, however, I found my access to the world of women to be much less than that of men. This was less because I was distrusted, than that I was recognized as a male and expected to behave as such. Therefore Karen—sometimes more willingly, sometimes less—often gave me glimpses of an extremely important part of village life: The domain of women in Kelantanese villages is much greater than either Islamic doctrine or state law would suggest.

Islam contains a variety of prescriptions and proscriptions affecting the public and private comportment of women. Generally these rules concern morality and proper behavior. One precept, however, affects both men and women equally, *khalwat*. This is a prohibition against an unrelated man and woman being alone together and is intended to assure that nothing of a sexual nature transpires between them. In 1968–69, while the interpretation of Islam and Islamic orthodoxy was a good bit looser than it is today, khalwat was still a common concern and effectively meant that I could not converse with women in private. Obviously this reduced my access to the attitudes and feelings of women about many of the more sensitive issues in village life. Fortunately I became accepted by several families so that it was possible for me to sit with a husband and wife and get the wife's perceptions on a variety of issues with which I was concerned. The presence of the husband must have had an influence on how the women chose to response, as, no doubt, did my own maleness. However, Kelantanese women are generally quite strong minded and are not generally shy about stating their own opinions, even when they disagree with their spouses.

The Woman Issue:
Strictures and Strategies

I consistently found Kelantanese women to be the most skilled of bargainers and quite aware of the complexities of finance. I also found that, despite some strictures emanating from Islam, they carried themselves with dignity and a calm assurance of their own importance. The value of women in traditional Kelantanese society and culture appears to antedate Islam by many years and may be partly a reflection of a wider cultural pattern throughout much of Southeast Asia. Indeed in Southeast

Asia, women generally have a status that compares favorably with many other parts of the world (Atkinson and Errington, 1990; Strage 1981; Winzeler 1974). The importance of Kelantanese women begins at birth and appears in many aspects of village life.

Female babies are welcomed by parents just as readily as males, and both are regarded as gifts from God (*hadiah Tuhan*). During her youth, a woman experiences many more strictures than a man, many of these reflecting Islamic ideals of modesty and chaste behavior. As she approaches puberty, a young woman may not travel alone, nor may she spend time in the company of an unrelated postpuberty male. Instead she spends time at or near home, helping with household chores and younger siblings. Her economic and social participation in village life is slight, but she is able to observe her mother and other older women who are quite active in these areas. Her parents often arrange her marriage, which she enters with her brideprice and whatever property she has inherited. Throughout her marriage she retains her rights to the property she brought with her, and should she become divorced, she is entitled to half of everything she and her husband have acquired during their marriage. As she bears children and grows older, her participation in the economic and social life of the village and her prerogatives increase.

A middle-aged, married woman is usually a more active participant in the economic and social life of the village than is her husband (Raybeck 1992b). She manages the household finances and sets the family budget. Although the husband is the principal worker in the rice fields, the wife helps at harvest time and with threshing. She also raises one or more cash crops for sale at the local market, and it is generally she, rather than her husband, who participates in the market. In addition women sell handicrafts that they and their husbands have made and such varied items as shellfish, candy, etc.

A wife's economic pursuits will take her to the market several times a week, where she encounters other women sellers and "middlemen," often "middlewomen," who help tie her into an extensive information network concerning prices, politics, local scandals, the availability of marriageable girls and boys, etc. Access to extradomestic information sources can strongly influence a woman's status. With such information, a woman can make responsible social decisions and can increase her participation in village affairs; without it, she is dependent upon others.

A married woman of middle age is freer to move about than is a younger woman, and many take up part- or full-time trading. A number of the older Wakaf Bharu women traded extensively across the border, and more than a few were engaged in the smuggling of the long-grain Thai rice that is popular in Kelantan. Such middle-aged women are freer to pursue other business concerns as well. A woman owned and ran the most popular coffee shop in the village, even though the local interpretation of Islamic morality holds that it is generally improper for women to frequent coffee shops.

One element that enables a woman to play such an active economic role is kindred support. Either the wife's or the husband's relatives, sometimes both, are usually nearby, and one or more relatives will watch the woman's children. Although kindred are obligated to provide such assistance, it is seldom necessary to voice the request, especially where grandparents are concerned.

Two women returning from the local Wakaf Bharu market in a tri-shaw. They sold a few goods, bought a few goods, and caught up on village gossip.

Although a village woman normally has to wait until middle age to acquire the status and freedom described above, there is a means of hastening at least the enjoyment of freedom—divorce. Divorce is extremely common in Kelantan, averaging well over 50 percent of marriages. A divorcée is relatively free of parental restrictions and can serve as head of her own household. She can obtain the assistance of kindred members, control her own property, contract debts, and generally take a more active role in village social life. Should she remarry, and most do, she, rather than her parents, will choose the husband and arrange the terms.

The traditional social prominence of women is reflected in a custom realized by many village men. As described earlier, when a man approaches middle age, he often adopts part of his wife's name. Thus our landlord, Mat Kadir, became Mat Mizin, taking his wife's first name. When I asked him why he had done so, he responded that it was to honor both his wife and tradition.

While the preceding description concerns women in rural villages, the situation in urban areas is similar. In Kota Bharu, the great central market is dominated by women who have come to buy and sell their goods. Women often own and/or manage the food stalls, jewelry stores, fabric shops, and assorted other business ventures that line the main and side streets of the capital.

Currently the major batik factory in Kelantan is owned and run by a woman who obtained a government loan, quit a position she held as a business clerk, and gradually built a small enterprise into a business that is known throughout the peninsula. This woman observed that Kelantanese women are "used to seeking their own living" (*cari makan sendiri*), and that this made them more independent and stronger.

Kelantanese men, comparing local women to those of other states, make observations such as, "Women here are more independent and self-reliant. They are used to earning a living." One banker even confided to me that he believed women were more industrious and reliable than men. He said that many bankers preferred to loan money to women because they were more likely to succeed than men and would repay their loans more promptly.

Like many women throughout Southeast Asia, Kelantanese women have active economic roles, participate in important family decisions, and are frequently household heads. At the same time they, as virtually all Kelantanese, are strongly Islamic, a religion that tends to favor male rights over those of women. Clearly there are potential and actual conflicts between the rules of Islam and the roles of Kelantanese women.

The relationship between Islam and the status of women is a complex one. Islam arose in the strongly patrilineal, patricentric Middle East, and its rules concerning women reflect a consequent male bias. When these rules are introduced into a country, such as Malaysia, where the indigenous status of women is comparatively high, culture conflicts can result. Over the years, the Kelantanese have become skilled at conforming to the tenets of Islam, while managing to preserve the integrity of their traditional social order. The manner in which they accomplish this yields significant insights into the ability of people to manipulate their own cultural circumstances.

There are three specific areas relevant to Kelantanese women's rights where Islam imposes its laws. These include the realms of inheritance, modesty, and divorce.

Islam is particularly concerned with the public behavior of women and specifies that a woman should remain properly covered when moving abroad, show deference to her husband, and maintain a modest demeanor. Further the Islamic khalwat rule forbids that a man and woman should spend time alone together unless they are married or closely related.

Rules regarding inheritance reflect a bias toward males. For instance a brother should receive twice the amount of property that his sister receives. It is expected that such rules will be carried out at the village level as a matter of course, but the religious court is always willing to enforce them when necessary.

The Islamic rules regarding divorce are clear and give males more prerogatives than females. A husband may divorce his wife simply by pronouncing a verbal formula and then paying a small fee to register the divorce. He need not supply a reason for the divorce. Until recently, under Islamic rules a wife could divorce her husband only if she could prove that he had consistently mistreated her, or that he had not supported her for six months or more. In either case the woman had to take her case before an Islamic court, and if her husband contested the issue, she might not obtain a divorce.

The Kelantanese view themselves and are viewed by others as devout Muslims. Islam is an important component of Kelantanese identity. At the same time, many of the behaviors and rules promoted by Islam are at odds with local custom. In particular the strictures placed upon women are often incongruent with the roles of married women. Thus we have a set of contending village influences that, by creating tensions and conflicts for both males and females, can jeopardize the harmony so important to Kelantanese villagers. The Kelantanese reduce the stress in these cultural inconsistencies by adopting various village-level strategies that maintain the letter of Islamic law but preserve the spirit of traditional village social organization and the approximate equality of women (Raybeck 1980–81).

Villagers, following what I believe to be pre-Islamic conventions, believe that women are as entitled to property as are men. Thus there are clear conflicts between Islam and traditional culture concerning the inheritance rights of women. However, there is a direct and effective strategy for dealing with the problem. Quite simply, as parents approach old age, they often give a premortem gift to their daughters. Following the parents' death, their property will be divided in strict accordance with Islamic law, with males receiving twice the share that females receive. However, when the inheritance is coupled with the premortem bequest, daughters receive what their parents perceive to be a fair portion. This may be less than, equal to, or greater than their brothers' shares, as was the case in the inheritances of Ismail and Khadija. Villagers, aware of how loyal Khadija had been, and how lax Ismail, regarded the settlement as quite fair, despite Ismail's receiving only a small plot of land while his sister got the bulk of their father's estate. Thus the rules of Islam were upheld and so was the villagers' sense of distributive justice (see Homans 1961).

Kelantanese, like other Malays, make a sharp distinction between public behavior and domestic behavior. In accord with Islamic convention, a Kelantanese woman dresses and behaves modestly in public, save that she wears a head covering rather than a veil. A woman is always fully clothed in public and displays deference to her husband through a respectful demeanor, including walking five paces behind him. Women also eat separately from men, and they visit public places, such as coffee shops, only infrequently if at all. The morality of women, especially young women, is judged according to such standards of public behavior.

At home, rules of modesty, particularly for older women, are relaxed. Women often go about informally dressed and even partially nude. Women at home may assert their opinions, disagree strongly with their husbands, and be the major decision makers in matters ranging from family finances to the choice of marriage partners for their children. Acknowledging that a woman should support her husband, a woman still views her marriage as an active partnership and will not generally tolerate being ordered about. Three women with whom I discussed this matter made the following observation: "A wife should be respectful toward her husband and speak to him in a polite fashion, but her words and needs should also be heeded. If this fails to be the case, voices will rise."

While Karen was neither Malay nor Islamic, there was a general expectation that she would comport herself appropriately in public. This meant wearing a head covering on religious holidays and when engaged in the series of visits that mark the end of such holidays. She agreeably acceded to this expectation but was less willing to walk several paces behind me—something I quite wisely did not press.

Karen also found herself invited to participate with women when feasts were being prepared and to eat with them in the kitchen during these feasts. As a result she was privy to the kinds of bantering and observations that Kelantanese women frequently make among themselves and which they shield from men, the common targets of some of their more trenchant observations and humor. I soon found that, despite her limited familiarity with the language, Karen was obtaining insights that I was denied. She also sometimes became aware of significant items of gossip well before I did. Happily she shared both insights and gossip with me, and my field notes are much the richer for them.

Karen often had to deal with questions without my assistance, and one of the most prominent was our childless status. We didn't want to admit that we were deferring a family, as that is not something Kelantanese would easily understand. Children are perceived as a blessing, and villagers perceive few plights sadder than a barren (*mandul*) couple. Women became sufficiently concerned about this issue that they would often ask us why we had no children. With our newly acquired skills, we both obfuscated and temporized. Our repertoire of unsatisfactory replies consisted largely of "it hadn't happened yet"; "we weren't sure of the cause"; and similar responses.

Karen also found herself subject to expectations concerning reciprocity. Our neighbor Cik Nab had earlier helped Karen through the intricacies of the market and had also demonstrated how to cook several Malay dishes. Following Karen's great success with banana bread, Nab began to hint that she would appreciate some tips on baking. Karen taught Nab to bake Western-style cake quite successfully. The result of this could have been foreseen. One afternoon I came home late to find a scene of major confusion and considerable activity. Karen was working in the kitchen with five women to create and bake seven loaves of banana bread. The cakes were completed, the women departed, and Karen collapsed in one of the rattan chairs. Her observations on the demands of fieldwork, and my tardy arrival, fit nicely with the general Kelantanese image of strong-minded women who "assert their opinions and disagree strongly with their husbands."

Karen also discovered the interest of women in gossip concerning family difficulties in the village, especially divorce. While women and men were both generally concerned with the interpersonal aspects of particular divorces, women often had better access to domestic information. Both sexes were also aware of the schism between social reality at the village level and Islamic rules surrounding divorce, which gave men a distinct advantage in initiating divorces.

The problem of unequal access to divorce is resolved through a well-known village stratagem. To some extent the high divorce rate of Kelantan reflects the tensions between the traditional village interpretation of women's status and the rules of Islam. The many young men who attend religious schools often absorb a variant of the ideal Islamic code for female behavior, while young women assimilate the example of their independent mothers. The variance between the ideal Islamic code for a wife's behavior and the actual village model of a wife's behavior can create conflicts that promote divorce.

Although men have greater jural access to divorce than do women, the latter can use social levers to accomplish this end. Because the Kelantanese are extremely sensitive to social affronts and strive to avoid embarrassing or malu situations, it is possible for a wife to construct a public performance that is so embarrassing to the husband that divorce is his only practical recourse.

During this period of fieldwork, there were twenty-nine divorces in the general area, all recorded as having been initiated by the husband. However, information that Karen garnered from women, and that I was supplied by the local Islamic priest and by other villagers, made it clear that more than one-third of the divorces were due to pressure from the wife.

The best example I have of the manner in which husbands can literally be forced to grant a wife a divorce came from a neighboring village. An extremely attractive and spirited young woman, Hasnah, had married in accordance with her parents' wishes. They had arranged a marriage with Haji Yacob, a wealthy man nearly sixty years old. The motives for both parties were quite clear to the villagers and, indeed, also well known in Wakaf Bharu. Hasnah's family was poor, and the brideprice offered by Yacob was M$700, a great deal more than the usual M$100–300 received by the bride's family. As for Yacob, he was quite clearly smitten, and there were a number of quiet jokes likening him to a rooster, the implication being that his reason was being ruled by his lust.

The marriage took place, and the two settled into Yacob's new house near the center of the village. A few months later it became known that Hasnah was unhappy with the union. Despite Yacob's continuing infatuation with his young bride, many people began to anticipate a divorce. Among Malays unhappiness is the major cause of divorce (Djamour 1959). Their expectations were given greater strength by a rumor that Hasnah had complained to her family, and that she had asked Yacob for a divorce on several occasions. Yacob, according to gossip, stolidly refused to grant Hasnah a divorce, thus setting the stage for a singular performance.

One afternoon, as women returned from the market and men from the fields, Hasnah stepped out on her front porch and turned to face the interior. In a loud voice she then upbraided her husband for his laziness and assorted other shortcomings. All of this took place in full view and hearing of passersby. Hasnah had clearly, indeed loudly, broken the public-domestic boundary in a fashion that was obviously intended to embarrass her spouse.

This event quickly became the centerpiece of gossip for several surrounding villages. It also represented an act that, while not common, had been known to occur before. When Hasnah emerged from her house the next afternoon, the path in front of the house contained an uncommonly large number of pedestrians. These were treated to a discourse quite similar to the one of the preceding day. Obviously Yacob had refused to divorce his wife. On the evening of the third day of Hasnah's "performances," Yacob was visited by several influential relatives who pointed out that his behavior was an embarrassment to them as well as to himself. On the morning of the fourth day, a disconsolate Yacob walked to his local Imam, where he paid a dollar to register a divorce that records would reflect as having been initiated by him.

It is fieldwork of the sort described here that leads anthropologists to be wary of official statistics. Had I trusted official accounts, I would be reporting that nearly all divorces were initiated by males. I am strongly committed to the importance of quantitative data, and I have recorded figures on divorce, marriage, and adoption for the Wakaf Bharu area. However, context is necessary to determine how such data should be interpreted and evaluated, and anthropologists believe that an appreciation of context is best developed through fieldwork.

The contrast between the Islamic strictures on females and the dignity, vitality, and social prominence of Kelantanese women reminds the observer that societies are complex and imperfectly integrated entities. Kelantanese are apparently quite capable of the kind of cognitive and social compartmentalization that enables them to adjust to the dissonant demands of their traditional customs, and of their adopted religious code. This ability has consequences for our understanding of cultural dynamics and for the often spurious consistency that characterizes our analytic models of ethnographic realities. We need to remember that the members of a culture are conscious participants in its code and are capable of devising a variety of conceptual and behavioral strategies to further their ends. The comparatively good status of Kelantanese women is the product both of their social contributions and of the cultural manipulations of both men and women. Without fieldwork, these manipulations would have been effectively invisible, as official records do not, and are not meant to, reveal them.

The Chinese Issue:
Ours Versus Theirs

Chinese did not enter the Malay Peninsula in significant numbers until the mid-nineteenth century. Prior to this period they were often transients who hoped to amass sufficient wealth to return home, buy land, and marry. In some instances they were traders who married Malay women and assimilated, at least in part, to Malay culture. Britain's development of the area trade and the concurrent expansion of tin mining greatly stimulated Chinese immigration, as did events such as the Taiping Rebellion in China. While most immigrants came to work in the mines, many quickly filled proliferating entrepreneurial positions and began to import wives from China. This increasing economic and familial stability encouraged the maintenance of Chinese culture, as did the establishment of Chinese schools.

Chinese prominence in the economic sphere continued while Malays, with the assistance of the British, played an increasingly active role in government, especially the civil service and police. The dichotomous involvement of each community has continued with each group expressing fear and distrust of the other (Roff 1967; Wang 1970). In 120 years, the Chinese population of the peninsula rose from approximately 1 percent to nearly 40 percent. In the process the communal tensions between Chinese and Malays increased and became quite well known to Southeast Asian scholars (Chu 1976; Nagata 1975; Strauch 1981; Tan Chee Beng 1984; Wilson 1967). It was apparent that the friction manifested in Malay-Chinese relations at the national level was also characteristic of villages, at least on the west coast of the peninsula, where appropriate field studies had been carried out (Swift 1965; Wilson 1967).

One of my research interests was interethnic relations, and I had chosen Wakaf Bharu partly because there was a significant Chinese minority present. My reading had informed me of the conflicts that prevailed between the two communities throughout Malaysia, and I was curious about the dynamics of interethnic relations in village Kelantan. Fieldwork, as I was to discover, once again resulted in a set of unanticipated perceptions. As a strongly Islamic state noted for its conservatism and for its support of the Malay rights party, PAS, Kelantan was widely held to be a bastion of anti-Chinese sentiment. This image was furthered by the knowledge that Kelantan is also more than 90 percent Malay. Initially I had expected village-level relations among Chinese and Kelantanese to demonstrate the same, or perhaps even greater, frictions as existed in villages on the west coast. This is not quite what I found.

Due in large part to their small numbers, most rural Chinese have adopted many aspects of Malay culture, especially in their public behavior. Erving Goffman, the sociologist who believes people are conscious of their performances, has made a useful distinction between what he terms "front stage," an area where a performance is given, and "backstage," a region where a performance may be abandoned or even falsified (Goffman 1959). Using this distinction for the behaviors of rural Kelantan Chinese, it is apparent that most of the adopted aspects of Kelantan Malay culture are front stage, while nearly all of the traditional Chinese culture is backstage.

Front stage or public behavior for rural Kelantan Chinese includes wearing traditional Malay clothing, speaking Kelantanese dialect, avoiding pork, and behaving in a manner congruent with budi bahasa, the language of courtesy. In the privacy of their homes, however, village Chinese will speak their own language (usually Hokkien); practice their own customs, such as ancestor worship; and eat traditional foods, including pork. Kelantanese have responded to these efforts by developing a novel set of cultural categories. Unlike Westerners, even Western social scientists, Kelantanese do not lump Chinese together in one racially based ethnic category. Instead Kelantanese distinguish three Chinese ethnic groups on the basis of cultural criteria. These criteria, however, more accurately reflect the Chinese behavior toward Kelantanese than cultural distinctions among Chinese themselves.

Kelantanese use the general term "Chinese" (*orang Cina*) to refer to a broad national category that includes all Chinese who dwell in other states as well as those Chinese in Kelantan who live in urban areas, maintain Chinese culture publicly, and are generally ignorant of, or insensitive to, budi bahasa and Kelantanese custom or adat. These Chinese are perceived not only as being different from Malays but also as being opposed to Malay interests, and as a possible threat to Malay and Kelantanese security. As I had anticipated, I found Kelantanese to be strongly prejudiced against this category of Chinese and suspicious of their activities, both political and economic. What I had not anticipated was the development of two additional categories.

Kelantanese refer to Chinese who exhibit Kelantanese cultural behavior "front stage," and who generally reside in rural areas, by the narrower term "Kelantan Chinese" (*orang Cina*

Kelantan). Generally Kelantanese do not view this category as threatening, but they are often suspicious of its members at the interpersonal level, as they are of most "outsiders."

Finally, Kelantanese term Chinese who manifest a "front stage" constellation of Kelantan cultural characteristics and who are coresident within the village as "Chinese of here" (*orang Cina sini*) or even "our Chinese" (*orang Cina kita*). This category of Chinese has often resided in a given kampong for as long as three generations. I discovered that Kelantanese villagers in Wakaf Bharu and elsewhere were much more positively disposed toward these Chinese than I had anticipated, given the literature I had read.

Initially both Karen and I had difficulty determining who was and was not Chinese in the village. Chinese walked, talked, and dressed like everyone else, and racial appearances were often muted. Once we became more familiar with the names of villagers this problem was reduced, as village Chinese retain their ethnic appellations. The accommodation village Chinese made to Kelantanese culture made it possible for Kelantanese villagers to relate to Chinese as individuals, rather than as simply representatives of a category. With improved communication came better interethnic relations. I discovered that village-level relations among Chinese were generally significantly better than those that had been reported for villages on the west coast of the peninsula (Raybeck 1980).

I became aware that for Kelantanese Chinese, the most significant distinction was the one between insiders and outsiders. Those who were insiders were often well accepted by village members and treated in a fashion that might surprise west coast Chinese and Malays. Thus, as described earlier, a Chinese villager from Wakaf Bharu who trained fighting bulls was supported by fellow villagers against Kelantanese from other villages. Indeed several Kelantanese spoke of him with pride, lauding his skill in training bulls and commenting on how his successes had enhanced the village's reputation.

In another instance a neighbor invited me to an Islamic feast, termed a *Kenduri Arwah*, a feast for all souls. Islamic prayers are chanted on such occasions and guests are well fed. I arrived to find approximately thirty adult males present. Chanting preceded the meal and lasted nearly an hour. (During this period most Kelantanese belonged to the Sufi sect of Islam, and rhythmic

Koranic chanting was believed to be a means of drawing closer to Allah.) As the chanting went on I noticed that the women standing in the doorway of the kitchen were watching me and whispering to one another. I became aware that, once again, my observations had also included some unanticipated participation. Rhythmic Koranic chanting can be very hypnotic and I found that, instead of sitting quietly in one of the circles, I was, like the others, swaying back in forth in time to the rhythm of the chants. The women were intrigued at that point because the chant was the basic "There is no God but Allah, and Mohammed is his prophet." According to Islamic doctrine, one can become a Muslim by making this statement with conviction. They were watching me to see whether I participated verbally, which, after becoming aware of the exigency, I declined to do.

After the chanting was concluded and we had begun to eat, a young Chinese man arrived on his motorcycle and was chided by his host for being late. The young man wore Western clothes but spoke excellent Kelantanese dialect and manifested a good knowledge of budi bahasa. I learned that he had earlier lived in the village and had rented a room from the host, but now resided in Kota Bharu. During his stay with the family he became quite close to both of them and used to buy the wife medicines and help the husband with his small rubber holding. He was seated in a side room where he was joined by the host, a few other guests, and me.

His presence was noteworthy because the occasion was a Muslim affair, and he was neither currently a villager nor had he been born there. Indeed, when I talked with some of the guests a few days later, several of them said that they found his presence a bit improper but that they had kept quiet out of respect for the host and hostess, whom they knew felt quite close to the young man. Indeed at one point the hostess had emerged from the kitchen and greeted the young man, referring to him as her adopted son.

Perhaps the best example I can provide of the degree to which Kelantanese villagers can accept and respect those Chinese who live among them comes from the funeral of Cho Bee, a store owner who had been born and raised in Wakaf Bharu. Cho Bee was a highly regarded member of the village, whom people often termed *baik hati*, acting from a genuine regard for others rather than from a concern with proper form. As a merchant he was generous in giving credit during the periods before the planting season, and he was also quick to offer assistance to several indigent members of the village who lacked kindred.

In late December of 1968, Cho Bee had a serious motorcycle accident after which he never regained consciousness. He died the next day, and my notes record the reactions of virtually all Kelantanese villagers:

> The Kelantanese reaction to the accident was that the whole thing was very *susah* [difficult] and a great shame because Cho Bee had been an "orang baik hati" or an "orang baik." I heard these terms used by literally everyone who spoke of him. One went so far as to say that it was always the good people who had the bad accidents. Many Malays were also disturbed by the fact that he left behind his first child, who was only three months old. A prayer service was held on the 25th for him, and Mat Kadir [my landlord and a well-regarded member of the village] came out, making a special trip from KB, to attend the services.

The funeral was held at 10 A.M. at the local Presbyterian church, of which he had been a member. Numerous Chinese relatives and friends entered the church and went through the funeral ceremonies. Following the service, something rather singular occurred. Kelantanese, as Muslims, are reluctant to enter another religion's place of worship. The Chinese knew this, and they were aware of how well regarded Cho Bee was by the people of Wakaf Bharu. The open casket was carried outside and placed on a small stand in front of the church, where Kelantanese could view the deceased. Nearly seventy Kelantanese villagers filed by to pay their respects, and several people wept openly. To anyone familiar with Kelantanese inhibitions on the open expression of emotion, a display like this is extremely impressive.

As far as I could determine, the people of Wakaf Bharu genuinely grieved for Cho Bee and took his loss personally. I have no doubt that this reaction reflected a real affection for the deceased. This event indicates the manner in which both Chinese and Kelantanese at the village level can relate to one another. The accommodations of the Chinese population have made communication between the two ethnic groups easy and common. As a consequence Kelantanese and Chinese view each other as individuals rather than simply as representatives of cultural categories, subject to stereotyping and marginalization.

This does not mean that relations across ethnic groups are always amicable, but rather that judgments of individuals are more likely to be based on personality and behavior than simply upon membership in a given ethnic category. Cho Bee's mother, a minor merchant known for her irascible nature and her stinginess, was nearly as widely disliked as Cho Bee was liked. Several Kelantanese spoke of her as being somewhat *jahat* (evil), a very serious condemnation. Interestingly, however, the accepted explanation for her behavior was not that she was "acting Chinese," but that she had been an adopted child and was poorly treated when young.

Had I conducted this research in some other fashion, perhaps by utilizing a questionnaire to survey attitudes toward Chinese, it is highly unlikely I would have uncovered the much more complex and textured nature of interethnic relations that characterizes Kelantanese village life. Fieldwork encourages anthropologists to stumble over reality rather than to skate across the smooth surfaces of generalizations and stereotypes. While the journey is often bumpier as a result, we believe we see more along the way.

10

Sunstroke

The most profitable approach to field research is characterized by a quality of continuing openness on the part of anthropologists. We are trained to try to reduce the weight of our own
cultural baggage, and depending upon the individual and the
situation, we succeed to a lesser or greater degree in this endeavor. We try to remain open to differing cultural interpretations
of events and to constellations of symbols that may be novel.
However, it is also important that we remain open to ourselves.
We need to be honest about our own foibles, our misperceptions,
and our needs.

In the preceding chapters, I have tried to describe, and even
to argue for, several qualities of fieldwork. I have suggested that
it is a gradual process that calls for patience, honesty, flexibility,
a good sense of humor, and a tolerance for uncertainty. While
recommending forethought and planning, I have also argued that
anthropologists should eschew detailed projections and rigid
schedules. The reason for this last contention is quite simply that
luck, both good and bad, can play an unexpected role in the
success of fieldwork. Sometimes events lead to unanticipated
windfalls of which the anthropologist can take advantage. Occasionally, however, occurrences are beyond both control and
sufferance. What follows is a description of both good and bad
luck, of manageable circumstances and unmanageable ones, of
situations where openness was of great utility and where it was
of little avail.

On Being a Mensch, Most Painfully Fêted

By January of 1969, after a year in the field, I was beginning to feel the press of time. I still had the semantic differential research to complete, and there were only six months remaining. Further Karen had been uncovering additional insights into women's lives, and I was developing a more finely grained appreciation of interethnic relations. It is true that the more you become familiar with a culture, the more you perceive how much more there is to learn. Certainly my rapidly expanding list of research concerns suggested some sort of Sisyphean success.

For some months prior, Yusof Ismail, my friend from the jaga, had been encouraging me to visit the home of his parents just across the Thai border. In Wakaf Bharu he lived with his grandparents, who looked after him and who arranged his marriage. Periodically, however, Yusof traveled to Thailand, where he visited with his parents and regaled them with a variety of tales concerning my clumsiness, Karen's cooking, and our public behavior. They had expressed an interest in meeting us and had extended an open invitation for a visit.

Because of my workload, I had continued to resist Yusof's blandishments, making a variety of excuses. Finally, however, it became apparent that this invitation was not simply an element of Kelantanese politeness, or even simply of curiosity on Yusof's part. Instead it had become important to him, partly because he genuinely wanted me to meet his family and partly because he had invested some face in asserting that he could bring about such a visit. One afternoon I accepted Yusof's invitation, not because I had research goals in mind but because he was a friend who had been of assistance to me and was someone to whom I owed a friend's obligation.

Three days later, on a bright and uncomfortably warm midmorning, Yusof came by to collect me. We had decided that I would make the trip "Malay style," which means two sarongs, one shirt, and one toothbrush . . . and no notebook. I greeted him in my fashion finery—flip flops, a bright batik shirt, and an older sarong. We walked down to the station and boarded the train for Sungai Golok. On the way, Yusof explained that his parents lived some three miles from Sungai Golok up the river in Kampong Pura-Pura,[31] a small village. He mentioned that there was no public transportation, nor were there roads, beyond the ubiquitous footpaths. However, he noted cheerfully, it was not a long walk. At this point I weighed 156 pounds and was suffering a bad cold. I received his news with enthusiasm that was quite well bridled, thank you very much.

We arrived in Sungai Golok in late morning and immediately set out for Kampong Pura-Pura. The first mile ran through thick, secondary jungle that provided plenty of shade, uncomfortable humidity, and insects of assorted sizes and dispositions. Just as I was cursing conditions, the terrain changed—it became markedly worse. The jungle ended and the last two miles followed a path that wound through a series of open fields and coconut orchards. Coconut trees are tall and skinny and provide negligible shade against the midday sun. I sweated, I poured, I lost quarts of water. Literally I was losing it so rapidly that the perspiration ran down my legs, wetting the tops of my flip flops, and making walking a much more difficult and slippery task than it should have been. We arrived at the village with markedly different presentations. Yusof appeared cheerful and energetic, with a light gloss of perspiration on his brow and upper lip. I, in contrast, was a sodden mass of rumpled clothing that continued to sweat profusely, raising concerns about heat prostration, or even insolation.

We went immediately to his house, where we were warmly greeted by his father and mother. Yusof suggested that we bathe and I immediately agreed, partly because I had no wish to offend and partly because I hoped the cool water would help to bring down my temperature. We each took bathing kains, old sarongs that have been torn or cut off so that they are knee length, and Yusof pointed out the well. I had been expecting a well in the front or back of the house as is customary in most places. This village, however, was impoverished and had only one rather large, central well serving the entire village. I appeared in all my pale, skeletal splendor in the middle of the village, wrapped in a strip of cloth, determined to try to bathe, yet to retain what remained of my dignity (read sarong). Within minutes there were more than twenty villagers standing about in a loose circle, gazing at this natural wonder and making unkind remarks about its lack of grace. There were some well-aimed jokes about the likelihood of my remaining clad, but I am pleased to report that, throughout this very awkward procedure, my modesty was maintained, however gracelessly.

The bath did help to stem the persistent perspiration, and Yusof and I returned to his family's house for lunch. Two things quickly became apparent. Yusof's family was quite poor, and they had gone to considerable expense on my account. The house was quite small and rather run-down. Unlike better houses, floors were of split bamboo rather than planking and there were no dividers to split the interior into separate rooms. The size of the house and its low ceiling made it oppressively hot, while the split bamboo provided a secure but very uncomfortable surface for sitting. The midday repast was served, as usual, on mats on the floor, but unlike the typical lunch, which consists of some cold leftover curry and rice, this one featured large bowls of freshly cooked rice and three curries. The Kelantanese staple curry is made from dried fish that has been soaked in coconut milk and cooked over a slow fire. It is strongly flavored, a good accompaniment to rice, and cheap. While there was a fish curry, it was made from fresh fish and carefully prepared. It was accompanied by a chicken curry and a beef curry. The latter in particular is quite expensive and generally served only on special occasions. The food was delicious and, despite my cold, I ate well.

Later that afternoon, Yusof and I accompanied his father to the railway line where he worked loading and unloading bags of rice. There we met two of Yusof's young friends, who, with some panache, took us around Sungai Golok and pointed out the various brothels and other quasi-legal and illegal aspects of town life. Yusof had informed them of my interest in values and deviance, and they surmised that my interest was somewhat more than academic. I was escorted into a brothel, introduced to several young Thai prostitutes, and told to take my pick! After demurring and explaining that I just wasn't interested, the persistent pair said they could remedy that with some very efficacious drugs, which would cost me only a few baht. It seems they were familiar with Western tourists in search of Sungai Golok entertainment and had locked me into a category from which no words could extract me. I finally gave it up, and Yusof and I returned to his parents' house.

I had realized that Yusof's family must have invested a fair portion of their weekly income in the meal they had prepared earlier. Sensitive to the honor that was done me, I had thanked my hosts profusely. This had an unintended consequence, when the family, impressed by my expressions of pleasure, decided to provide a really special repast for that evening. Yusof and I bathed one more time at the central well. The audience for my second performance rivaled the first, though they seemed somewhat less concerned that I might lose my kain.

We entered the house, changed into proper sarongs, and sat down for the evening meal, whereat the anthropologist was most painfully fêted. There was a delicious, highly spiced chicken curry. I had mentioned in passing that I liked "hot" food, and Yusof's mother may well have exhausted the house's supply of chili peppers in preparing the dish. There was a more delicately seasoned mutton curry, another expensive entree. Finally there was the crowning glory, the culmination of culinary cleverness—*sotong sardine*.

This will require some explication. Literally, "sotong sardine" means canned squid. At that time, eating tinned food was a hallmark of a progressive posture, somehow intertwined with modernization. This particular dish consisted of eight canned squid that had been stuffed with a mixture of glutinous rice and *budu*. The whole was then covered with budu and slowly baked. You're probably wondering of what budu consists. I shall tell you, but please remember this is professionally motivated.

Budu is made utilizing a hollow bamboo tube, one end of which is closed. This is filled two-thirds with fresh coconut milk and one-third with *ikan bilis*, a small member of the herring family related to anchovies, save that the flavor is more intensely fishy. Once the bamboo tube is filled, a wood stopper is inserted in the open end and the tube is placed in direct sunlight where it sits, and sits, and. . . . The fish quite naturally rots and joins its enhanced flavor with that of the fermenting coconut milk. The result is a most singular sauce beloved by most Malays and viewed as quite a delicacy.

Budu is rated by the number of days it remains in the sun. The budu I had been served was ten-day-old budu . . . good stuff! The closest approximation I can make to the smell and texture of budu derives from memories of crossing cow pastures back in New Hampshire. It was and remains the rankest comestible I have ever encountered. I believe it raises fundamental questions about the category "edible."

Yusof's mother smiled proudly as she placed the platter with its eight little denizens before us. Yusof's father smiled generously as he dished each person one sotong, except of course the honored guest, who received two. I smiled tightly and sat staring stonily at my plate, sniffing the food before me. I knew the expectations of my hosts, I was sensitive to my role as a visitor in their home, and I appreciated the traditional Kelantanese roles of courtesy and etiquette that obligated me to partake. But the odor!

It is with no small amount of pride that I report my consumption of one sotong and most of another. I finally surrendered, citing my bad cold and a full stomach. My hosts were inclined to credit my tale of illness, given my increasing pallor throughout the meal. (The sotong did *not* become more palatable with practice.) I rank this accomplishment as among the bravest things I have done. Cobra killing pales in comparison.

Following supper, Yusof and I visited with folks in the village and then returned to his parents' house to sleep. The one open room of the house served as a shared bedroom once the "beds" were put in place. A traditional Kelantanese bed is termed a tikar, a sleeping mat. It is made of woven pandanus fronds and is fully an eighth-inch thick. When placed on a split bamboo floor, it enables anyone resting upon it to discern each edge, point, and irregularity below. Further, shifts of weight call forth a timpani of associated clicks and clacks, as the bamboo strives to realign itself in the least comfortable fashion possible. As the honored guest I was supplied with the newest tikar in the house, just like a Sears SuperFirm Special but without the springs, padding, or comfort.

I took my place against the back wall of the house and stretched out my bony body in search of Lethe. Yusof spread his tikar beside mine, and the other members of the household took their accustomed places. I soon discovered that, while the household lacked mosquito nets, it had a plentitude of mosquitos. They strove mightily throughout the night to prevent me from sleeping and were ably assisted by the cries of Yusof's young sister, who had a fever, and the coughs of Yusof's mother, who had tuberculosis. Yusof and the members of his family seemed quite inured to this situation and, rather callously, promptly fell asleep. After some six hours of tossing, turning, swatting, and scratching I was contemplating the benefits of narcolepsy when, somewhere around five o'clock, I lost consciousness. (This seems, somehow, a more appropriate phrase than "fell asleep.") Half an hour later, I made a distressing discovery. The house adjoined the village *balaisah*.

Small villages that cannot afford a mosque often have a balaisah, a simple structure that serves as a chapel. The balaisah in Kampong Pura-Pura was simply a house that served as a place of worship and from which the faithful were called to prayer. The prayer call was accomplished in the traditional Malay fashion with a large, open-ended drum (*geduk*). It is struck several times for each of the five prayers, so that villagers will know when they should prostrate themselves toward Mecca. As you may recall, the first prayer of the day, Suboh, is said at dawn. In this balaisah the drum was suspended by two ropes from beams on the front porch. The open end of the drum was (I measured it!) three feet from the pandanus mat wall behind which I had so recently lost consciousness. I regained consciousness.

The morning of the second day, I accompanied Yusof's father to the warehouses where he often worked. He complained that he only made a couple of dollars for a full day of hard labor but noted he could occasionally improve his income with smuggling. As his words penetrated my semisomnolent state, I realized that this trip might provide unanticipated dividends. He introduced me to some of the more active smugglers in the area, cautioning me to be discreet, as they were influential men (*orang besar*) and were known for their courage and actions (orang berani). It seems that Yusof had informed him of my interest in smuggling in Wakaf Bharu and of the difficulties I had encountered trying to pursue the network beyond Sungai Golok. Thus these meetings were not happenstance but instead resulted from the desire of Yusof's father to assist me in my research. Over the next two months, with his assistance, I gradually gained a fuller picture of the smuggling network that moves everything from rice to prostitutes across the border.

That afternoon, after yet another special meal, Yusof and I walked back to Sungai Golok, boarded a train, and returned to Wakaf Bharu. I arrived home sweaty, exhausted, and with a worsened cold. The trip had been experientially quite costly, but it had also resulted in unforeseen benefits that were to add greatly to my research.

This example nicely illustrates one of the curious facets of fieldwork: nadirs are often zeniths in disguise. Initially it is damnably difficult to assess the consequences of any given situation. Anthropologists believe their insights into another culture improve with increasing familiarity and understanding, and they do. But that improvement is never all that we would like it to be, and we need always to remain open to surprise. However, while surprises can often result in research benefits, the converse also remains possible.

The Race Riots of 1969

During February through May of 1969, much of my time and attention was devoted to the approaching election. Malaysia achieved its independence in 1957 as a constitutional monarchy. National elections had been held at irregular intervals in 1955, 1959, and 1964 but not since. However, one was scheduled for May of 1969, and this important social and historical marker was absorbing everyone's attention.[32]

I have mentioned that the village was factionalized and contained loyal supporters of both UMNO, the United Malays National Organization—which, as the major partner in the Alliance Party, governed nationally and had control of all states save Kelantan—and PMIP, the Pan Malaysian Islamic Party (also termed PAS)—which controlled Kelantan's state government. As the election gradually approached, village social life underwent something of a transformation. The clientele of coffee houses changed somewhat as a given kedai became associated with one or the other party. In these kedai, gossip about politics and political maneuvers became the central concern, displacing all but the most sensational of village occurrences. Many villagers who wished to remain publicly uncommitted became even more circumspect in their behavior and their utterances. These would often frequent kedai that were putatively neutral in the political arena. Three identifiable subsets of villagers emerged from the interplay of political preferences and village social patterns. Those dedicated to UMNO, those supporting PMIP, and those who wished to remain uncommitted, probably the largest group of villagers.

The issues before the voters were clear and quite distinctive. UMNO promised increased development and modernization, while critiquing the insularity of PMIP's leadership. PMIP promised continued defense of traditional Kelantanese culture and opposition to foreign (Chinese) interests. PMIP criticized the ruling party for its neglect of Kelantan's economic needs. The stage was set for a contest between modernization and improved interethnic relations versus traditionalism and an emphasis on Malay rights.

The approaching election of 1969 would test the fortunes of both parties and would also serve as something of a referendum on the Alliance-controlled government. Throughout the following months, the Alliance manifested a rational, calculating, and pragmatic approach to the election that, in several ways, seemed rather Western in style. In contrast the PMIP relied upon traditional images and social means to present a somewhat more impassioned message regarding ethnic identity, as well as political concerns.

As the election drew closer, Alliance undertook a new strategy. The government promised the voters of Kelantan that, should the Alliance take the state in the approaching election, the state would receive M$548 million in development. Alliance was smart enough to realize that this figure would be too abstract for most voters to comprehend. (Just how many truckloads of money was that?) Hence it provided a detailed list of pending development projects. As a result, each village was aware of exactly how it might benefit from Alliance's success. Projects ranged from paved roads, electricity, and piped water, to health centers, new schools, and even new mosques.

This ploy was widely regarded by the PMIP as an attempt to purchase the election. Datok Asri, the Prime Minister of Kelantan at the time, termed the offer "daylight political bribery" (*Straits Times* 4/16/69). Many villagers viewed the government's promises as encouragement to abandon traditional Kelantanese values in favor of progress and a closer relationship with the Chinese.

UMNO, aware that PMIP was trying to capitalize on Islam (Kessler 1978:35 ff.) and on UMNO's connections with the Chinese, did what it could to minimize the damage (Clutterbuck 1985). It derided the economic accomplishments of the PMIP in Kelantan and argued that it was not the sole party of Islam. The government emphasized its plans to construct new mosques, and whenever possible it used religious personages as spokespersons in Kelantan. Two days before the May 10 election, Tun Razak, the Deputy Prime Minister of Malaysia, flew to Kelantan where he opened a new mosque and, not too parenthetically, gave a speech praising the role of the government in, among other things, promoting Islamic interests.

Alliance could not deny its connection to the Chinese, but it attempted to reduce concern about this issue. At one political rally I attended, the speaker told listeners that the connection to the Chinese party had always been useful and that people shouldn't worry about the Chinese, because Malays firmly controlled the army, police, and government bureaucracy. In other instances UMNO representatives actually spoke harshly about the Chinese

(Kessler 1978:136). The strategy was generally to clarify the material promises of the government; then spend most of the time belittling the accomplishments and the nature of the PMIP.

The strategies employed by UMNO and the Alliance revealed a good deal of general political sophistication but also displayed a surprising insensitivity to traditional Malay culture. Most of the serious errors committed by UMNO and its representatives reflected an inability to decenter from a modernized west coast perspective and to take seriously the values and worldview of traditional Malay peasants.

The Alliance controlled the media and made good use of print, radio, and television sources to emphasize the material progress that had occurred under Alliance leadership. Its representatives in Kelantan were careful to use the designation UMNO rather than Alliance, since the latter term tended to remind Malays of the political ties to Chinese and Indian interests. However, as soon as UMNO representatives began direct campaigning in Kelantan, their political myopia became apparent.

The majority of UMNO representatives presented themselves to villagers as important personages—in their dress, in their demeanor, and via often imposing entourages conveyed by shiny limousines. Such dramatic displays are appropriate for royalty and those connected to royalty, but they are not appropriate within a village context. Many of the villagers with whom I spoke observed with resentment that the UMNO people were "putting on airs," and that they seemed to think that they were better than others.

At the village level, most Kelantanese remained concerned about UMNO's alliance with the Chinese. One of my neighbors noted that he preferred PMIP because being a good Malay was most important to him. He was worried that, if they won the election, UMNO would start selling land to the Chinese. He said, "I feel that Malaysia is the inheritance of the Malays, but if the Chinese own all the land, where is this inheritance?" He didn't mind the idea of the Chinese buying land in the cities, as long as they didn't encroach on the countryside. He said that his principal concern was not progress, but the protection of Malay interests and "Malay life ways."

There were significant UMNO misjudgments at both the national and local levels. At the national level, UMNO spokespersons tried to link the PMIP to the Malaysian Communist Party

(Ongkili 1985). Since the MCP was almost totally Chinese in membership and, due to Communist doctrines, opposed to Islamic authority, this charge was not entertained by Kelantanese villagers, whether PMIP supporters or UMNO sympathizers.

UMNO representatives who made speeches in urban and rural areas invariably spoke of progress, but they did so by citing the thousands of dollars that would be spent in that particular location to bring about various material improvements. Most villagers were not favorably impressed, and a number openly voiced their disquiet that the national government was trying to buy them and their cultural heritage—a concern that PMIP did all it could to promote in its own speeches.

An excellent example of the kinds of presentation errors made by UMNO speakers occurred at a political rally in Kota Bharu just two days before the election. The speakers were nearly all university students, and the objective seemed to be to demonstrate the success they had achieved through the support of the national government and UMNO. They talked of the value of education as preparation for the future, of the greater capability of UMNO to meet pending challenges, and of the importance of UMNO to the young and to coming generations. The following is an extract from my field notes:

> Megat Ramli gave a very well reasoned and intellectual speech in which he made some remarkably dumb political blunders. He mentioned that he was a student of Zainal Abidin Wahid, who had spoken the night before for PAS, but that he could not agree with his politics. He then went on to point out that it was the Chinese and English who had opened up Singapore and Penang and brought prosperity to Malaysia while the Malays were just sitting around in their kampongs (Brilliant!). Since then the Malays have shared in the increasing prosperity. He also pointed out that the Malays have profited from government projects financed largely with taxes drawn from the Chinese businessmen.

Not only was Ramli clearly insensitive to Kelantanese pride, he publicly opposed his teacher. Traditional Kelantanese view the teacher-student relationship as akin to that of apprentice-master. Teachers are seen as wiser and more experienced, and students are expected to defer to them in most matters. It is understood that a student is in a teacher's debt, and the kind of public disagreement that Ramli articulated discredits the student far more than the teacher.

With the approach of the election there were several signs that the Alliance's bid to take over Kelantan was in trouble. Undecided people in Wakaf Bharu and elsewhere were becoming increasingly disenchanted with the rather obvious means that UMNO and the Alliance were employing to curry favor among the voters. Perhaps more instructive, those masters of the political scene—the bookmakers of Kota Bharu—were changing the odds on an Alliance victory. Early in the pre-election process, book-makers were giving odds of 7–10 against an Alliance victory. With two weeks to go, the odds fell to 1–2, a political prognostication of some certitude.

At the local level the activities of both parties focused on information gathering, as well as direct campaigning. In Wakaf Bharu both parties attempted to assess the political sympathies of fellow villagers. This was a difficult task because Kelantanese were very reluctant to openly commit to a political position, lest it disagree with one held by a fellow villager and lead to interpersonal friction. A query concerning political preferences was typically met by such already familiar comments as "My head is cloudy," "I haven't decided yet," and my personal favorite, "I'm still sitting on the fence." PMIP supporters pursued their assessment of this situation via the time-honored means of gossip. UMNO supporters in Wakaf Bharu were, however, more innovative.

UMNO party workers, aware of the reticence of villagers to discuss politics with adults, trained young boys between the ages of five and ten to investigate political sympathies. The boys were encouraged to encounter villagers during their work and to question them about their political beliefs in as ingenuous a fashion as possible. They would then be paid M10– 25 cents for each position they could identify.

Since many villagers were illiterate and not well versed in political platforms, boys were taught to direct their question to the visual symbols that were used to represent each party. A young boy would encounter a man working in a rice field and inquire, "Which is better, the ship with a sail or the (crescent) moon and star?" These symbols had been chosen by each party for their associations, as well as for their clarity. UMNO employed the ship symbol on its political fliers and posters indicating that all were in the same ship sailing into a progressive future. PMIP used symbols that clearly identified itself with Islam.

UMNO's strategy was employed in several villages in addition to Wakaf Bharu, and initially it worked quite well, but village gossip quickly discovered the ploy which, thereafter, became quite counterproductive. Most villagers strongly disapproved of the duplicitous technique, and increasingly they judged UMNO political activists to be violating the trust and mutual support that covillagers are expected to accord one another.

In the last few weeks prior to the election, there were a number of egregious Alliance blunders, though none of these occurred in Wakaf Bharu. Elsewhere, however, UMNO leaders organized youth groups, referred to as *Pemuda-Pemuda Tahan Lasak*, which translates roughly as capable youths. These young people, virtually all males, were associated with Malay progress and with leadership in Malaysia's future. However, the role played in local politics by these groups quickly belied the lofty rhetoric surrounding their formation. There were numerous instances when groups of youths identified as Pemuda-Pemuda Tahan Lasak disrupted PMIP political rallies, roughed up opposition politicians, and even began fights with local PMIP supporters. Such behaviors, especially in a village context, are in direct opposition to strongly held Kelantanese values concerning the maintenance of harmony.

PMIP representatives demonstrated their sensitivity to their audience by speaking Kelantanese dialect, by using Islamic references, and by associating themselves with valued elements of Kelantanese culture (see Kessler 1978:35 ff.). Listeners were reminded of the importance of maintaining the Islamic-oriented, traditional lifestyle despite challenges from "outside." UMNO contributed to this strategy with their offer of development funds for the state, should it elect UMNO candidates. The PMIP was able to respond that the Alliance wanted to purchase the Kelantanese birthright, a charge that seemed increasingly believable in light of UMNO's persistent references to material incentives.

All of this activity was occurring as April ended and May began, presumably our last month in Kelantan. We were scheduled to depart Malaysia on June 16. Understandably I felt myself to be under considerable pressure. I had been completing the collection of semantic differential responses, while still trying to follow political developments. As a result Karen, who was engaged in recording the semantic differential responses, and I were both harried and short on sleep.

The election occurred on May 10 and heralded some unanticipated and undesired changes for both Malaysia and our circumstances. As predicted by the bookmakers, PMIP retook Kelantan without difficulty and also made gains in other states. Elsewhere in the peninsula, the Alliance lost ground to other parties as well, notably the progressive Chinese-oriented Democratic Action Party (DAP). Many Malays were very upset about what they saw as a threat to their position in society. Until then there had been an uneasy balance between Chinese and Malay interests, with Malay control of the political apparatus offsetting the economic prominence of the Chinese. The election seemed to raise fundamental questions about the future role of Malays in their own society.[33]

On May 13, rioting broke out in Kuala Lumpur between Malays and Chinese. DAP supporters were noisily celebrating in the streets when they encountered some resentful Malay youths. Fighting broke out and provided a focus for communal tensions that were already exacerbated by the recent election and ensuing rumors of political change. Very shortly there were outbreaks of violence in Kuala Lumpur and in several other major cities on the west coast.

In Wakaf Bharu, news of the troubles first arrived via the ubiquitous transistor radio. We learned with other villagers of the violence elsewhere, and that curfews had been declared in the west coast states of Selangor, Penang, and Perak. We felt quite estranged from the news of trouble elsewhere in the peninsula, but this was not true of our coresidents. Both Malays and Chinese had friends and relatives scattered throughout the Peninsula, and both groups treated the news of the riots as a significant threat to their own interests. Interestingly while Malay supporters of UMNO and PMIP were interested in the potential interethnic threat posed by west coast Chinese, there also remained a good deal of tension between the two camps. I was to discover that this was a good sign and a reflection of the comparative absence of interethnic tensions in the village.

The radio continued to provide heavily edited coverage of the troubles. Two days later the government said that forty people had been killed and more than a hundred injured. However, it also made a strong plea for blood donors, and there were reports from radio sources outside Malaysia that the death toll was well in excess of 100. By that evening the government had acknowledged 70 deaths, 277 injured, 70 cases of arson, and Prime Minister Tengku Abdul Rahman had declared a state of emergency. His initial announcement of the Emergency also called for voluntary mobilization by all loyal young men and suggested the riots were part of a Communist-inspired attempt to take over the country. This argument was never pursued, but a strict curfew was enforced, and the usual organs of government were replaced by a National Operations Council headed by the then Deputy Prime Minister, Tun Razak.

The dispassionate nature of the preceding does little to capture the tensions of the time. Perhaps the following rather telegraphic excerpt from my field notes of that day does a better job:

> By morning death toll report up to 42 (Radio Vietnam again reported over 100 dead). They are, of course, giving no idea of how many Malays and how many Chinese are dead.
>
> Emergency calls kept going out for nurses, ambulance drivers, etc. to report for work. Also calls for blood donors— would seem to indicate the number of injured is more than the 114 they claim.
>
> Planes are still running from KL to east coast, but not between KL and Penang, etc. on west coast. Train from Singapore is going only as far as Gemas.
>
> Tengku on about 10, declaring a state of emergency throughout the country, calls for voluntary mobilization of all loyal young men, says the uproar is communist-inspired attempt to take over the country.
>
> Reported tolls: 75 dead, 277 injured, 70 cases of arson (38 of these were houses). Curfew extended to Negri Sembilan and Malacca (from last night).

The Emergency had several highly visible results in the Wakaf Bharu area. Armed soldiers appeared and were stationed on main roads. A roadblock, replete with armed soldiers and police, was established at the main bridge linking the Wakaf Bharu area to Kota Bharu. Banks were closed, businesses impaired, and postal service interrupted. Despite these alterations, my friends continued to be concerned about reported troubles elsewhere, but they showed little concern that such events could transpire in Wakaf Bharu. Karen and I, while not concerned about our well-being, became quite worried about our planned departure in mid-June. Once again, funds had been delayed, and we had earlier written American Express in an effort to have money waiting in Kuala Lumpur, the center of the riots. We immediately wrote again requesting the transfer of funds to Singapore.

The government continued to maintain tight control of newspapers and radio and supplied only the sketchiest information concerning the troubles. Since many villagers feared for loved ones, the result was a series of proliferating rumors concerning events on the west coast. These stories generally featured thorough and grisly descriptions of atrocities perpetrated against a speaker's ethnic group by members of another ethnic group. The locus of these tales was usually Selangor, where most of the trouble was known to be occurring. The structure of these narratives could remain constant across ethnic groups while the ethnic identity of the characters involved could be dramatically transformed. From a Chinese merchant in Kota Bharu, I received a detailed account of how a young Hokkien woman in Kuala Lumpur was bound with barbed wire, raped, tortured, and finally burned to death by Malay youths. Two days later I encountered the same tale, save that this time it was related by a Kelantanese and featured a young Malay girl who had been bound, raped, and immolated by Chinese youths.

Kelantan was exempt from the curfew that had been declared in several west coast states, but all public gatherings were banned and competitions were cancelled. Still, urban areas such as Kota Bharu seemed to impose voluntary curfews, as large numbers of Malays and Chinese elected to stay home after dark. In Kota Bharu, areas where there was a concentration of Chinese mounted their own evening patrols. The Malays, secure in their greater numbers, took no such precautions.

The few instances of violence that did occur in Kelantan were limited to Kota Bharu and a few other urban centers. All five of the breaches of order I was able to substantiate involved Kelantanese acting against Chinese, save one. An attempt was made to burn down a food stall owned by an unpopular Indian, but it was thwarted by neighboring Kelantanese who doused the fire. The Kelantanese involved were almost exclusively youths, many of whom were members of urban gangs, while the Chinese involved were all urban dwellers who were visibly Chinese in their front-stage behavior. Although other violent acts probably occurred, I found no evidence of a pattern of overall organization, nor did there seem to be support for such behavior, even on the part of urban Kelantanese.

Throughout Wakaf Bharu there was considerable interest in events on the west coast, but little tension between Kelantanese and Chinese in the village. It seems the strength of the interpersonal ties I had witnessed, through events such as the funeral of Cho Bee, was sufficiently strong to withstand the current vicissitudes. My field notes of this period give some sense of the conflicting undercurrents relating to Kelantanese-Chinese relations:

> Interesting to note Hussein's comments on the local Chinese in regard to possible trouble here. He says they are all orang sini, and their *turun-menurun* [descent] is here. He says they are all pretty baik hati, and he doesn't really expect anything to happen. Yet at the same time he expressed fear that, if there is trouble, other Chinese here might poison the local water supply. He was quite serious about this. Obviously he has ambivalent feelings about this. The feeling is that, if there were trouble here, this was a strong possibility.

Nonetheless during the entire period of the troubles, there was only one incident of interethnic violence in Wakaf Bharu, and that, curiously enough, tended to suggest good rather than problematic interethnic relations. The occurrence is perhaps better relayed through my field notes, which demonstrate not only the incident, but how one goes about trying to accurately ascertain facts surrounding a highly charged issue:

Wakaf Bharu   Thurs. 5/15/69

> At 6:15 this afternoon Shamsudin, the Tok Imam's son, was involved in a fight with the son of Lo Sam, a local *tukang mas* [goldsmith], who lives in the kedai area just down the entrance road a little way. According to Yusof Daud (actually Che Gaya was the one who saw it), Shamsudin was standing with two friends on the road when the Chinese kid came by on his bicycle; he pointed to himself and his two friends and went—"*satu, dua, tiga*"—and then pointed to the Chinese boy and said "*topek*" [a derogatory reference to his ethnicity], and he repeated this a couple of times. Finally the Chinese

boy got off his bicycle, walked over to Shamsudin, at which point Shamsudin gave him a push, and after that they started to fight. According to Yusof, the way he saw it—Shamsudin challenged the Chinese boy—"*Dia cabar anak Cina.*" The fight was broken up by some adult Malays who were on hand, and they parted them.

Lo Sam, the father of the boy, was born in HK. He started out here in Singapore, then moved to Pahang, then finally to Kelantan. Che Gaya, who was listening to Yusof and my conversation, said "*Dia orang luar.*" [He's an outsider.] Immediately after this Yusof clarified his background. "*Dia sudah warga negara sini,*" in other words, he's already become a citizen here. Although he was born and raised outside of Kelantan. In this way they (Kelantanese) draw the distinction between a Chinese of Kelantan who is an orang sini, and therefore different from Chinese on the west coast. I've been told this several times by different people—that the Chinese here are much more Malay than the Chinese on the west coast.

*** ******

Fri. nite 5/16/69

The first person to shout "topek" at the Chinese boy was not Shamsudin, but Hussein b. Ja'afa, who is the anak saudara of Mat Zain, husband of Che Nab bidan [the village midwife]. After he had yelled "topek" all three joined in and yelled "topek" at the Chinese kid. Then the event described occurred. This last information was supplied by Che Gaya with Che Nab bidan agreeing in the presence of Mat Zain.

*** ******

Sat. eve. 5/17/69

I told Hussein about the incident with the Tok Imam's son. He hadn't heard it before but he didn't seem very surprised. He said he had advised Mat Yusof not to associate with Shamsudin anymore. After I related the tale, Hussein gave me the following information: He says that part of the trouble is due to the Tok Imam himself, who, while being a good person, doesn't jaga [oversee] his anak enough, in fact more or less lets him do what he wishes.

This event provides good support for the argument that Kelantanese and Chinese at the village level perceive one another as individuals, rather than simply as members of a category. The Chinese youth was the son of a comparative newcomer to the village, while the Kelantanese youths involved included the son of the highly respected local Imam. Nonetheless, Kelantanese sympathies did not follow ethnic divisions. Instead what I encountered was a highly contextualized set of judgments reflecting a familiarity with all of the parties involved and a concern with proper behavior more than with partisanship.

Note that my initial notes also contained a serious error concerning who did what to whom. This was clarified later in conversations with other parties. In particular, the agreement of the midwife and her husband concerning their nephew's role in the altercation greatly increased my confidence in the accuracy of the report, as did Hussein's later commentary concerning the prior misbehavior of the Imam's son.

While the Kelantanese of Wakaf Bharu made fine distinctions concerning local Chinese, they remained nervous about the rumors emanating from Kuala Lumpur and sought scapegoats. Shortly after the riots, one woman who was concerned about the welfare of a nephew living in a Chinese area of Kedah stated, "If one of my relatives was killed I would try to hurt or kill one of their group (*kaum*)." I was disturbed by her statement and began naming local Chinese, asking whether she would care to attack them. Several others present smiled, and she began to laugh, protesting that "village Chinese are like people here—we are of one heart."

The Chinese of Wakaf Bharu seemed aware that there was little danger from coresident Kelantanese. Like geese in a duck pond, their behavior remained casual, and I perceived no alterations in their patterns of interaction. Indeed some Chinese seemed to show a surprising disregard of the possibility of problems.

Three days after the riots began, I attended a local evening performance of Thai music and dancing. There were about two hundred villagers present, about one-third of whom were Chinese. In the midst of the performance, two Chinese who appeared drunk and were heckling the performers got into a fight with several of the performers. Kelantanese in the audience helped to separate the combatants and remonstrated with the Chinese for being drunk and for disturbing everyone. I heard one older

Kelantanese villager stating vehemently that such behavior was not good and a violation of village harmony (ta' baik, ta' sesuai). However, beyond pointing out the dangers of drinking, neither he nor anyone else present seemed to treat the occurrence as a peculiarly Chinese mistake.

While this incident impressed me with both the equanimity of the Kelantanese and the thoughtlessness of the Chinese, the next evening provided an even more dramatic example underlining the security of village Chinese in Kelantan.

At dusk, four days after the riots started, I was sitting on the front porch of a friend's house discussing rumors and gossip when three shots rang out. Shooting is seldom heard in villages as, unlike the United States, the government makes it difficult to obtain a gun permit, and both guns and ammunition are quite expensive. In all of Wakaf Bharu, I knew of only three firearms, all small-bore shotguns. To my surprise, the shots attracted no interest. Passersby did not stop and cock their heads. My companions didn't even comment on the shots. I seemed to be the one person who was visibly discomfitted and nervous. My companions observed that it was probably just someone hunting. The next day I discovered that an elderly Chinese had borrowed a shotgun from a Kelantanese friend, and without seeking permission, he had entered the Imam's durian orchard to hunt bats. When I asked the old man why he had carried out this seemingly ill-considered and perilous act, he responded in a fashion that reminded me of Mr. Paska' Hopi several years and thousands of miles ago: "I wanted to make some soup."

Twilight

While Kelantanese and Chinese villagers were dealing well with the difficulties created by the Emergency, Karen and I were encountering unexpected problems. By the end of May we had only two weeks remaining. We had begun the process of packing and mailing equipment, clothing, and books, but the post office was only open at erratic hours, and there were disconcerting rumors about disruptions in delivery service. Certainly we were aware that some of our own mail had been delayed or had gone astray, but with no other options, we decided to mail our goods and burn incense—an act recommended by a Chinese friend who knew of our worries.

Karen worked assiduously to box, wrap, and package a variety of goods, which I loaded on the Yamaha and transported to the post office in Kota Bharu. I returned bearing the same packages. It seems that there were a series of recondite rules regarding the mails, especially those concerning registered packages of the sort we wished to send. First, the address had to be written directly on the paper. Second, the package had to be secured with string side to side and top to bottom. Finally, the package had to be sealed with wax. As we cheerfully destroyed one of our white candles, Karen joked that they would probably require red instead of white wax. Ho, ho, ho . . . they did.

I worked feverishly to complete the collection of semantic differential protocols. Not surprisingly, several of the earlier semantic differential responses were, upon close inspection, unusable. Things go awry. This was particularly true of my two smaller samples, prostitutes and taxi drivers. If I was to have a sufficient number of respondents in each group, I had to locate more participants immediately. This was narrowly accomplished amidst the distractions of packing and the tumult following the riots. As our date of departure rapidly approached, we found that we had accomplished most of our objectives save one—our money to cover the expenses of the trip home had yet to arrive.

We had valid air tickets and anticipated no legal difficulties in leaving a country that had imposed some travel restrictions, but our financial resources were nearly exhausted and we needed money for such necessities as hotels, airport taxes, and the purchase of departure gifts. I had been trying to arrange the transfer of US$700 via American Express to Kota Bharu. Given the Emergency there seemed to be unanticipated difficulties with this project . . . *quelle suprise*! There was one clerk at the Chartered Bank in Kota Bharu who had been working on our money transfer, and I counted on his expertise and familiarity to help us remain solvent. Naturally, two weeks before we were to leave, he took a vacation and left for Singapore. None of the other bank employees seemed familiar with our plight—or particularly concerned about it.

A few days later a bank officer agreed to try to trace the funds by calling American Express's major in-country institution, the First National City Bank in Kuala Lumpur. The effort of phoning elicited several apologies from assorted operators, but no connection. Two days later, on the fourth of June, contact was made with the First National City Bank, and they reported no record of any transfer. We then contacted Chase Manhattan by phone, as they were the U.S. institution involved in the transfer of funds to Kuala Lumpur. They informed us that the US$700 order had arrived but been cancelled. We hoped that this meant the funds were being transferred to Singapore as originally requested, but to be certain, we sent cables to both Ithaca and Kuala Lumpur to try to ensure this outcome. If you are beginning to get a foreboding about the ultimate outcome of these endeavors, you have profited from the preceding pages.

During the last two weeks our days and nights were filled with both work and socializing. Leave-taking in Kelantan is not something lightly essayed. There are a valued set of conventions concerning proper behavior, if one is to avoid creating embarrassing (malu) faux pas. Thus we attended a variety of feasts in honor of our departure. Despite the paucity of time, none of these could be declined without creating difficult and uncomfortable situations. We ate, consumed, ingested, partook of, and devoured. Our bloated bodies scuttled between social engagements in the evening and a variety of bureaucratic offices during the day. Karen completed the mailing of our belongings, and I finished my research. Well, strictly speaking, one does not finish fieldwork. Instead I acknowledged that I had run out of time and no more could be accomplished.

We spent the last few days in a round of ritualized visits. At each friend's house we would review some of our shared memories and leave small presents, including a photo of the two of us. Usually we were also given small presents meant as reminders of our stay. Because of our dwindling funds, we gave only three significant gifts. Young Yusof Ismail, my frequent companion, and Hussein, our helpful and knowledgeable next-door neighbor, were both given watches. Yusof Daud, who had been a constant

Karen and I attired in our finest Malay garb prior to engaging in a round of feasts marking our departure from Kelantan. Her dress and my "cummerbund" are made of *songket*, an expensive cloth into which silver, and sometimes gold, threads are woven. Copies of this photo were left with numerous friends in Wakaf Bharu as mementos. As late as 1993, there were still several copies posted in various locations to apprise me of how much I had aged in the intervening 24 years. ▶

source of support and assistance, received a camera and some film with a request that he occasionally mail us pictures of his family. We also gave each of their wives—Nab, Ro'fiah, and Gayah—a blouse and an attractive piece of Javanese batik. We also disposed of most of our household goods as gifts, or as inexpensive purchases. We would have liked to have given away our stove and bed to Hussein and Nab, and our Yamaha to Yusof Daud, who had expressed an interest in obtaining the cycle. Unfortunately we had genuine need of money to see us out of the country, and we sold these major items for nominal amounts.

The last day in the village was a difficult time, not simply because we still had details to attend to but because we were leaving good friends. I shall forego a description of the several tearful farewells and mention only one episode.

We were loading a beca we had hired to carry our bags to a rest house in Kota Bharu, from which we would depart the next day. As we tied down the last bag, Rahimah, a young girl from a poor family, whom Karen had been tutoring, came running up and placed a small wooden box in Karen's hand, then turned and ran off crying. Inside the box was a small silver ring with a blue stone, and a note with a Malay saying: "Far from view, but close at heart" [*Jauh dari mata, dekat hati*].

Concluding Comment

The preceding sentence is an appropriate place to end this chapter, but there remains one rather sensitive issue I wish to discuss. It has been alleged by a number of people, both within and outside the profession, that anthropologists exploit those whom they study. Certainly some of the history of anthropology during the colonial period can be cited in support; and, more recently, I expect that a few anthropologists unintentionally, and fewer purposefully, may well have been guilty of abuses. However, I strongly doubt that such a case can be made for most of us, or for the profession as a whole.

We are not drawn to this craft out of a desire to exploit others, but rather from a desire to understand them, and sometimes from an optimistic search for meaning beyond that which our own culture provides. Our greatest success in understanding the "other" comes when we defeat ourselves, and the "other" disappears—to be replaced by friends, acquaintances, and a range of individuals, some of whom are disliked and some of whom become lifelong friends.

11

Sundown

Return Culture Shock

Karen and I left Kelantan from the Kota Bharu airport at 11:00 A.M. on Monday morning, June 16. Hussein, driving his nephew's car, picked us up at the rest house where we had been staying and drove us to the airport. You may recall that Hussein had feared to borrow his nephew's car because of the possibility of embarrassment. This was the first time he had done so, and we felt appropriately honored.

At the airport we were surprised by the presence of Yusof Daud, Yusof Ismail, and many other villagers, who had somehow arranged transportation. Tearful farewells were said, along with promises to stay in touch. The plane actually left on time, and we boarded as our friends watched. Our appearances that day were somewhat contrastive. Karen looked good in a Western-style dress made of batik, while I, attired in chinos and a loose-fitting short-sleeve shirt, simply appeared Ichabod-like. In addition, we were both laden with the results of eighteen months of field research.

Protecting field notes and other research results, such as photographs and tapes, is something about which anthropologists become justifiably paranoid. These resources represent the sometimes painfully acquired fruit of considerable time and effort. Their loss is a truly terrifying prospect, and most anthropologists take steps to ensure the security of their research findings. Our paranoia is provoked by tales of anthropologists who lost their notes or had them confiscated just before leaving the field. This had occurred to G. William Skinner, one of our Cornell professors, just before he was due to depart mainland China.[34] To his credit, he returned to Cornell, learned Thai, and then conducted a seminal study of overseas Chinese in Thailand (Skinner 1958).

I had no desire to emulate Skinner's daunting accomplishment, so Karen and I had been careful to mail home copies of most field notes and some film negatives. However, what remained were a variety of tapes; numerous rolls of film; some unprocessed, uncopied semantic differential materials . . . and the original field notes. As we clambered aboard the plane, I had two airline bags depending from my neck and carried another bag filled with papers, five-by-eight-inch cards, and assorted other materials. Karen carried two bags, which contained her journals and a variety of field records. We made an attractive couple.

We flew to Kuala Lumpur, changed planes, and then flew to Singapore in search of our money. An official at American Express informed us that, yes, the money order had come in, but that it had subsequently been cancelled. He was sorry but didn't see what he could do to assist us in our penurious plight. This last straw was too much. I became a bit wroth, while Karen delivered a succinct but thorough summary of our last eighteen months and then broke down in tears. Her approach was by far the more effective one. After a few uncomfortable minutes, the official said he would see what he could do and left to confer with someone. He returned and informed us that American Express would advance us some money in Singapore, and we could repay it in New York. We were extremely grateful both to him and to American Express for their trust and assistance. It is worth noting that our salvation came not from bureaucratic procedure but from the initiative of an employee that rejected such procedure.

From Singapore we flew to Hong Kong to visit a close friend, and then on to Los Angeles. During the flight across the Pacific we discussed our plans for our return, as we looked forward to seeing friends and loved ones from whom we had been absent for two years. We also eagerly anticipated a return to a culture with which were familiar and comfortable. Our mistake.

When you depart for a foreign culture you anticipate that things will be different, that you will need to make adjustments and accommodations to novel and even strange circumstances. Despite this expectation a degree of culture shock almost always accompanies a prolonged period of stay abroad. Over time you adapt to the new circumstances and may even come to enjoy the experience enormously. Nonetheless there is always the knowledge that "home" is somewhere else; it contains different people and is characterized by different patterns of behavior and belief. During fieldwork, anthropologists can experience nostalgia for the familiar and even pronounced bouts of homesickness (DeVita 1992).

When anyone, anthropologist or other, returns after an extended period abroad, there is an expectation that one is coming "home." You expect to encounter behavior with which you are comfortable and situations which, because of their familiarity, require little conscious examination. These expectations are wholly human and, in the absence of daily contact with home, very understandable. They are also more often frustrated than realized.

The problem of return culture shock has two sources; one in the traveler and one in the home culture. Travelers, including anthropologists, are apt to simplify memories of their own culture and even to engage in some selective remembrances of its virtues. This is termed a "halo effect" and is quite natural, especially during periods of nostalgia or ennui. However, it can result in an unreasonable set of expectations concerning both the simplicity and the comfort of the native culture. The other source of difficulty stems from changes that occur in your own culture over time. When you are away, your memory of the familiar may be selective, but it does not alter to incorporate changes, either anticipated or unanticipated. Cultures, however, always change. Sometimes change is incremental and slow, and sometimes it is quite dramatic and rapid. Simple cultures tend to alter gradually, while complex ones often undergo significant transformations in brief periods of time. There is no culture that changes more rapidly than that of the United States. Indeed we are one of very few peoples in the world who seem to value change for its own sake (Bellah et al. 1985; Morris 1956).

Karen and I were aware that there had been changes in the culture of the United States. We had listened to armed forces radio, read the international edition of *Newsweek*, and corresponded with friends. We knew that there had been some significant alterations, but our knowledge was of an abstract, cognitive nature. We comprehended the changes, but we didn't apprehend them. That is, we understood there were significant innovations to which we had not been a party, but we had no way to "feel" what these might mean.

We had been away from the United States for two years, including all of 1968, probably the most disquieting year of the decade. During that time Czechoslovakia was invaded by the Warsaw Pact; the number of troops deployed by the United States in Vietnam exceeded five hundred thousand; the Tet Offensive occurred in January of 1968 and was to have enormous impact on how America subsequently perceived that tragic conflict; the My Lai massacre occurred, further scarring our image of ourselves; and, owing largely to the effort of young people working on behalf of Senator Eugene McCarthy, President Johnson announced he would not seek a second term.

From a distance it appeared that U.S. culture was becoming immersed in violence. Cornell, our university, made the front cover of *Newsweek* when a group of armed black militants led by a student, Thomas W. Jones, took over the student union.[35] The year was most starkly marked when Martin Luther King, Jr. and Bobby Kennedy were both assassinated. I remember my confusion when I tried, largely unsuccessfully, to explain to my Kelantanese friends how it was that anyone in America could obtain and use firearms, and that there would always be a few who would abuse this right. Their response was a simple question: why would people wish to make this possible? Despite having been raised in rural New Hampshire and owning several firearms myself, I had no good response for this query. Twenty-five years and numerous headlines later, I still lack a convincing answer.

Not all news was catastrophic. There were advances in the sciences and in the arts. The musical *Hair* had become a hit and was leading a small revolution in the theater. This was also the period of the Apollo launches, including a successful circumnavigation of the moon.

When Karen and I stepped off our plane in Los Angeles, we were met by close friends who took us to their home, fed us, and encouraged us to sleep in, in order to help shake the jet lag that always accompanies trips of such magnitude. The next afternoon, they treated us to a Los Angeles performance of *Hair*. This was akin to taking two acrophobes for a walk up the slopes of Mount Fuji. It is fair to observe that we were not wholly prepared for this undertaking. We had just spent eighteen months living in a culture where both genders remained modestly covered, clothing extended to the ankles, and public demeanor was invariably reserved and polite. I had already been bemused by the prevalence of miniskirts, which for some reason made a greater impact on me than on Karen. *Hair*, with its colorful language, upbeat music, strident assertiveness, and nudity, made a most singular impression. It was almost as though we were watching a caricature of American culture, with its emphasis on personal freedom, expressiveness, and cheerful disregard for constraining convention.

Somewhere in the first two days of our return we experienced the visceral realization that the home we were encountering was not the home we had left. I have always considered myself a very adaptable person, and I was surprised by the degree to which this realization discomfitted me. "Home" was something that had been inarticulately anticipated as a haven for rest and recuperation. Certainly friends and relatives contributed to this goal, but for two weeks, each day always contained some jarring experience or perception. However, evolution has worked diligently to ensure that we can adapt to a wide range of circumstances, and so we did.

Obviously the longer one is away from home and the greater the amount of change that occurs, the longer the period of return culture shock is apt to be. Surprisingly, however, this is seldom a protracted period. Generally return culture shock dissipates in two weeks or less, as returning travelers become accustomed to the alterations that have transpired during their absence.

Present-Day

The State

It has been twenty-eight years since Karen and I first entered Kelantan, and much has changed. Since the riots of 1969, Malaysia has embarked on a systematic program of development. For the last several years the country's GNP has grown at the enviable rate of 8 percent. Most of the increases in employment and standard of living have occurred on the west coast. Kelantan has tenaciously remained a bastion of Malay culture and a stronghold for the conservative, Islamic PMIP. Consequently the national government has been slow to improve the circumstances of Kelantanese. In May of 1995, they once again repeated past mistakes by promising the state greatly increased development, a new university, and other improvements, if only the people would elect a state government in accord with the ruling National Front Coalition, guided by the still powerful UMNO. Once again, though their national victories were greater than any since independence, they lost badly in Kelantan.

Lately an increase in the influence of Islamic fundamentalism has led to some assaults on traditional Kelantanese culture. Within the last year, such traditional entertainment forms as the shadow play (wayang kulit), top spinning, and kite flying have either been banned or inhibited. Traditional curing ceremonies (*main puteri*) and *mak yong*, a form of opera indigenous to the area, have also just been banned. There are also a series of efforts to curtail the freedom of women. Those women with whom I have spoken recently are not pleased with these attempts. An excerpt from field notes of two years ago:

> We talked longer about religion, and she clarified her views on Islam and current changes in its practice. She is quite annoyed with *dakwah* [the fundamentalist movement] and their posturings. She mentioned that there are those who think they are better than others because they are dakwah, yet many of them are comparatively ignorant of religious matters. She said they are unfamiliar with *hukum* [used here to mean religious law]. She also noted that there were some who didn't even pray regularly though they continue to posture.

And from a male during the same research:

> He seemed displeased with some aspects of the Islamic resurgence that has occurred over the past years. He notes that now, people who wear uniforms can alter those in order to add religious elements. He clearly did not approve of this development. He added that people who objected to such headgear changes were accused of being against Islam. He stated that the interpretation for acceptable behavior had become more narrow and less tolerant.

The power of the fundamentalists in Kelantan is not unlike that of some in our own society who claim special access to the moral high ground. To oppose such individuals is to oppose morality, or in the case of the Kelantanese, Islam. I am perturbed by these developments partly because they contravene some elements of Kelantanese culture that I have always thought admirable. Historically, Kelantanese have subscribed to what they sometimes term a broad path (*jalan lebar*) and, like the Javanese (Anderson 1965), have been accepting of a range of behaviors and beliefs, so long as these were not threatening to village interests. The Kelantanese, like other Malays and many Indonesians, subscribed to the concept "Other fields, other grasshoppers" (Lain padang, lain belalang). Only two years ago one older man, upset with the narrow and exclusive worldview promoted by dakwah members, expressed to me his conviction, "There is only one God, but there may be many roads to him."

Currently the state government of Kelantan is contemplating the introduction of the Hudud, those conservative Islamic laws that mandate the removal of various portions of the anatomy for a range of offenses. Despite the fact that these laws will impose significant restrictions on women and curtail a variety of freedoms currently enjoyed by many Kelantanese, they are not being opposed by villagers. My recent research indicates that villages either support this initiative, believing that anything originating in Islam cannot be bad, or they fear opposing it for reasons already stated. If implemented, these laws and other corollary changes will significantly alter the status of women and may threaten the pacific nature of interethnic relations as well.

Although the state government has been careful to assert that the new regulations will pertain only to practicing Muslims, Chinese are already experiencing new restrictions on their behavior, including the consumption of alcohol and the holding of public celebrations. Recently, in October of 1995, the Municipal Council of Kota Bharu banned all public song and dance performances, whether performed by Muslims or non-Muslims. These alterations have yet to affect village Chinese, who are much more integrated into the local culture, but it seems likely that the proposed changes will impede the formation of close interethnic bonds. At the very least, it will be highly unlikely for a Chinese to attend a Muslim feast, or for Muslims to appear at a Christian funeral: both events that transpired in 1968.

Wakaf Bharu

The village has grown from a modest marketing community of two thousand to a burgeoning entrepreneurial center of some eight thousand. It has a new health clinic and a secondary school, which is attended by most village children through the sixth form, or until they are about nineteen. There is also an enlarged police station, established principally to deal with the continuing problem of smuggling. Former footpaths are now paved roads, and the central market has spilled over into areas that had been residential. Cars are common and motorcycles are ubiquitous, but they must still contest the right of way with chickens and the occasional water buffalo. The latter are gradually being replaced by small, walk-behind tractors that are used to till rice fields. Most homes are still traditional in design, though pandanus walls are far less common than wooden planking. Some houses are of brick and stucco, fully enclosed, and even air conditioned. Public utilities such as electricity and water are everywhere, and virtually all houses sport antennae for their Sony Trinatrons.

The advent of television has made a significant impact on village social life. There is currently less visiting after dinner and somewhat less concern with village gossip. Traditional hospitality is still offered whenever people drop by, but visitors may also be treated to a television show in progress. There is greater knowledge of the world beyond the village but, correspondingly, somewhat less knowledge about the village itself. Part of this is due to the absorption with television and part to the turnover in village population. The growth in the village is due largely to immigration as people move in to take advantage of the active market and of the rail connection with Thailand.

Attitudes toward change and modernization are generally positive, even when it is acknowledged that there are significant costs to progress. Following are two brief excerpts from my field notes of 1989, my first research in Malaysia after a ten-year hiatus:

> I am quite impressed with changes in the pace of life here, especially in WB, which seems to have undergone more changes than most places. In KB traffic is thick, fast, and pays nominal attention to the rules. When things are really crowded there is a tendency to ignore red lights and to push through intersections anyway. The walking pace in the city remains slow, but that is easily attributable to the heat.

People throng stores all over the city, though their purchases seem to be mainly small scale.

In WB, where there is also a good deal of traffic and continuing construction, the pace of life seems to have definitely picked up, and it has been defended by some villagers as part of *kemajuan* (progress). I have also had people explain that they no longer have time enough to practice the old skills. There is still leisure but it exists principally for the unemployed, of whom there is still quite a large number. Those with jobs, including kids going to school, seem to be busy a good deal of the time. What leisure time there is is usually spent watching TV. Several shows a day are drawn rather eclectically from U.S. TV and range from *Mission Impossible* to *Family Ties, Facts of Life, Head of the Class, Murder She Wrote*, to occasional movies, especially those featuring violence, such as *The Terminator* and westerns. My present impression is that those who rush about are no longer disparaged very much, but I am not sure how representative WB is of the larger culture.

Attitude Toward Progress   5/4/89

This A.M. in WB I mentioned to Mat Mizin about the noise in the village. He corrected me, calling it kemajuan and seemed to believe that it was something of an improvement. Later in the conversation, however, he contrasted the quiet of the village with the noisy city. Attitudes seem a bit conflicted, but there is pride in the progress.

Old Friends

If there have been changes in the state and in the village, there have also been changes in the circumstances of my friends. Mat Mizin, formerly Mat Kadir, our landlord, has returned to Wakaf Bharu, taken up residence in the house he once rented to us, and has continued to be a prominent member of village social life. Currently he has constructed several small houses that he rents out, and he serves as the head of Wakaf Bharu's PMIP chapter.

Mat Halimah died in 1984. He was a pleasant and helpful man who, together with Halimah, his wife, had been very good to both of us. He is the one who, with the assistance of Halimah, was able to identify 184 relatives, their places of residence, means of livelihood, and approximate ages. He had been working in a distant garden, where he was bitten by a cobra, still the leading cause of accidental death in Kelantan. After having been bitten, he tried to return home by bicycle, an unwise and costly effort, as the exercise accelerated the spread of the toxin. Halimah has remained single and lives in a small apartment over a garage in Wakaf Bharu.

Young Mat (whose full name is Mohammed bin Su) of the jaga, one of my key informants, is no longer young and is now referred to as Pak Mat, Uncle Mat, a term denoting both age and respect. He has been married for twenty-seven years, and he and his wife now have twelve children, the oldest of whom is twenty-six and a school teacher in Tanah Merah. To Mat's pleasure, his children live with or near him, and both he and his wife have continuing access to their grandchildren. By Kelantan standards Mat is considered to be "wealthy," meaning that he has many healthy children who have become good citizens. Mat currently rents a kedai in the market district, from which he runs a very successful general store. Mat takes pleasure in the progress that the village has experienced and is well liked and respected by many villagers. He remains warm, friendly, and outgoing.

Yusof Ismail, of the jaga and perhaps my most valuable young informant, has not fared as well as his friend Mat. Yusof was always headstrong and this, together with a history of unpaid debts, has led many villagers to distrust him. He has gained a good deal of weight and currently lives in Thailand, near Sungai Golok, with a new young wife. He now has three wives, Rofiah, his first wife, still resides in Wakaf Bharu, while a third wife is in a distant village near Tanah Merah. He makes a sporadic income from intermittent activities, several of which are not approved by villagers. Rofiah receives no maintenance from Yusof and works to support her family, including her aging mother.

My good friend and neighbor, Hussein, succumbed to a form of lung disease that was never fully diagnosed. He died some eight years ago, leaving Nab, his son Yusof, and adopted daughter Ruslinah with the kedai, but with little else. Nab ran the shop by herself for years, as Yusof had married and moved out of Kelantan. Ruslinah, a bright and talented young woman, applied herself to her studies and was trying to enter the National University near Kuala Lumpur.

In my last visit, in 1993, I was touched to find the kedai virtually unchanged from what it had been in 1969. On the back wall was a yellowing, faded picture of Karen and me dressed in Malay finery, which we had given Hussein and Nab as a remembrance. The shop still sold one of nearly every item one might need, and the main income was still derived from grated coconut to be used in the preparation of traditional curries.

In 1993 Nab was sick with diabetes and, during the latter part of the fieldwork, most of my visits with her were in the hospital. She was visited daily by Ruslinah, who spent most of her nights sleeping in a chair next to Nab. Knowing that Nab did not write very well, when I left I gave her a small radio and tape recorder, asking her to occasionally make a taped message that Ruslinah could send to me. Unfortunately that never occurred, and I received a letter from Ruslinah in 1994 informing me that Nab had died of diabetes.

Yusof bin Daud, now retired from his position as village clerk, had a stroke in 1989, just six months before I again arrived in Wakaf Bharu. When I saw him, he had lost the use of his right hand, and movement in his right leg was greatly impaired. His spirits were good though, and he was determined to follow a regimen of exercise in an effort to improve his condition. During that fieldwork stint, Yusof's youngest son, Roslan, served as a very able field assistant, helping me gather both data and people with whom I could work. Yusof had made the haj some years earlier and was now entitled Haji Yusof. He was, as earlier, a respected member of the village from whom others often sought advice.

When I returned in 1993, I was delighted to find Yusof's health much improved. His right hand still had very limited movement, but he could now walk about with the aid of a cane. His energy was back, his attitude was positive, and he was enjoying the role of gentle patriarch, as most of his children were married and had already had several children themselves. Yusof, in better health, was determined once again to be of significant assistance. One of my research topics involved songbird contests, a topic on which he is something of an expert. Roslan, with Yusof's new car, drove Yusof and me to several bird contests, where Yusof introduced me to judges and carefully explained the rules and procedures, also supplying a wealth of background on the purchase and training of birds.

My favorite memory of that field stint, was May 31, Hari Raya Haji, the first day celebrating the conclusion of the haj. It is customary for children to return to their parents' homes for this celebration. In Malaysia this currently means an outpouring of cars from urban areas and trips of often considerable distance to villages of origin. For Yusof and his wife, Cik Gayah, this meant that, in addition to their nearby children, they would see others from some distance. I will not detail here all of the accomplishments of Yusof's children, but their positions range from immigration officer, to accountant, to research chemist. For the next few days Yusof's house was filled with pleasant reminiscences, laughing children, and a plentitude of good food. I was invited to the major celebration, during which a cow was slaughtered in the traditional fashion and the meat shared amongst relatives and the needy.

During the ensuing meal, I discovered that I too had been transformed by time. Throughout earlier visits since 1969, I had been referred to as Cik Lah, Mr. Abdullah. Now with my white beard, bald pate, and distinguished wrinkles about the eyes and mouth, I had become Pak Lah, Uncle Lah. As was the case for Mat, this term denoted both respect and *age*. I recalled the respectful manner in which I had approached the various Paks I had known during my first fieldwork, and I recognized that my position in Kelantanese society had been altered simply by the passage of time. Linguistic markers of this sort help to differentiate among villagers and add texture to life's many rites of passage. At least that is what I told myself to assuage my somewhat dented American ego.

The day before I was to leave Kelantan for the United States, Yusof asked me to come to his house for a feast in my honor. I had already purchased my going-away gifts for him and for Gayah, but I added some pieces of kain for other members of the family. Prior to the meal, I gave Yusof his present—a motor-driven Pentax that he could use with one hand. He took several pictures of the feast during the evening, and I have some copies for remembrance.

The meal was a delicious affair, as Gayah was already aware of what I most liked and went to some pains to design the menu around my tastes. There was a spicy soup made from the neck bones of a cow, a spiced beef and vegetable dish, two kinds of fish, and a really hot chicken curry. Every time I looked away from my plate, someone added food to it. I ate all I possibly could and finally surrendered, sprawling sideways on the floor to demonstrate my plight. An amused but pleased Gayah suggested that I may indeed have eaten enough.

As I was ready to leave, Yusof retired into a back room. One of his sons suggested that I wait, as he was seeking something. He had already given me two handsome pieces of batik, one for Karen, who had not accompanied me, and one for Alethea, our daughter. He had also tried to give me one of his son's awards, which was a fine gesture but not one that I was comfortable accepting. He emerged from the back of the house carrying a box that contained men's jewelry that he had acquired during his pilgrimage to Mecca. He selected a plain silver ring with a large red stone, of the sort that Malay men like, and gave it to me. It is sitting on a shelf above my computer as I complete this chapter.

The Validity Issue

In the process of writing about fieldwork, I have also had to describe the Kelantanese, or at least my impressions of the Kelantanese. As a reader you must be aware that any description of another people and culture by an anthropologist or by anyone is, to some degree, suspect. People not reared in a given culture are limited in their ability to comprehend that foreign reality. All impressions are filtered through one's own cultural background and prior experience. Thus the image a reader receives of another culture is not only secondhand, it represents, to a greater or lesser degree, a transformation of the original.

Currently there are postmodern anthropologists who argue that the degree of transformation is such that ethnographies are better treated as texts, as creations of authors rather than as descriptions of other peoples. I readily admit the core of their argument, that ethnographies invariably involve a subjective perception of another culture. But that is true of all perceptions. Perception is an active, selective process for most organisms, including humans. All our perceptions, even fundamental visual cues, involve transformations (Kaufman 1974; Segall et al. 1966). We are not video cameras, passively recording the world around us. Instead we determine our focus, select our particular subject matter, and highlight some elements more than others.

In a real sense, the important question is never one of validity or truth. Truth exists in the realm of mathematics and in the philosophy of logic, not in perceptions of reality. For those who would understand the world about them, the question is not one of truth, but of utility. Do our investigations deepen our understanding, further our ability to ask more refined questions, and lead to better predictions of events? If so, then the research is justified. If not, it remains but sophistry.

Are the Kelantanese just as I have described them? Undoubtedly not. Yet I persist in the conviction that this effort is not simply a text, but rather a reasonable descriptive approximation. I know there are elements of the culture to which I never became privy, and I suspect that I may have placed undue stress on some elements of Kelantanese culture, especially those that contrast so dramatically with my own culture. I may have overemphasized the importance of village harmony and the nurturing nature of village social life. Certainly I did not give equal weight to the continuous rounds of gossip and personal criticisms that are found in any small village. Nonetheless I stand by the core of my description and my choice of those aspects of Kelantanese culture that I have argued are central. Happily I have quantitative data from the semantic differential to support my perceptions (Osgood et al. 1975; Raybeck 1974), and concordance with the work of others (Gosling 1964; Scott 1985; Wilson 1967). However, perhaps the best test of my assertions will come later, when some of my Kelantanese friends have read copies of this book and communicated their impressions of its accuracy to me.

The Benefits of a Good Tanning

Most people change over time. Some, exposed to significant alterations in their daily patterns, can change markedly. Not surprisingly, fieldwork, with its curiously complex demands and rewards, can be expected to change the practitioner. Having returned from eighteen months of reasonably successful fieldwork in the tropics, I discovered there had been changes in myself as well as in the culture we had left. For a year and a half Karen and I had experienced life as members of a minority. Please do not misunderstand my meaning here. I am not suggesting that we underwent anything like the social disadvantages and cultural stigma that American minorities often encounter. On the contrary we were comparatively advantaged and often accorded a status we did nothing to earn. But we were a minority, a tiny enclave of two, set apart. Regardless of the warmth and support of our Kelantanese friends, there was always the awareness that we could not fully belong, that we were objects of curiosity (and occasionally amusement), and that, despite the genuine, enduring friendships that were formed during that period, there was always a chasm, compounded of cultural distance and personal backgrounds, that could be bridged but neither closed nor ignored.

Reflecting on that first fieldwork, and on subsequent research in Kelantan, I find that, just as my instructors had mysteriously suggested, there have been some significant personal profits that owe more to life's celebration than to the mind's cerebration. I gained a better sense of my own strengths and weaknesses, discovering I could accomplish things I would not have expected, and that I possessed some equally surprising frailties. I also was forced to encounter the limits of effective action and to realize that there are times and circumstances when uncertainty can not be readily resolved. The greatest change I found in myself was both personal and philosophical. I was, in some very important ways, less certain of myself and my opinions. I found I was more willing to entertain alternatives than I had been prior to fieldwork. I had been trained to take a relativistic perspective toward other peoples and other cultures, and now I found that this perspective had seeped into the way in which I viewed much of what went on around me.

During the heated times of the Vietnam war, my increased ability to decenter and to try to see more than one side of an issue made me few friends. Conflict, whether armed or simply intellectual, pushes positions to extremes. The middle ground is difficult—even dangerous—terrain, yet it is the only position from which both sides can be viewed at once. I am not trying to suggest that my fieldwork experience turned me into an indecisive moral relativist, but I do think that it greatly widened my approach to issues and gave me greater access to the complexity that characterizes real human behavior and beliefs.

Now having completed the circuit of fieldwork, I find I am in the position of my early instructors, trying to persuade others of the value of the experience. I have sought to convey in this little book some of the practices, the difficulties, and even the mystique of fieldwork. I remain uncertain of the degree of my success, but if you have garnered some sense of the personal and intellectual utility of field research, then I am pleased to have made the effort.

Notes

[1] As you may have realized, while this book deals with several aspects of field-work and fieldwork techniques, this will involve neither a technical discussion of fieldwork nor an exhaustive discussion of the variety of appropriate research methods. There are several good books that treat these concerns, such as Pelto and Pelto (1978) and Russell Bernard (1988, 1994).

[2] Anthropology's interest in futuristic extrapolations is not a new one (Tax 1960, 1977). Recently a number of anthropologists, science fiction writers, and NASA types have been cooperating on a project called CONTACT, which seeks to develop future scenarios concerning problems that we are about to encounter or may possibly encounter as the result of events ranging from environmental changes to contact with extraterrestrial intelligence.

[3] Anthropology, for all its romance, suffers visibility problems. Few people are familiar with the names of anthropologists beyond those of Margaret Mead and Lévi-Strauss. Those of you who are undergraduates or lay readers will have to accept my assessment of the Cornell anthropologists, but I assure you that their names and contributions are recognized by virtually all anthropologists. Indeed, a few, such as Victor Turner, have worldwide reputations, having made major substantive contributions to the field.

[4] Works that illuminate the roles of kinship in American social life include *American Kinship: A Cultural Account* by David Schneider and *All Our Kin* by Carol Stack. Both are interesting, well written, and provide good insights into some of the important yet little appreciated influences of kin connections.

[5] Readers interested in this issue can consult work by Nagata (1984) and by Raybeck (1980–81, 1992).

[6] So that you will be apprised of my biases and have some sense of the direction this book takes, I should inform you that I have come to share this assessment in large degree. However, I would not argue, as would some, that it is necessary to carry out fieldwork in a foreign and preferably exotic land in order to enjoy such benefits.

[7] There are several good examples of fortuitous alterations in fieldwork contained in *The Humbled Anthropologist: Tales from the Pacific*, edited by Philip DeVita (1990), and in *The Naked Anthropologist: Tales from Around the World*, another collection of fieldwork essays by DeVita (1992) that contains a precursor of this book.

[8] All members of society need opportunities to relax from the pressures of public performances and, occasionally, to engage in soft deviant activities (Goffman 1959; Murphy 1964). Phrased more bluntly, we all need opportunities to pick our noses. To some extent we all need privacy; access to what Goffman terms

"backstage areas," where public performance demands can be circumvented and even subverted (Goffman 1959). In many societies, like Kelantan, privacy may be troublesome to secure and, when gained, may be viewed with considerable suspicion and even disapproval. The difficulty in obtaining privacy in small-scale social units is particularly acute, due to such factors as high visibility of members, persistent demands for social participation, and comparatively easy access to interpersonal information (Raybeck 1991a).

[9] The spelling of Malay terms throughout this book follows the current orthography, which was initiated several years after the fieldwork period described here. The prefix Encik, abbreviated Cik, is similar to Mr., Mrs., Miss, or even Ms. in that it is used for an adult, but, unlike our practices, this reference is not gender specific. Malay naming customs are based on Islamic practices, where a son or daughter is termed "name, son (bin) or daughter (binte) of father." Thus Hussein's father was Ahmad and his full name is Hussein bin Ahmad. Likewise his son, Yusof, is Yusof bin Hussein. There are no persisting family names, and such common first names as Yusof, Mohammed, Abdullah, and Hussein abound. If you suspect that this might raise certain problems with attempts to collect genealogies, devise a village census, or simply keep one's field notes straight, you are quite perceptive.

[10] During the initial fieldwork period described here, a Malay dollar was valued at approximately US33 cents. This mattress cost slightly more than twelve dollars.

[11] This is accomplished through scalar rating procedures and a factor analysis of the resulting information. Semantic differentials have been constructed for more than thirty language-cultures and, in each instance, the strongest resulting factor that accounted for the greatest amount of variance has been an evaluative factor relevant to ethical judgments of goodness and badness. The strength of this factor, plus the open-ended manner in which the factors are derived within a cultural context, make the semantic differential particularly appropriate for investigations into people's attitudes concerning values and deviance (Raybeck 1975). Furthermore the semantic differential permits individual responses and group responses to be analyzed separately, which facilitates a comparison of beliefs and attitudes held by the members of identifiable "sub"cultures.

[12] Adjective pairs, employed in the scalar ratings, and their factor loadings are generated by members of the culture and are not imposed via translation procedures. The only operational assumption implicit in the construction of the semantic differential is that people across cultures find the principle of opposition to be meaningful, and that they can make meaningful judgments on a seven-place scale. For the former, there is good evidence concerning the cross-cultural commonality of antonymous relations (Raybeck and Herrmann 1990), and were the latter not the case, the data would yield only noise rather than factor structures.

[13] For a good discussion of types of sampling procedures and associated concerns, I recommend Bernard (1994:73ff.)

[14] The results of semantic differentials administered orally and in writing were checked to make sure that they were comparable. The method of collection appeared to introduce no bias into the result.

[15] I chose several of these concepts because my fieldwork led me to expect that they were value related. They included such obvious choices as Islam, relatives (waris), and village society (*masyarakat kampong*) as well as other concepts designed to provide texture and background to the responses (Raybeck 1975:110 ff.). One of these concepts was "I, myself" (*saya sendiri*), chosen so that the villagers' responses to this concept could be placed in the context of their other judgments.

[16] It is imperative that instructions be translated accurately and in a language that is accessible to the reader. I was once again indebted to Amin Sweeney, who ensured the accuracy of the final product.

[17] Please remember that although I sometimes employ the present tense, the period referred to here is January 1968 through June 1969. The circumstances of taxi drivers, as well as the economics described here, have changed markedly.

[18] The responses of the taxi drivers proved to be very useful and, as I had hoped, were between the students and the villagers in perceptions concerning traditional culture and modernization (Raybeck 1975).

[19] For an example of questionable anthropological behavior, you might wish to consult *The Rise and Fall of Project Camelot: Studies in the Relationship between Social Science and Practical Politics* (Horowitz 1967).

[20] Nonetheless my profession has generated just such a list, which is, despite good intentions, quite inadequate as a practical guide to making ethical decisions in the field (American Anthropological Association 1971). It is the *Principles of Professional Responsibility*, the official code of ethics for the American Anthropological Association. It contains a number of prescriptions and proscriptions, some of which are too specific to be of much use in the complexities that constitute fieldwork.

[21] The yellow shirt is significant because yellow is the color associated with royalty and is not commonly worn by villagers. The young man was probably marking himself as an orang berani who didn't mind breaking conventions.

[22] The names of villagers have, thus far, been accurate. The names of the principals in this section have, for obvious reasons, been altered.

[23] Unlike Westerners, Malays believe that the liver rather than the heart is the seat of emotions. Thus the literal translation of this phrase would be a "person of good liver."

[24] Such premortem bequests are not unusual, as they provide parents with a means of circumventing the rules of Islam that dictate that a male child shall receive twice what a female child inherits.

[25] Reports of what transpired differed somewhat because individuals tended to favor one or another of the principals. It does seem clear that Ismail interfered with Ali's grandchildren, but the extent of that interference may have ranged from a verbal remonstrance to striking the child and threatening his life.

[26] The local Kota Bharu paper, which was quite critical of the national government, carried a column called enam-sembilan that disparaged the ruling Alliance party.

[27] The cost of raising fighting bulls has increased markedly. Some bulls are reputed to cost more than M$40,000. This rather impressive expense linked to animals can be found elsewhere in Kelantanese culture. Songbirds, which are very highly regarded even today, may cost as much as M$10,000–M$50,000. The most

expensive bird of which I heard was a spotted dove that in 1993 cost its owner M$70,000. He then reportedly refused an offer to sell it for M$100,000.

[28] I happily recommend Savishinsky's book, *The Trail of the Hare: Life and Stress in an Arctic Community*, as a well written and absorbing study of a hunting and gathering band.

[29] Kelantan now has an irrigation system that allows two plantings of rice per year. This has greatly altered the traditional rhythms of village life, as has the increasing presence of Sony Trinatrons.

[30] Both Karen and I are very grateful for the monetary support we received. The National Institute of Mental Health (Grant MH 11486) and the London-Cornell Project, quite simply, made the research possible.

[31] For reasons that will soon be obvious, the names here, including that of the village, are fictitious.

[32] In 1969, the Alliance party, a coalition entity consisting of the United Malays National Organization (UMNO), the Malayan Chinese Association (MCA), and the Malayan Indian Congress (MIC) controlled every peninsular state save Kelantan and maintained a large enough political majority in Parliament to amend the constitution unilaterally. This situation had obtained for several years, and the Alliance party was very interested in continuing its virtual reign.

[33] Here is not the place to discuss the details of the election results or the subsequent changes in the social and political life of Malaysia. These have been well described elsewhere (Funston 1980; Gullick 1981; Milne 1976, 1981; Ongkili 1985; Ratnam and Milne 1970; Rudner 1970; Vasil 1980; Wang 1970).

[34] We graduate students who took his courses or did research under him were convinced the *G.* stood for God, such was his manner and his reputation for demanding the most of his students. The tales of his performance in the field did little to allay our suspicions.

[35] Time writes changes for us all. Thomas W. Jones, the black militant who led the armed occupation of the student union at Cornell in 1969, is now president of a pension fund. In 1993 he was appointed to Cornell's Board of Trustees. Two years later, at the university, he endowed a five-thousand-dollar prize that rewards efforts to foster interracial understanding and harmony.

References

American Anthropological Association. 1971. *Principles of Professional Responsibility*. Washington, DC: American Anthropological Association.

Anderson, Benedict R. O'G. 1965. *Mythology and the Tolerance of the Javanese*. Ithaca: Modern Indonesia Project, Southeast Asia Program, Dept. of Asian Studies, Cornell University.

Atkinson, Jane Monnig, and Shelly Errington, eds. 1990. *Power and Difference: Gender in Island Southeast Asia*. Stanford: Stanford University Press.

Banks, David J. 1983. *Malay Kinship*. Philadelphia: Institute for the Study of Human Issues.

Beals, Ralph, and Harry Hoijer. 1965. *An Introduction to Anthropology*. New York: Macmillan.

Bellah, Robert N., et al. 1985. *Habits of the Heart: Individualism and Commitment in American Life*. New York: Harper & Row.

Bernard, H. Russell. 1988. *Research Methods in Cultural Anthropology*. Newbury Park, CA: Sage Publications.

———. 1994. *Research Methods in Anthropology: Second Edition: Qualitative and Quantitative Approaches*. Thousand Oaks, CA: Sage Publications.

Bodley, John H. 1982. *Victims of Progress*. Palo Alto, CA: Mayfield Publishing Company.

Bonvillain, Nancy. 1995. *Women and Men: Cultural Constructs of Gender*. Englewood Cliffs, NJ: Prentice Hall.

Brettell, Caroline B., and Carolyn F. Sargent, eds. 1993. *Gender in Cross-Cultural Perspective*. Englewood Cliffs, NJ: Prentice Hall.

Brown, Donald E. 1991. *Human Universals*. New York: McGraw-Hill.

Campbell, J. K. 1967. *Honour Family and Patronage: A Study of Institutions and Moral Values in a Greek Mountain Community*. Oxford: Clarendon Press.

Chan, Su-ming. 1965. Kelantan and Trengganu, 1909–1939. *Journal of the Malaysian Branch of the Royal Asiatic Society* 28:159–98.

Chu, Chi-hung. 1976. Ethnicity, Partisanship, and Legislative Activity in Malaysia. *Legislative Studies Quarterly* 1:551–61.

Clutterbuck, Richard L. 1985. *Conflict and Violence in Singapore and Malaysia, 1945–1983*. Boulder, CO: Westview Press.

Cole, Michael, and Sylvia Scribner. 1974. *Culture and Thought*. New York: John Wiley & Sons.

DeVita, Philip R., ed. 1990. *The Humbled Anthropologist: Tales from the Pacific*. Belmont, CA: Wadsworth Publishing Company.

———. 1992. *The Naked Anthropologist: Tales from Around the World*. Belmont, CA: Wadsworth Publishing Company.

Djamour, Judith. 1959. *Malay Kinship and Marriage in Singapore*. New York: Humanities Press.

Downs, Richard. 1967. A Kelantanese Village of Malaysia. In *Contemporary Change in Traditional Societies*. Vol. 2, *Asian Rural Societies*, ed. Julian Steward, pp. 107–86. Urbana: University of Illinois Press.

Firth, Rosemary. 1966. *Housekeeping Among Malay Peasants*. New York: Humanities Press.

Foster, George M. 1965. Peasant Society and the Image of Limited Good. *American Anthropologist* 67:293–315.

Funston, N. John. 1980. *Malay Politics in Malaysia: A Study of the United Malays National Organization and Party Islam*. Kuala Lumpur: Heinemann Educational Books (Asia).

Gaffin, Dennis. 1991. Faeroe Islands: Clowning, Drama, and Distortion. In *Deviance: Anthropological Perspectives*, ed. Morris Freilich, Douglas Raybeck, and Joel Savishinsky, pp. 191–211. New York: Bergin & Garvey.

Goffman, Erving. 1959. *The Presentation of Self in Everyday Life*. New York: Doubleday Anchor Books.

Goodenough, Ward. 1956. Componential Analysis and the Study of Meaning. *Language* 32:195–216.

Gosling, L. A. Peter. 1964. Migration and Assimilation of Rural Chinese in Trengganu. In *Malayan and Indonesian Studies*, ed. J. Bastin, and R. Roolvink. Oxford: The Clarendon Press.

Gullick, John M. 1981. *Malaysia: Economic Expansion and National Unity*. Boulder, CO: Westview Press.

Hägerstrand, Torsten. 1988. Time and Culture. In *The Formulation of Time Preferences in a Multidisciplinary Perspective*, ed. Guy Kirsch, Peter Nijkamp, and Klaus Zimmermann, pp. 33–42. Brookfield, VT: Gower Publishing Company.

Homans, George C. 1961. *Social Behavior: Its Elementary Forms*. New York: Harcourt, Brace & World.

Horowitz, I. L., ed. 1967. *The Rise and Fall of Project Camelot: Studies in the Relationship between Social Science and Practical Politics*. Cambridge: MIT Press.

Hutterer, Karl L., A. Terry Rambo, and George Lovelace, eds. 1985. *Cultural Values and Human Ecology in Southeast Asia*. Ann Arbor: University of Michigan Press.

Jones, James M. 1988. Cultural Differences in Temporal Perspectives: Instrumental and Expressive Behaviors in Time. In *The Social Psychology of Time: New Perspectives*, ed. Joseph E. McGrath, pp. 21–38. Beverly Hills: Sage Publications.

Kaufman, Lloyd. 1974. *Sight and Mind: An Introduction to Visual Perception*. New York: Oxford University Press.

Kessler, Clive S. 1977. Conflict and Sovereignty in Kelantanese Malay Spirit Seances. In *Case Studies in Spirit Possession*, ed. Vincent Crapanzano and Vivian Garrison, pp. 295–331. New York: John Wiley & Sons.

———. 1978. *Islam and Politics in a Malay State: Kelantan, 1838–1969*. Ithaca: Cornell University Press.

Kluckhohn, Clyde. 1951. Values and Value Orientation in the Theory of Action: An Exploration in Definition and Classification. In *Towards a General Theory of Action*, ed. Talcott Parsons and Edward A. Shils. New York: Harper & Row.

Kluckhohn, Florence, and Fred Strodtbeck. 1961. *Variations in Value Orientations*. Elmsford, NY: Row, Peterson and Co.

Laderman, Carol. 1991. *Taming the Wind of Desire: Psychology, Medicine, and Aesthetics in Malay Shamanistic Performance*. Berkeley: University of California Press.

Latif, Rabiah, and Christopher Spencer. 1981. The Time in Bukit Perah: A Field Study of Time Reckoning in a Kampong in Kelantan (Malaysia). *The Eastern Anthropologist* 34:207–12.

Levine, Robert V. 1988. The Pace of Life across Cultures. In *The Social Psychology of Time: New Perspectives*, ed. Joseph E. McGrath, pp. 39–60. Beverly Hills: Sage Publications.

Malinowski, Bronislaw. 1967. *A Diary in the Strict Sense of the Term*. Trans. Norbert Guterman. New York: Harcourt, Brace & World.

McGrath, Joseph E., and Janice R. Kelly. 1986. *Time and Human Interaction*. New York: The Guilford Press.

Milne, Robert Stephen. 1976. The Politics of Malaysia's New Economic Policy. *Pacific Affairs* 49:235–62.

———. 1981. *Politics in Ethnically Bipolar States: Guyana, Malaysia, Fiji*. Vancouver: University of British Columbia Press.

Montagu, Ashley. 1957. *Man: His First Million Years*. New York: Columbia University Press.

Morris, Charles. 1956. *Varieties of Human Value*. Chicago: University of Chicago Press.

Munroe, Robert L., and Ruth H. Munroe. 1994. *Cross-Cultural Human Development*. Prospect Heights, IL: Waveland Press.

Murphy, Robert F. 1964. Social Distance and the Veil. *American Anthropologist* 66:1257–74.

Nagata, Judith. 1975. *Pluralism in Malaysia: Myth and Reality.* Leiden: E. J. Brill.

———. 1984. *The Reflowering of Malaysian Islam: Modern Religious Radicals and Their Roots.* Vancouver: University of British Columbia Press.

Nash, Manning. 1974. *Peasant Citizens: Politics, Religion, and Modernization in Kelantan, Malaysia.* Athens: Ohio University.

Ong, Aihwa. 1987. *Spirits of Resistance and Capitalist Discipline: Factory Women in Malaysia.* Albany: State University of New York Press.

Ongkili, James. 1985. *Nation-Building in Malaysia, 1946–1974.* New York: Oxford University Press.

Ortner, Sherry B. 1974. Is Female to Male as Nature Is to Culture? In *Woman, Culture, and Society,* ed. Michelle Zimbalist Rosaldo and Louise Lamphere, pp. 67–87. Stanford: Stanford University Press.

Ortner, Sherry B., and Harriet Whitehead, eds. 1981. *Sexual Meanings: The Cultural Construction of Gender and Sexuality.* Cambridge: Cambridge University Press.

Osgood, Charles E. 1964. Semantic Differential Technique in the Comparative Study of Cultures. *American Anthropologist* 66:171–200.

Osgood, Charles E., William H. May, and Murray S. Miron. 1975. *Cross-Cultural Universals of Affective Meaning.* Urbana: University of Illinois Press.

Osgood, Charles E., George J. Suci, and Percy H. Tannenbaum. 1957. *The Measurement of Meaning.* Urbana: University of Illinois Press.

Peacock, James L. 1968. *Rites of Modernization: Symbolic and Social Aspects of Indonesian Proletarian Drama.* Chicago: The University of Chicago Press.

Pelto, Pertti J., and Gretel H. Pelto. 1978. *Anthropological Research: The Structure of Inquiry.* New York: Cambridge University Press.

Ratnam, Kanagaratnam J., and Robert S. Milne. 1970. The 1969 Parliamentary Election in West Malaysia. *Pacific Affairs* 43:203–26.

Raybeck, Douglas. n.d. Kelantanese Divorce: The Price of Kindred and Village Harmony. Unpublished Manuscript. Author's possession.

———. 1974. Social Stress and Social Structure in Kelantan Village Life. In *Kelantan: Religion, Society and Politics in a Malay State,* ed. William R. Roff, pp. 225–42. Kuala Lumpur: Oxford University Press.

Raybeck, Douglas. 1975. *The Semantic Differential and Kelantanese Malay Values: A Methodological Innovation in the Study of Social and Cultural Values.* Ph.D. Diss., Cornell University.

————. 1980. Ethnicity and Accommodation: Malay-Chinese Relations in Kelantan, Malaysia. *Ethnic Groups* 2:241–68.

————. 1980–81. The Ideal and the Real: The Status of Women in Kelantan Malay Society. *Women and Politics* 1:7–21.

————. 1986a. The Elastic Rule: Conformity and Deviance in Kelantan Village Life. In *Cultural Identity in Northern Peninsular Malaysia*, ed. Sharon Carstens, pp. 55–74. Athens: Ohio University Press.

————. 1986b. Kinesics and Conflict Management in Kelantan, Malaysia. Paper presented at 85th Annual Meeting of the American Anthropological Association.

————. 1989. On Wings of Waxed Paper: Kite Flying in Kelantan, Malaysia. *The World & I* November:652–63.

————. 1991a. Deviance, Labelling Theory and the Concept of Scale. *Anthropologica* 33:17–38.

————. 1991b. Hard versus Soft Deviance: Anthropology and Labeling Theory. In *Deviance: Anthropological Perspectives*, ed. Morris Freilich, Douglas Raybeck, and Joel Savishinsky, pp. 51–72. New York: Bergin & Garvey.

————. 1991c. To Seek Their Own Living. *The World & I* November:666–77.

————. 1992a. The Coconut-Shell Clock: Time and Cultural Identity. *Time & Society* 1:323–40.

————. 1992b. A Diminished Dichotomy: Kelantan Malay and Traditional Chinese Perspectives. In *In Her Prime: New Views of Middle-Aged Women*, ed. Virginia Kerns and Judith Brown, pp. 173–89. Chicago: University of Illinois Press.

Raybeck, Douglas, and Douglas Herrmann. 1990. A Cross-Cultural Examination of Semantic Relations. *Journal of Cross-Cultural Psychology* 21:452–73.

Roff, William R. 1967. *The Origins of Malay Nationalism.* New Haven: Yale University Press.

Rokeach, Milton. 1973. *The Nature of Human Values.* New York: The Free Press.

Rosaldo, Michelle Zimbalist, and Louise Lamphere, eds. 1974. *Woman, Culture, and Society.* Stanford: Stanford University Press.

Rudner, Martin. 1970. The Malaysian General Election of 1969: A Political Analysis. *Modern Asian Studies* 4:1–21.

Rutz, Henry, ed. 1992. *The Politics of Time.* Washington, DC: American Anthropological Association.

Salleh, Mohamed b. Nik Mohd. 1974. Kelantan in Transition: 1891–1910. In *Kelantan: Religion, Society and Politics in a Malay*

State, ed. William R. Roff, pp. 22–61. Kuala Lumpur: Oxford University Press.

Savishinsky, Joel S. 1974. *The Trail of the Hare: Life and Stress in an Arctic Community*. New York: Gordon and Breach Science Publishers.

Schneider, David M. 1980. *American Kinship: A Cultural Account*. Chicago: University of Chicago Press.

Scott, James C. 1985. *Weapons of the Weak: Everyday Forms of Peasant Resistance*. New Haven: Yale University Press.

Segall, Marshall H., Donald T. Campbell, and Melville J. Herskovits. 1966. *The Influence of Culture on Visual Perception*. New York: The Bobbs-Merrill Company.

Skinner, G. William. 1958. *Leadership and Power in the Chinese Community of Thailand*. Ithaca: Cornell University Press.

Stack, Carol B. 1974. *All Our Kin: Strategies for Survival in a Black Community*. New York: Harper & Row.

Strange, Heather. 1981. *Rural Malay Women in Tradition and Transition*. New York: Praeger.

Strauch, Judith. 1981. *Chinese Village Politics in the Malaysian State*. Cambridge: Harvard University Press.

Swift, M. G. 1965. *Malay Peasant Society in Jelebu*. New York: The Athlone Press.

Tan Chee Beng, ed. 1984. *Ethnicity and Local Politics in Malaysia*. Singapore: Department of Sociology, National University of Singapore.

Tax, Sol, ed. 1960. *The Evolution of Life: Its Origin, History, and Future*. Chicago: University of Chicago Press.

Tax, Sol, and Leslie G. Freeman, eds. 1977. *Horizons of Anthropology*. Chicago: Aldine.

Vasil, R. K. 1980. *Ethnic Politics in Malaysia*. New Delhi: Radiant Press.

Wang, Gungwu. 1970. Chinese Politics in Malaysia. *The China Quarterly* 43:1–30.

Wilson, Peter. 1967. *A Malay Village and Malaysia: Social Values and Rural Development*. New Haven: HRAF Press.

Winzeler, Robert. 1974. Sex Role Equality, Wet Rice Cultivation, and the State in Southeast Asia. *American Anthropologist* 7 6:563–67.

Wolf, Eric R. 1966. *Peasants*. Englewood Cliffs, NJ: Prentice Hall.

Zerubavel, Eviatar. 1981. *Hidden Rhythms: Schedules and Calendars in Social Life*. Chicago: University of Chicago Press